Safeguarding Our Common Future

SUNY Series in Environmental and
Architectural Phenomenology

David Seamon, editor

The SUNY series in Environmental and Architectural Phenomenology presents authored and edited volumes that emphasize a qualitative, descriptive approach to architectural and environmental experience and behavior. A key concern is scholarship, education, planning and design that support and enhance natural and built environments that are beautiful, alive, and humane. A clear conceptual stance is integral to informed research and design, and the series gives first priority to phenomenological and hermeneutical approaches to the environment but also sponsors other styles of qualitative, interpretive research.
Volumes in the series include:

David Seamon, editor
Dwelling, Seeing and Designing:
Toward a Phenomenological Ecology (1993)

Robert Mugerauer
Interpretations on Behalf of Place:
Environmental Displacements and Alternative Responses (1994)

Louise Chawla
In the First Country of Places: Nature, Poetry and Childhood Memory (1994)

David Seamon and Arthur Zajonc, editors
Goethe's Way of Science: A Phenomenology of Nature (1998)

Herb Childress
Landscapes of Betrayal, Landscapes of Joy:
Curtisville in the Life of Its Teenagers (2000)

Safeguarding Our Common Future

Rethinking Sustainable Development

Ingrid Leman Stefanovic

State University of New York Press

Published by
State University of New York Press, Albany

© 2000 State University of New York

All rights reserved

Printed in the United States of America

For information, address State University of New York Press
State University Plaza, Albany, N.Y., 12246

Production by Michael Haggett
Marketing by Fran Keneston

Library of Congress Cataloging-in-Publication Data

Stefanovic, Ingrid Leman
    Safeguarding our common future : rethinking sustainable develop-
ment / Ingrid Leman Stefanovic.
        p.   cm—SUNY series in environmental and architectural phe-
nomenology)
    Includes bibliographical references and index.
    ISBN 0–7914–4651–4 (hc.: alk paper)— ISBN 0–7914–4652–2
(pbk.: alk. paper)
    1. Sustainable development. 2. Human ecology. 3. Ethics, Modern.
4. Phenomenology. I. Title. II. Series.
HC79.E5 L45 – 2000
338.9'27'01—dc21   99–054570

10 9 8 7 6 5 4 3 2 1

To my father,
who helped me find the direction
and to my husband and children,
who keep me on course.

Contents

Illustrations

Acknowledgments

I wish to thank David Seamon for his invaluable support in my preparation of this book. His editorial assistance and overall guidance were offered with a spirit of grace and friendship that far outreach any normal expectations.

My thanks extend also to the Department of Philosophy, University of Toronto, and the Social Sciences and Humanities Research Council, who provided, through a grant-in-aid, financial and logistical support in the preparation of this work.

I am especially pleased to acknowledge the opportunity provided to me by the Netherlands School for Research in Practical Philosophy to present summaries of my research to faculty and colleagues. Particularly helpful comments were provided to me in an intensive, working session with the Dutch Association on Philosophy of Nature and Environment, although, of course, they remain completely absolved of responsibility for any shortcomings of this book.

Finally, I am grateful to my family for their patience, understanding, and support throughout the process of writing.

Editor's Introduction

In *Safeguarding Our Common Future*, philosopher Ingrid Leman Stefanovic asks perhaps the single most important question facing humankind in the twenty-first century: How are we to live with our natural and built worlds in such a way that both they and we are sustained and flourish?

Throughout her book, Stefanovic's practical and conceptual baseline for exploring this question is *Our Common Future*, the influential account of environmental and socioeconomic sustainability written by the World Commission on Environment and Development in 1987 and better known as the *Brundtland Report*, after Norwegian commission chairperson Gro Harlem Brundtland. In developing the concept of "sustainability," the report's authors sought to delineate a way of living economically and ecologically that would provide for humankind's present material and psychological needs without sacrificing the ability of future generations to meet their own needs.

In her book, Stefanovic develops a careful rethinking and enlargement of the report's definition of sustainability, drawing on the ideas of phenomenology, especially as presented by German philosopher Martin Heidegger. Her aim, she writes, is "to overturn taken-for-granted assumptions of sustainable development so that we might more genuinely respond to unlimited needs within the reality of finite constraints."

In the first part of her book, Stefanovic lays out the taken-for-granted assumptions that *Our Common Future* makes about sustainability. More broadly, she demonstrates how these assumptions are grounded in the dominant Western worldview through which nature and the environment are currently conceptualized, mostly in a tacit, unquestioned way. The core of this dominant view, she argues, is an objectivist-subjectivist division that interprets the nonhuman world in two contrasting ways, neither of which allows that world to be fully what it is. On the one hand, the objectivist lens of the positivist scientist understands nature as an unaware, material stuff that can be measured, manipulated and used as a "standing reserve," usually unthinkingly. On the other hand, the subjectivist lens of the post-structural scholar or many contemporary artists views nature as a malleable, passive realm with no inherent meaning and thus justifiably amenable to the arbitrary interpretation of the human interpreter. In both perspectives, the nonhuman world has little to say in the meanings that human beings impose upon it but, instead, is forcefitted into a particular mindset or point of view.

In part II of her book, Stefanovic sets the groundwork for an alternative conception of sustainability, drawing on phenomenological insights. She emphasizes the need to understand environmental problems holistically yet also argues that conventional scientific efforts are unable to deal with the whole other than as a collection of parts. She then considers how a phenomenological interpretation might lead to an environmental understanding that can illumine the "referential whole within which we are situated."

In other words, might there be, asks Stefanovic, some other way of understanding whereby nature and environment could be allowed a space to be what they are before they are automatically conceived in objectivist or subjectivist terms? This new style of seeing is what Stefanovic identifies, after Heidegger, as *originative thinking*—a style of empathetic looking by which the thing to be understood is given room to be both what it is in itself and what it is in relation to the larger whole of which it is part. Stefanovic's hope is that such a new mode of understanding might allow for nature and the environment, whether natural or built, to be seen in a fuller, more accurate light and thereby be better appreciated and cared for.

Finally, in part III, Stefanovic examines how originative thinking might contribute to an enlarged sense of sustainability. One of her central conceptual foci is the phenomenon of place and implacement, which she believes provides a foothold for grounding environmental responsibility and action in relation to particular individuals, groups and localities. Places, Stefanovic argues, arise "in the very interplay between self and world." The ontological primacy of place, therefore, might become the starting point for place-based environmental ethics out of which, more spontaneously and without direct control or predetermination, might arise more sustainable ways of living.

Most broadly, Stefanovic argues that what we do is what we understand and that our environmental actions will change only when we see our world and ethical obligations to that world in a different way. Stefanovic concludes that, most essentially, the basis for ethical action must shift from an emphasis on "traditional liberal attitudes and self-determined concerns of autonomous individuals" to a recognition that, through the ontological primacy of place, "individual human beings are fundamentally already implaced in a complex array of sociocultural, economic, technological, regulatory and environmental relationships."

As with much phenomenological thinking, Stefanovic's argument is a return to beginnings—what, in other words, are the essential lived foundations of a responsible environmental ethic and a sustainable repertoire of environmental actions and, in turn, how can these lived foundations be adapted for specific individuals, groups, regions and cultures? In this sense, Stefanovic's book is especially valuable in the way that it seeks to integrate different literatures and perspectives that are typically held apart: Heidegger's discussions of Being, dwelling and technology; the phenomenological research on place; conventional philosophical approaches to environmental ethics; and real-world efforts to facilitate specific environmental policies through the dominant objectivist approach.

In drawing together these separated points of view, Stefanovic builds a useful bridge between theory and praxis, helping us to realize that how we picture and relate to the world shapes that world in one way rather than another. Finding a way to allow our world, especially the natural world, to become a place sustainable and sustaining for both present and future is the possibility toward which *Safeguarding Our Common Future* illuminates the first crucial steps.

David Seamon
Editor, SUNY series in Environmental and Architectural Phenomenology

Introduction

We must co-exist for until we do,
The Trees will continue to stand alone,
In their majesty and ancient wisdom,
Bearing witness to our crimes
As we slaughter them. Oh, Love,
Let us see their tears.
—Kirstin Miller, "The Trees"

Miller's testimonial invites us to reflect on the value of nature, for the sake of our love of the trees themselves. At the same time, while we bear witness to the tears, we know that we must affect the natural world, simply by virtue of existing. Human development imposes environmental costs that seem necessary, particularly if technological society is to promote a higher quality of life for increasing numbers of people worldwide. The challenge of reconciling the demands of development within the graces of nature constitutes the most pressing task facing humanity today. This task of learning to live sustainably on the earth, in the hope of safeguarding our common future, is the subject of this book.

More than a decade ago, the World Commission on Environment and Development published a landmark document that argued for a balance between socio-economic progress and environmental care. Their report popularized the notion of sustainable development as "development that meets the needs of the present without compromising the ability of future generations to meet their own needs."[1] This definition made its way into academic publications, government policies, environmental programs, and even cocktail conversations. The phrase has been reported in countless documents, so much so that, today, the generalized message of sustainability may appear to mean nothing specific at all. Perhaps the term has been reused and recycled beyond repair.

This book wishes to suggest the exact opposite view. The essence of sustainability is vital and its fundamental message deserves our continued attention. At the same time, it is probably the right moment to rethink some essential assumptions that underlie our interpretations of environmentalism. Not long ago, such challenges would have been met with technical solutions. Consider how in 1946, a Canadian news magazine heralded the prospects of harnessing atoms for peace. We were promised that "power pills will keep planes in the air and ocean liners endlessly plowing the seas, without need to refuel; all industrial production will be geared to atomic energy which will be almost as free as air, until everything from homes to baby buggies will be within pocketbook range of the humblest Zulu tribesman."[2]

Today, we are less naive about the possibilities of technological progress. Still, we continue to hope that electric cars will reduce harmful effects of polluting vehicles and that computerized technologies will somehow solve complex environmental problems. Certainly, technology promises to improve our quality of living and to contribute to sustainable solutions. We have come to a growing awareness, however, of the environmental setbacks brought about by many technological advances as well. The nuclear industry, glorified in the quotation from 1946, has caused its own set of environmental problems associated with the disposal of waste and the perils of nuclear accidents. Science is reaching some limits in predicting environmental risks and no amount of technological manipulation can solve problems in the face of such scientific uncertainty.

In this technological age, sustainable development clearly becomes more than a technical issue. It is also, in fact, a philosophical matter. Fundamental questions of ethics, logic, and metaphysics underlie our analysis of environmental impacts and inform our patterns of decision-making. Philosophers can help us to understand how we perceive a wide array of environmental problems, what we value and how we think through appropriate programs of action. This volume takes a step in the direction of exposing some of the philosophical issues that may have been taken for granted in many discussions of sustainable development to date.

For a number of years, I have attempted to bridge philosophy with environmental and architectural concerns. Philosophers have much to offer to other disciplines concerned with improving our overall quality of life. This volume presents—and attempts to enlarge upon—the work of a central figure in modern philosophy, German phenomenologist Martin Heidegger. Heidegger believed that contemporary, technological society has lost a genuine sense of belonging to our natural and built places. He argued that we have come to value material things at the expense of understanding both the relationship between entities and the context within which those entities are comprehended in the first place. His writings support the need for a rethinking of human dwelling and for a broader interpretation of the meaning of thinking itself.

After all, environmental decision-making is first and foremost a process of thinking, as a condition of enlightened action. As we develop policies and plans for sustainable development, basic beliefs and value systems frame the very questions we ask in the first place. The job for philosophers is to shed light on inconsistencies in our patterns of thinking. One way of doing this is to expose taken-for-granted assumptions, value judgments, and even cultural paradigms and language structures that condition our way of seeing the world.

Phenomenology is particularly helpful in investigating such issues. It specifically aims to illumine not only what is explicitly said in policy-making and program development, but also what remains unsaid. Sometimes, hidden worldviews that structure our ways of thinking are so much a part of who we are that it becomes a special challenge to expose those paradigms in particular. Phenomenology is dedicated to precisely such a task of illumining our fundamental ways of thinking about our world.

Some critics may claim that, in examining ways of *thinking*, phenomenology is simply a descriptive account of *subjective* experiences of reality. These critics are mistaken. The phenomenological method aims to shed light on the dynamic *relation between* human interpretation and a complex world that, in its mystery and complexity, inevitably exceeds mere subjective projections. In its origins, phenomenology evolved in reaction to a metaphysical tradition that tried to explain the question of Being in universalizing terms as grounded in either a reified, idealistic subject or the static reality of an external, objective world. Instead of investigating exclusively subjective experiences or objective, value-free facts in isolation from one another, phenomenology examines the relation between human beings and their world, *before* philosophers engage in any theoretical abstractions that divide or separate their lived experiences from the world within which these experiences find their meaning and their ground.

By recognizing the relation between human beings and their world as dynamic and changing, phenomenologists will be suspicious of grand solutions to environmental problems that are presented as static, definitive accomplishments, immune to the effects of history and time. Sustainable development will inevitably be closer to a continuing challenge than a conclusive state to be attained once and for all. Just as they are wary of metaphysical attempts to ground philosophy in a substantive, indubitable and eternally plausible explanation of the meaning of existence, phenomenologists will avoid the pretensions of constructing grandiose, systematic solutions to complex environmental problems.

At the same time as they avoid universalizing answers to questions of sustainable development, however, phenomenologists will attempt to avoid a collapse into mere skepticism or relativism. The postmodern era has awakened us to the importance of history, and of different interpretations of the meaning of life that evolve through plural, cultural perspectives. These postmodern insights are important when it comes to appreciating diverse approaches to sustainable development that arise among different peoples of the world. On the other hand, simply recognizing and describing plural interpretations often leaves us empty-handed when it comes to guidance in environmental decision-making.

Phenomenology aims to maneuver between two extremes: On the one hand, it tries to avoid the naïveté of assuming that simplistic, unilaterally imposed and universal answers to complex environmental problems can be conclusively defined once and for all in an accomplished state of sustainability. On the other hand, phenomenology is also uneasy with a postmodern skepticism that simply accumulates plural interpretations of the world. The aim, instead, for phenomenology is to remain open to cultural and ontological diversity, while at the same time seeking some essential moments where horizons of interpretation converge and patterns of thinking reveal pathways for positive, collective, environmental action.

The Organization of the Book

Seeking to advance such a phenomenological task, this volume is divided into three parts. Part I is entitled "Problems with Current Thinking about Sustainable Development." The first chapter locates phenomenology in a postmodern era and argues for a central role of philosophy in reflections on sustainability. Chapter 2 describes calculative thinking and shows how it predominates in contemporary assessments of what is real and what is true. Chapter 3 indicates how this mode of thinking has come to distort current interpretations of our relations to other people, to the environment, to the city and, ultimately, to the meaning of sustainable development.

Part 2 is entitled "Foundations of Phenomenological Thought." It moves beyond the critical stance of the previous part to propose a new way of "originative" thinking, introducing the reader to phenomenological ontology and to the possibility of phenomenological ethics. I argue that we need to move beyond reductionist, calculative paradigms of sustainability to a more holistic way of thought. As chapter 4 shows, holism is not an unproblematic notion. Nevertheless, chapter 5 proposes a phenomenological interpretation of holistic thinking—one that recognizes both the need to synthesize as well as to take into account Heidegger's notions of no-thingness, absence, and ontology. The final chapter of this part addresses the question of the possibility of a phenomenological ethics. If philosophy can contribute to our understanding of taken-for-granted ways of thinking about human beings and the environment, then the possibility exists for phenomenology to illumine an *ēthos* that is supportive of sustainable development.

Part 3 aims to provide some "Phenomenological Guidelines for Sustainability." Chapter 7 proposes that environmental care is grounded in a primordial belonging to place. Place is understood, however, not simply in terms of geographical location but in terms of the ontological notions of dwelling and implacement. Chapter 8 is a preliminary excursion into the field of phenomenological, environmental ethics as place-based. Chapter 9 argues that originative thinking can inform a more holistic discussion of sustainable development indicators. Chapter 10 describes cases where phenomenology has informed specific projects relating to problems of sustainability. It ends with a discussion of how phenomenological thinking and place-based ethics offer clues for a re-evaluation of the aims of environmental education.

Heidegger has suggested that "to save" means more than protecting from danger. It also implies a safekeeping and a recalling of essential origins. In safeguarding our common future, we are faced with special challenges of promoting human development while preserving ecological foundations. Unique difficulties for decision-making arise in a postmodern era, where plural interpretations of right and wrong and skepticism about the possibility of absolute truth claims may overwhelm us and simple, universalizing solutions to daunting environmental problems are often inadequate.

Nevertheless, we cannot afford to be bewildered by this complexity. Nor can we be complacent in the face of diverse, competing demands that appear irreconcilable. Phenomenology presents us with a way of thinking that respects the reality of change and flux. It also aims to provide direction by reflecting on converging threads of meaning and essential connections among apparently competing truth claims. It is my hope that the phenomenological reflections in this volume will help to expand our way of thinking about sustainable development and invite more discerning action when it comes to dwelling more respectfully and with care on this earth.

PART I

*Problems with Current Thinking
about Sustainable Development*

1

The Challenge of Sustainability
in a Postmodern World

The children know. They have always known. The children see.
—Maurice Sendak

To describe childhood simply as the age of innocence is to delude ourselves. Un-encumbered by customs and social artifice, the vision of the child is ingenuous but not unenlightened. Often, the child's experience is a disclosure of the world in its primary and immediate givenness. The tedium of replicated experiences is yet to accumulate. In its place, life still resonates with the grace of originary revelation. When Plato tells us that philosophy begins with wonder, perhaps it is this very resonance that he recalls.[1] Certainly, Nietzsche will reflect that the child is "innocence and forgetfulness, a new beginning, a sport, a self-propelling wheel, a first motion, a sacred Yes."[2] In the place of lofty speculation and theoretical constructs, the task for philosophy may be simply *to see* the world more originatively than we normally do.

What might one accomplish with such childlike reverence? To paraphrase philosopher Martin Heidegger, perhaps the question concerns not what *we do* with such seeing but, rather, what might such seeing *do with us?*[3] Today, the eyes of our children gaze upon a world where they no longer play unprotected from the sun. Asthmatic inhalers clear the air for our daughters and sons, and for an increasing number of their friends. Favorite swimming holes—brooks, streams, and lakes—now store our wastes. Environmental degradation no longer remains a mere slogan of green fundamentalists, but envelops our children worldwide.

In this epoch, where environmental concerns bring together world leaders for global summits and where recycling becomes a natural part of our lives, we hear more and more how "sustainable development" policies will help to assure our children a healthier world. The concept of sustainable development alerts us to the dangers of focusing shortsightedly upon gratification of our present needs at

3

any cost. Defined by the World Commission on Environment and Development as "development that meets the needs of the present without compromising the ability of future generations to meet their own needs," the notion of sustainability implies a long-term moral imperative to attend with greater care and insight to the preservation of our natural and built worlds.[4] At the 1992 United Nations Conference on Environment and Development, representatives of the global community met in Rio de Janeiro to publicly express their commitment to precisely this goal of sustainable development.

Though diverse in form, the aspirations of those who seek sustainable development are often noble ones. On the other hand, too rarely are popular conceptions founded in a reverent, philosophical vision of existential wonder. More typically, a false security arises through piecemeal quantification that seeks the calculation of equilibrium in place of harmony and balance. Costs and benefits become exclusive measures of equity and justice. Environmental management techniques seek quick-fix solutions rather than the wisdom of long-term care. No longer is there talk of persons but of human "resources."

It is time, in my view, to stop and rethink some common paradigms of sustainable development. A first step is to stretch our imaginations beyond the comfort of unquestioned assumptions and to critically analyze them from new vantage points. I recall a game from my own childhood, where I would dream of what it would be like to live in an overturned world. My soul wandered on the ceilings, balancing on chandeliers. I reeled along sloping rafters and stepped over the tops of door frames between rooms. Where in this vast inverted universe I might end up by stepping out of the front door—this question was too incredible to conceive. When I encountered the Hegelian image of philosophy as the world stood on its head, these memories returned to me.[5] Taken-for-granted worlds only become evident when exposed from alternate perspectives.

This book aims to overturn taken-for-granted assumptions of sustainable development so that we might more genuinely respond to unlimited needs within the reality of finite constraints. This latter notion of constraints is troublesome to many of us. Recounting a final childhood memory takes me back to New Year's Day, 1960, when I was only seven years old and I recognized, in that first experience of the dawn of a different decade, that time was passing. A sudden weight descended upon my youth as I saw that my being in the world was not forever. Time was not an eternal resource to be thoughtlessly squandered. My world was not to be taken for granted. I knew then that life had some inviolable limits.

The aftermath of such a recognition was not a morbid gazing at the end but, rather, a renewed appreciation of the gift of life. If the concept of sustainability may sensitize us to an awareness of some limitations, the challenge will be to pursue development with increased humility and respect of our planet. The Chinese proverb tells us that with every crisis comes an opportunity. Increasingly, we accept that the environment is in a state of crisis. At the same time, the concept of sustainable development holds the promise of new opportunities for learning and for change. This book is one attempt to build upon this promise, for the benefit of our own children, as well as for generations to come.

Philosophy and Sustainable Development

Since the publication of *Our Common Future* in 1987 by the World Commission on Environment and Development (WCED), the term "sustainable development" has come to have a central place in environmental policy-making.[6] The concept has found support from both environmentalists as well as economists and public policy makers who hope that human needs can somehow be met indefinitely into the future, with minimal negative impact upon the natural world.[7] In the words of the WCED, sustainable development "requires the promotion of values that encourage consumption standards that are within the bounds of the ecologically possible and to which all can reasonably aspire."[8]

There are some individuals who see the notion of sustainability as signifying an original and fundamentally innovative direction in environmental thought. Dr. George E. Connell, chair of the National Round Table on the Environment and the Economy in Canada, wrote a letter recently to the Prime Minister in which he stated that "there is no question that sustainable development requires new models of decision-making, new systems of measurement and assessment."[9] Similarly, Ranjit Kumar, Edward Manning, and Barbara Murck of the Centre for a Sustainable Future in Toronto maintain that with a new era of sustainability, "a new world order is emerging, just as revolutionary as that following the Industrial Revolution or the Social Revolution of the last century."[10]

On the other hand, other commentators trace the spirit of the concept at least as far back as the ancient Greeks. Learning from Aristotle, Herman Daly and John Cobb define *oikonomia*, the root of economics, as "the management of a household so as to increase its value to all members of the household over the long run."[11] They contrast *oikonomia* with *chrematistics*, "the manipulation of property and wealth so as to maximize short term monetary exchange value to the owner."[12] Old or new, the concept of sustainable development as "positive socioeconomic change that does not undermine the ecological and social systems upon which communities are dependent" today has prominent influence over environmental and development policy.[13] Moreover, while the concept of environmental care may be as old as civilization itself, it is clear that modern technological society places new demands upon us—demands that will require new ways of interpreting our changing world.

To be sure, mechanisms for implementing sustainability, as well as physical design parameters of sustainable communities, remain elusive. This fact in itself, however, may not be as problematic as it appears at first glance. One might persuasively argue that it is a dangerous illusion to assume that we can provide an exact, technically complete roadmap on our way to achieving sustainability. Rajni Kothari points to the hazards of reducing environmentalism to a technological fix. He laments the fact that, once again, "manager technocrats" are charged with developing technical solutions: "Economic growth, propelled by intensive technology and fuelled by an excessive exploitation of nature, was once viewed as a major factor in environmental degradation." Ironically, that same paradigm of economic growth and technological progress "has suddenly been given the central role in solving the environmental crisis."[14]

Kothari distinguishes between sustainable development as a "narrow economic ideal" and as an "ethical ideal," arguing that environmental jargon often serves as a cover for the very sort of economic activity that caused environmental destruction in the first place.[15] It is only in a rethinking of our value systems and ethical paradigms that there is some hope for moving toward sustainable development that is also just on an economic, social, and political level. Economist William Rees echoes this sentiment when he writes that

> [planners] will acquire maximum leverage by shifting the focus of their efforts from changing the environment to changing human minds and redesigning social institutions. For sustainable development . . . *the need is more for appropriate philosophy than for appropriate technology.*[16]

To examine the philosophical foundations of sustainability is no small task. On the other hand, in the absence of philosophical enquiry, many of our attitudes and judgment calls remain ungrounded and lacking in rigor. Philosophy is not a free-floating, academic exercise in abstract concepts. Rather, if the aim of philosophical analysis is to bring to light the structure of our beliefs and to ultimately guide us in substantiating our decisions, then philosophy becomes the prerequisite for wise environmental policy formulation and decision-making. Philosophy provides the opportunity for articulating the foundations and groundwork in building toward more thoughtful and comprehensive sustainable development programs.

Phenomenology, Science, and Metaphysics

The philosophical approach that inspires this book is phenomenological. Phenomenology has been cast in many molds since its founder, Edmund Husserl, presented his own, unique "transcendental" phenomenological method.[17] From the hermeneutics of Ricoeur and Gadamer, to the existential perspective of Merleau-Ponty and Sartre—and finally, to the ontology of Heidegger, phenomenology has answered to a variety of philosophical questions and a single, unified methodology appears elusive.[18] In Heidegger's own words, "there is no such thing as *the one* phenomenology, and if there could be such a thing, it would never become anything like a philosophical technique. . . . The only thing that is truly new in science and in philosophy is the genuine questioning and struggle with things which is at the service of this questioning."[19]

Despite diverse interpretive arenas, common threads of meaning can, nevertheless, be seen to weave their way among the different thinkers. For one thing, phenomenology is profoundly nondogmatic. Husserl described himself as a "perpetual beginner," meaning that philosophy could never be, properly speaking, a static accomplishment but was, essentially, open to further questioning and to the evolution of thought. Rather than present conclusive "theories," Husserl's own "investigations" avoided the pretense of categorical philosophical doctrines or treatises, engaging instead in a perpetual rethinking and, sometimes, even rejection of previous works. Similarly, Martin Heidegger describes his own philosophical journey as being "on the way," rather than conclusively established at any single point in time.[20] Spiegelberg is, therefore, right to describe the course of phenomenology as a *movement*, rather than the development of a single doctrine.[21]

There are at least two reasons why phenomenology chooses this route against dogmatic theoretical assertions. First, I would argue that phenomenologists are wary of the immodesty of some scientific methods that would presume to be capable of an absolutist, value-free grasp of objective facts. Second, this wariness comes from an overall disillusionment in the aspirations and consequences of western metaphysical thought. Let me address each of these points in turn.

We cannot deny that we live in an epoch where, for many people, science defines what is real and true. Clearly, science has advanced knowledge in the modern world, including our understanding of such topics as the disappearance of rainforests, the ecological effects of over fishing and the extent of damage to the ozone layer by chlorofluorocarbons. At the same time, we must not forget that exercising scientific judgment requires the *interpretation* of facts. Facts are not merely value-neutral, ahistorical entities that the expert divines once and for all. The meaning of a fact depends on the question you ask and on the context that is presupposed in order to ask the question in the first place.

Phenomenologist Martin Heidegger has spoken of the "greatness and superiority of natural science during the 16th and 17th centuries"—a greatness that rests in the fact that "all scientists were philosophers. They understood that there are no mere facts, but that a fact is only what it is in light of the fundamental conception, and always depends upon how far that conception reaches."[22] More recently, scientific thinking has come to presume that "it can manage sufficiently with facts, or other new facts, while concepts are merely expedients which one somehow needs, but should not get too involved with, since that would be philosophy."[23] A dichotomy is, therefore, set up between apparently objective, empirically verifiable and immutable factual knowledge on the one hand, and subjective, historically variable philosophical opinions and values on the other.

Environmental philosophers, together with more enlightened scientists, today recognize, however, that this rift between facts and values is misplaced.[24] Consider a telling example relating to energy policy. While scientists may accumulate facts relating to the quantity of resource depletion or costs of generating plants, those facts lead to very different policies, depending upon whether they are being interpreted within the context of the priority of supply or demand. From the point of view of supply, many argue that, since we are running out of energy, we require new energy sources (such as from nuclear fission breeder reactors). From the perspective of demand, development of "appropriate technologies" and strategies to increase energy efficiency—better home insulation, increased transit use, and solar power—would be judged as more suitable energy policies.

While the set of facts may, in both cases, be the same, it is inevitable that human judgment will color the interpretation of those facts.[25] Scientific "facts" do not subsist in the realm of eternal truths, separate from human judgment but, on the contrary, only appear as true on the strength of the human interpretation that makes them meaningful in the first place. When anyone presumes to be in a position to conclusively prove, once and for all, a theory about the natural world, phenomenologists remain skeptical, because they know that it is in the nature of understanding that it can never attain to an absolutist grasp of that world. A more modest view recognizes, in the words of environmentalist Robyn Eckersley, that "nature is not only more complex than we presently know, but also quite possibly, more complex . . . than we *can* know."[26]

Why have we, in modern times, come to have such faith in the immutable power of scientific facts? The answer to this brings us to our second point, namely, that phenomenologists avoid the comforts of closed systems and dogmatic theoretical constructs because of a disillusionment in the course of the western metaphysical tradition itself. Heidegger's phenomenological investigations showed how metaphysics, from the time of the ancient Greeks, has supported a worldview that idealizes absolute certitude and the comfort of timeless truths—and it is such a metaphysical presupposition of the nature of reality that grounds the culmination of the tradition in science.

According to Heidegger, Plato inadvertently sowed the seeds of a tradition that, of necessity, moved toward ever increasing abstraction and a loss of the very wonder that he had argued was the source of genuine philosophical thought. Beauty, order, and the good for Plato subsisted in a world of ideal forms, in some manner separate from the everyday world of becoming and flux. "It was in the Sophists and in Plato that appearance was declared to be mere appearance and thus degraded. At the same time Being, as *idea*, was exalted to a suprasensory realm. A chasm, *chorismos*, was created between the merely apparent essent here below and real being somewhere on high."[27]

This distinction between an eternal, transcendent realm of universal truths and mundane existence persisted throughout the Middle Ages, when philosophers sought structure and meaning in theological revelation and divine law. The "definitive preeminence of the supersensuous" is grounded now in God the Creator, whose revealed truth is proclaimed by Church doctrine.[28] As *doctrina*, truth is, in principle, capable of being collected within the *Summa*, that is, the systematic collection of the entire heritage of ahistorical, doctrinal views espoused by theology and absolutely bound to the teachings of the Church.

Heidegger's argument here is that the equation of truth with the eternal and supersensible, unchanging universe was present at the origin of metaphysics, and persisted through the Middle Ages, even beyond the modern disillusionment with religion. With the decline of the religious worldview, the way was opened for a grounding of reality and truth in human beings—especially, the enduring truths revealed to human rationality. Now sense and intelligible order were to be attained by way of human reason and scientific logic.[29] Descartes' aspiration to invest philosophy with the certitude of a science was only further testimony to the search for order in rational principles. The power extended by technology to human beings similarly corroborated the appearance of human, calculative mastery over the environment as a whole.

At the end of this metaphysical tradition, phenomenologists despair of the worldview that places truth beyond history—whether such a worldview grounds truth within the realm of the supersensible world of ideals, or within the hierarchical order of divine creation, or, finally, within the dogmatic assertions of scientific rationality. There is a sense in which western philosophy has tired itself out in abstractions at the end of the metaphysical tradition, becoming strangely irrelevant to the challenges of daily human life. As philosophy strives to attain the certitude of science, metaphysics itself collapses into a reductionist mode of thinking that no longer admits poetic inspiration or artistic revelation within the domain of the academic discipline.

Phenomenology is, in some sense, a vocal reaction to and rethinking of the essence of the metaphysical tradition that we, of necessity, inherit in our modern world. Seeking to reawaken us to what Edmund Husserl called the richness of a lived-world "of essences of mental processes which are not abstracta but instead concreta," Husserl's aim in developing phenomenology as a "strict science" was to suspend all epistemological and metaphysical presuppositions to reveal the "things themselves" (*Sachen selbst*) as they are presented to us in our original and immediate experience of the world, prior to the construction of theories, dogma or preconceived hypotheses.[30]

Martin Heidegger, Husserl's student, inherited from his teacher the famous maxim of phenomenological thought: "To the things themselves!"[31] In his own unique language, Heidegger argued that the aim of phenomenology was "to let that which shows itself be seen from itself in the very way in which it shows itself from itself," namely, unadulterated by abstractions or unwarranted judgments.[32] By shedding light on the taken-for-granted, prepredicative origins upon which explicit theoretical reflection and scientific understanding are grounded, phenomenology emerges, according to Husserl, as "the secret nostalgia of all modern philosophy" and ultimately, as "first philosophy" itself.[33] Similarly for Heidegger, it is phenomenology as ontology that offers a way to uncovering the most fundamental, hidden ground of all questioning, that is, the meaning of Being itself.[34]

Phenomenology in a Postmodern World

As the twenty-first century draws to a close, phenomenology finds itself at the end of an era where the death of God is superseded even by the death of reason. Two world wars and the capability of global destruction serve as reminders that rational principles teeter at the edge of an inexplicable void and the mysteries of human passion. Strangely, in an era of overwhelming technological dependency and computerized mastery over the world, our doubt in the very power of reason that steered us to the current condition manifests itself both in New Age mysticism and postmodern skepticism. The death of a transcendent God momentarily opens the possibility of an alternate foundation in the principles of human reason. When it becomes evident, however, that human beings are guided by passions and instincts instead of simply intelligible principles, the measure and order grounded in immanent reason itself is threatened.

There are many thinkers who celebrate this moment in history. Freed from the authoritative shackles of metaphysical deity and abstraction alike, the possibility presents itself of a renewed awareness of our historical rootedness. Philosophy has finally recognized the futility of its pretense to being a universal science. In this respect, there is some promise of its recovering a sense of self by remaining open to the concreteness of the lived world—a world interpreted from within, rather than in terms of imported categories and rationalizations. Instead of seeking to impose a static, universal metaphysical structure upon the synergism of the natural world, the way remains open for a more receptive *listening* to the rich, variegated revelations of temporal meaning of a complex and dynamic cosmos. It is this very receptivity and openness that is celebrated by phenomenology itself.

Yet in the abandonment of intelligibility and reason lies a danger as well. The postmodernist fashion refuses the "consolation of correct forms."[35] War is declared on totality by postmodern thinkers who proceed to "work without rules."[36] In an era that lacks some of the structures of past centuries, the risk is that disorder may reign. The withdrawal of reason may manifest itself not only in the horrors of Nazi Germany, Rwanda, or Yugoslavia. As Werner Marx points out, another insidious danger looms, and this is the danger of indifference.[37] In a world with no reason and no apparent order or purpose, apathy may reign. Such apathy may find concrete expression in a disinterest for one's community, for other people, and for the environment. In the end, this disinterest threatens the very meaning of selfhood and the dignity of being human.

Inasmuch as it recovers the wonder that philosophy has forgotten, phenomenology offers a way of thought that neither collapses into a war against reason, nor abandons the concrete essence of the lived world. One of its primary tasks is to articulate essential meanings as they appear to human understanding. It seeks to discern underlying patterns of meaning that may not be self-evident but that permeate our efforts to interpret the world in which we find ourselves. In aspiring to more than a fixed system of theoretical conclusions, the phenomenological movement is a way of seeing the world that is never definitive but still aims to crystallize some essential truths in their historical and cultural rootedness.

While the phenomenological investigations of this volume make some appeal to experience instead of to abstract theoretical constructions, this does not mean that the book is merely one person's subjective account of elements of sustainability. It is a common misconception to conclude that phenomenology is simply an arbitrary, first-person recounting of facts as experienced by a lone subjectivity. For instance, in his otherwise thoughtful introduction to an anthology of phenomenological works, Robert Solomon describes phenomenology as a "first-person description . . . of one's own consciousness of the world."[38] This kind of account will then lead geographers like Hok-Lin Leung to conclude that "humanistic streams such as phenomenology . . . focus on consciousness."[39] Phenomenology, consequently, for this author "has severe limitations as a 'scientific' method because it emphasizes the unique, often at the expense of generalizations and verification."[40]

The problem with this kind of characterization of phenomenology is that it sets out a dichotomy between objective analysis of facts vs. arbitrary, subjective storytelling. As going beyond the metaphysical dualism of subject and object, phenomenology seeks to describe the originary belonging of human being-in-the-world that is ontologically prior to any subject/object split.[41] Phenomenology seeks to avoid both the immodesty of supratemporal, generalized claims about the world, but it equally avoids merely relativistic, first-person storytelling where "just anything goes."[42]

Thomas Nenon has it right, in my view, when he explains that phenomenology is about "the possibility of certain kinds of experiences which any reader should be able to recreate imaginatively on his or her own and thereby see that the possibility for such an experience is universal, even if the reality is not."[43] The phenomenological method is not, properly speaking, inductive, as it does not seek to catalog the frequency of experiences or to determine statistical correlations between past and future events. Nor is phenomenology a deduction of universal norms from logically necessary principles. Rather, "it exhibits possibilities *as* possibilities that any human being could undergo without claiming that in either a logical or empirical sense, they necessarily follow from certain other conditions."[44]

While the present volume, then, cannot presume to provide a cure-all manual of solutions to complex, interdisciplinary issues of sustainable development, the work takes the reader on a phenomenological journey that seeks to unearth some taken-for-granted assumptions and to provide some alternative visions of the essence of sustainability. Hopefully, readers will be led to critically examine some of their own assumptions and to see the world from alternative perspectives. These new perspectives, then, should serve to guide us along unique pathways that each of us travel in the effort to achieve sustainable development, locally and globally.

Paradigms, Attitudes, and Sustainable Development

Taking the cue from phenomenology, the goal of this book is to rethink "sustainable development" by questioning the foundations of current interpretations. Our attitudes are not something that we consciously superimpose upon our everyday activities. On the contrary, taken-for-granted assumptions shape the way that we view the world, and implicitly guide our decision-making on environmental matters. We may borrow a Cartesian image here: our thinking on environmental issues is like a tree.[45] The individual disciplines, from economics to chemistry, are like the branches. The trunk integrates these disciplines in the synthesis of ecology. The roots of the tree, however, take their nourishment from the soil of paradigms and attitudes that while hidden, nevertheless provide for the very existence of the tree. Unless we seek to comprehend better the essence of that soil, perhaps even modifying its structure, there is a growing fear that the tree itself can no longer be sustained.

A recent case in Canada shows the importance of taken-for-granted beliefs in environmental policy.[46] In 1985, the Canadian Minister of Agriculture cancelled the registration of the herbicide "alachlor," which had been used by Canadian corn and soybean farmers since 1969. Alachlor's original registration had been based upon toxicological studies performed by the scandal-ridden Industrial Biotest Laboratories, whose methods and results had been shown in some cases to be invalid. Consequently, the supplier, Monsanto Canada Inc., was asked to submit replacement studies to the Health Protection Branch (HPB) of Health and Welfare Canada. Based upon these new reports, as well as studies presented to HPB and to the Environmental Protection Agency in the United States, Health and Welfare Canada concluded that "alachlor is one of the most potent carcinogenic pesticides presently in use, and should be removed from the market as soon as possible."[47]

What is significant about this case is how the identical set of laboratory studies were differently interpreted by the various parties involved in the final policy decision. On the one hand, the government argued that the very *possibility* of carcinogenic risk was sufficient to warrant removal of alachlor from the market. Here, risk was seen as unacceptable in terms of an "absolute" standard of safety, independent of other relative risks or benefits. Risk assessment was also based on worst case scenarios: the safety of alachlor was to be based on those rare cases when protective clothing of applicators might not be worn or might for some reason be ineffective.

On the other hand, Monsanto countered that more attention needed to be paid to the *actual* degree of carcinogenic risk. The mere possibility of risk was to not to be considered in isolation from benefits and relative risks. For instance, economic benefits of alachlor to farmers had to be included in the risk assessment as well. Ultimately, the herbicide was not reinstated, even though the Review Board agreed with Monsanto that, while alachlor had been shown to be an *animal* carcinogen with tests on rats, it could only be considered a "potential" rather than "probable" human carcinogen.

Altogether, this case shows how risk assessment—based upon the identical set of "objective" scientific "facts"—nevertheless may result in a broad range of interpretations of the significance of those same facts. The phenomenological task, in such instances, would include illumining the taken-for-granted assumptions that impact, indirectly though pivotally, upon our explicit deliberations on environmental risk analysis.

Consider another example—one that sheds some light on the importance of prethematic attitudes underlying the suburbanite's well-cataloged dependency upon the automobile. The use of the car can be described operationally in terms of a factual inventory of how often the car is driven, for what purpose, for what duration, and so on. We can, in this way, delineate observable characteristics of the utility of the car for the suburbanite, which is often the task of the traffic engineer.

Yet we avoid in such descriptions what automobility *means* experientially for the lover of cars. Observing how and when others use their cars tells us something about car use, but it is not the whole story. In fact, although I may rationally "know" all the good reasons why I *should* leave my car at home and take the bus instead, I may deceive not only others but myself when I offer less than compelling rationales for taking the car. It is the task of phenomenology to seek to shed light on the deeper, experiential significance of what, in describing auto hegemony, Durning refers to eloquently as "carcooning."[48] I have found it illumining to run an experiment in a number of my environmental classes over the years, where I ask students to imagine that they have won a windfall lottery and can purchase the car of their choice. Later, they are inevitably embarrassed to recall their wildly enthusiastic descriptions of the automobile of their dreams—the very car that, on other occasions, they criticize as unsustainable.

But it is not only academics who recognize the need of a rethinking of hidden assumptions if we are to move toward our goal of sustainability. Public policy makers say much the same thing. Consider the example of the phenomenon of urban sprawl. The detrimental consequences of suburbs have been cataloged by numerous authors. The fundamental dependency upon the automobile is recognized to result in increased traffic congestion and environmental deterioration. Disappearance of prime agricultural land, increased infrastructure costs, and decline of the traditional nuclear family all point to the fundamental unsustainability of sprawl associated with traditional subdivision development.[49]

Because of these direct costs, many governments are adopting policies to encourage increased densities within urban and suburban communities. In Canada, and particularly in Southern Ontario, there is widespread government support for "intensification"; in the United States, a parallel concept is "growth management."[50] A serious obstacle to implementation of intensification policies, however, is being encountered in ratepayer opposition to any increase in housing density.[51] A 1991 poll suggests that on average, 39 percent and 36 percent of Canadians, prefer to live in "older" and "new" suburbs respectively, while only 22 percent prefer the downtown or inner city.[52] Consequently, in a discussion paper entitled "Reflections on Sustainable Planning," the Canadian Institute of Planners offers a number of specific recommendations:

- Review historical ideas, such as the garden cities. Why did they go wrong? What can we learn?
- Clarify the basis of public choice. Find out why people prefer low density suburbs.
- Use that information to make concentrated cities more liveable. Once you overcome the technical problems, how do you make concentrated cities attractive so that people will *want* to live there?[53]

Similarly, in the United States, the 1996 report of the President's Council on Sustainable Development recommends changes in fiscal planning that will help to counter sprawl. At the same time, the council explicitly recognizes that many Americans still do appear to prefer lower density suburban living to more technically sustainable, higher density alternatives and it encourages planners to take such preferences most seriously.[54]

As much as the public *explicitly* may recognize the technical environmental costs and unsustainability of low density development, on a more subtle level of attitudes, values and choices, that same public often is not prepared to choose the more sustainable alternatives associated with increased densities. Moreover, in the absence of a fundamental shift in public attitudes, governmental policies directed toward "intensification" risk remaining purely academic.

Similarly, in *Our Common Future*, the World Commission on Environment and Development recognizes the need of changing human values and attitudes toward the environment and development.[55] Inasmuch as inequality is cited by the commission to be the planet's main environmental and development problem, the affluent are charged with an obligation to adopt different lifestyles more in tune with the planet's ecological means: "Making the difficult choices involved in achieving sustainable development will depend on the widespread support and involvement of an informed public."[56] The crux of the problem, however, is clearly articulated when the question is asked: "How are individuals in the real world to be persuaded or made to act in the common interest?"[57]

Certainly, modifying human attitudes will require new strategies relating to education, public awareness, and institutional development. Before we make attempts to *change* human attitudes, however, we need to achieve a more comprehensive *understanding of the foundations* of such attitudes. This is where philosophy—and specifically phenomenology—may offer a significant contribution in seeking to bring those attitudes to light. It is important to remember, however, that these worldviews that phenomenology seeks to describe are more than individually willed, explicitly recognized opinions that one chooses to uphold following a lengthy process of reflection. Very few people take the time to carefully articulate and substantiate their value systems. I would argue that, even those individuals who do so, can never fully specify every moral precept because explicitly formulated judgments always occur within the *implicit* context of a human horizon of understanding. For instance, the very language we use "frames" the world in a structured way so that communication may occur. Although the frame is the condition of the possibility of understanding, it itself is not part of the picture. It must always serve as the ground of the explicit articulation. Otherwise, the articulation could not occur.

Kuhn persuasively demonstrated how tacit knowledge in the form of shared "paradigms" grounds meaningful discourse.[58] Although it may not be always evident, shared expectations regarding criteria for truth, language, rules, and standards for practice affect the evolution of acceptable methodologies within any particular tradition. Such paradigms provide the context for communication until the breakthrough of a genuine revolution overturns one worldview in favor of another.[59]

We may not often deliberate about the meaning and significance of these taken-for-granted horizons of understanding. The task of such self-reflection is hardly straightforward. Consider Gadamer's insight that, in the study of language, "we are seeking to approach the mystery of language from the conversation which we ourselves are."[60] Language may be learned but when it is appropriated as one's own, it defines our very Being-in-the-world. As such, language is not normally critically reflected upon but, rather, constitutes the very ground of our meaningful encounter with the world.

All in all, we all have our own personal opinions about people, events, and entities in our world. We each are able also to articulate our own set of explicit values on certain issues. More than this, we are culturally embedded and historically defined in terms of our taken-for-granted paradigms that serve as a framework for rules and principles guiding our actions. Even the language that we use to assign meanings provides the most fundamental, taken-for-granted horizon of understanding. We may not often reflect upon these implicit contexts of meaning. When we do so, however, we recognize that we simply could not *be* in their absence.

A major task for phenomenology is to help shed light on the foundations of deeply rooted human motives relating to sustainability and on how they are embedded in taken-for-granted historical and cultural worldviews. Accordingly, part I of this book begins the phenomenological journey by critically examining the calculative foundations of current paradigms of sustainable development. Part II provides an alternative horizon for discussions of sustainability from the perspective of phenomenology. Part III addresses the feasibility of holistic approaches to planning in a postmodern era and discusses how phenomenology may affect our understanding of sustainability beyond *Our Common Future*.

Overall, the reader may expect some overturning of commonly accepted values. A call may sound for coming to terms with certain finite demands that we would prefer to deny. Some results will necessarily remain inconclusive. On the other hand, we may hope to make some progress in raising awareness and in uprooting some unsustainable patterns of living. It is in an effort to reawaken philosophical questioning of the foundations of a sustainable future that this book has been written.

2

The Brundtland Report and Limits of Techne

Sustainable development seems assured of a place in the litany of development truisms,
but to what extent does it express convergent, rather than divergent, intellectual traditions?
—Michael Redclift, *Sustainable Development*

When an original text emerges as a seminal work, its very richness incites a variety of interpretations. In the repetition of the messages, the original work is sometimes enlarged. In other cases, the popularized perspectives diminish the innovation and significance of the initial text. In 1987, the World Commission on Environment and Development prepared their seminal work entitled *Our Common Future*.[1] In a very real sense, this book can be seen as one of the most significant in our century because it presented visionary descriptions of central problems and opportunities of sustainable development.[2]

But the book did more. It focused public attention on these issues, as no document before had done. To be sure, other discussions had addressed the concept earlier.[3] It was, however, the *Brundtland Report* (as it came to be called, in recognition of Norwegian commission chairman Gro Harlem Brundtland) that popularized sustainable development as "development which meets the needs of the present without compromising the ability of future generations to meet their own needs."[4]

While the term is now commonplace, some distinctive accomplishments of the report have been downplayed in ensuing appropriations of the original text. For instance, the commission wisely chose to avoid forecasts for the future or rigid, top-down blueprints for action. Fifteen years earlier, The Club of Rome had published *The Limits to Growth*, similarly seeking to examine "the complex of problems troubling men of all nations."[5] The foundation for the conclusions of The Club of Rome's "Project on the Predicament of Mankind," however, was the fearless, if not presumptuous, development of a "formal, written model of the world."[6] Ultimately, the authors did admit that "[w]e would not expect the real world to behave like the world model in any of the graphs we have shown,

17

especially in the collapse modes."[7] Yet the underlying dependency upon computerized technology and mathematical models, as well as the forecasts of global disaster, seemed to have the insidious effect of portraying the image of the "expert" who, once and for all, had fordained the end of the world.

By contrast, eight years later, former chancellor of the Federal Republic of Germany Willy Brandt, chaired a commission that produced *North-South: A Program for Survival*. In a more conciliatory and constructive tone, the report presented a dialogue among eighteen commission members from five continents. Despite disparate convictions, they were able to come to "share a common vision of the kind of world we hoped for."[8] Recognizing that the "shaping of our common future is much too important to be left to governments and experts alone," the commission appealed to a broad range of groups, from youth and women to technicians and managers, to work collectively to free humankind from dependence and oppression and to achieve "freedom, justice and solidarity for all."[9]

This book was positive and hopeful: "hope itself is the most important element in overcoming obstacles."[10] In many respects, this publication foreshadowed the careful approach of the Brundtland Report, which avoided the pretensions of "expert predictions," seeking instead to "serve notice" of the need for change and to suggest "*a pathway* by which the peoples of the world may enlarge their spheres of co-operation."[11] Rather than concocting a sectoral, specialist's vision of another utopian or dystopian reality, *Our Common Future* aimed to illumine underlying conditions for sustainable human progress and survival, paving the way for the implementation of more comprehensive ecological policies and programs. Some critics felt that it was precisely because the Brundtland Report did not present an expert's manual of do's and don'ts, that too little was specified in a precise way. As Dunstan, Jope, and Swan reported, "in the speak-easy world of politics, sustainability is popular precisely because of its lack of meaning."[12] Yet these same authors recognized, as did the Brundtland Commission, that sustainability is more than a set of techniques that can be mechanically applied according to edicts from a handbook. Just as being a respectful person cannot be accomplished by some set of precise rules, there are no preset standards that lead to sustainability.[13] That the Brundtland Report was sensitive to the limits of imposing top-down models or other uncompromising solutions to complex problems, is very much to its credit.

More significantly, *Our Common Future* recognized the limits of sectoral, one-dimensional approaches and the importance of interconnections in the struggle to delineate sustainable programs of action. "The environment does not exist," they wrote, "as a sphere separate from human actions, ambitions, and needs."[14] The commission clearly acknowledged the links between environmental, economic, social, and political factors:

For example, the rapid population growth that has so profound an impact on the environment and on development in many regions is driven partly by such factors as the status of women in society and other cultural values. Also, environmental stress and uneven development can increase social tensions. It could be argued that the distribution of power and influence within society lies at the heart of most environment and development challenges. Hence, new approaches must involve programmes of social development.[15]

This broad interpretation meant that problems of sustainability are neither bounded by sectoral disciplines nor by local regions but, rather, are global in character.[16] In the words of Canadian member of Parliament Charles Caccia at a WCED Public Hearing, "how long can we go on and safely pretend that the environment is not the economy, is not health, is not the prerequisite to development, is not recreation?"[17] As for discussion of an environmental or energy or development crisis, "they are all one."[18]

Again to the commission's credit, the report recognized that sustainable development is not to be understood as a fixed state of harmony but, instead, involves a process whereby changes must accommodate both present and future needs.[19] Rather than construct a static or exhaustive picture of the future, *Our Common Future* recognized the role of time and change within discerning sustainable programs of action. The report appreciated that sustainability was not a consummate, hypostatized *end product*, to be once and for all achieved in any idyllic community. Instead, by virtue of *temporal process*, continuing challenges relating to the unprecedented growth of cities would mean that new pathways to sustainability would continue to evolve:

> Security must be sought through change. . . . We have no illusions about "quick-fix" solutions. We have tried to point out some pathways to the future. But there is no substitute for the journey itself, and there is no alternative to the process by which we retain a capacity to respond to the experience it provides.[20]

The commission also emphasized that, on the way to sustainability, *local* processes were crucial in determining appropriate solutions, in parallel with broad global concerns. Recognizing how standardized interpretations risked remaining oblivious to the nuances of many regional problems, the commission noted the importance of being open to the specific needs arising by virtue of local conditions. While technical assistance was still required from central agencies, local customs, urban patterns, social priorities and environmental conditions deserved foremost respect.[21]

Significantly, there was explicit recognition of a fact that many environmentalists had denied over the past several decades—the inevitability of the "urban revolution." Since 1950, the number of people living in cities has almost tripled. In the less-developed world, the figure has quadrupled to 1.14 billion.[22] The Brundtland Commission saw that the solution to ecological problems arising from increasing urbanization trends could no longer consist of a romanticized call for a "return to nature," in the remnants of a frontier mentality. Instead, the necessary interrelation between urban and ecological concerns was explicitly recognized: "Rural and urban development strategies and approaches should be complementary rather than contradictory."[23]

It is worth remembering that in 1972, the United Nations organized the first major conference on the environment in Stockholm; three years later, the Habitat Conference on Human Settlements convened in Vancouver. One could logically infer, then, that environmental and settlement issues were disparate concerns. Indeed, to this day, that heritage of separateness remains, in the sense that UNEP (United Nations Environment Program) and UNCHS (United Nations Centre for Human Settlements) operate as distinct entities with independent mandates. Yet *Our Common Future* wisely emphasizes that "environment and development are not separate challenges; they are inexorably linked. Development cannot subsist upon a deteriorating environmental resource base; the environment cannot be protected when growth leaves out of account the costs of environmental destruction."[24]

Overall, the Brundtland Report constitutes a rethinking of values relating to such issues as urbanization; the role of women and indigenous peoples; economics; and definitions of justice and equity.[25] The report makes important contributions to these and many other issues through a comprehensive approach motivated by a genuine search for a balanced and positive treatment of a broad range of concerns. Other past reports have unilaterally forecast that all ultimate "limits to growth on this planet will be reached sometime within the next one hundred years."[26] *Our Common Future* takes a less dramatized, measured approach when it sensibly concludes that, while there are ultimate limits, nonetheless, "[d]ifferent limits hold for the use of energy, materials, water and land."[27] There is the possibility that the "accumulation of knowledge and the development of technology can enhance the carrying capacity of the resource base" as much as there is the possibility of a total apocalypse within finite constraints.[28]

The encouraging outcome of the Brundtland Report is that it offers some promise of survival and environmental enhancement within the balanced vision of sustainability. This in itself becomes a courageous move in an era where optimism is viewed as mere naïveté.[29] The gift of *Our Common Future* is, in the end, the immeasurable gift of increased awareness, and indeed, the very rare gift of purpose, of elemental challenge, and of hope.

Questioning Assumptions

Yet, as much as it accomplished, the Brundtland Report is not beyond reproach. The commission members set a course but, in so doing, one can argue that they merely provided a scaffold upon which further work and thought were to be founded. Or is it the case, perhaps, that the scaffold itself needs reconstruction?

Despite the broad and pervasive influence of the Brundtland Report, support for it has not been unequivocal. Many environmentalists have openly and actively condemned it, denouncing the underlying ethic as primarily based upon western, Eurocentric standards. While *Our Common Future* recognized that some of the most urgent challenges are in the developing countries, critics charge that members of the commission failed to address the broader implications of their own statements.[30] Overall, the Brundtland Report is seen to constitute "an enthusiastic and unquestioning reaffirmation of the system, lifestyles and values that are causing the problems under discussion."[31]

The very term "sustainable development" has been the focus of much criticism, inasmuch as it has been repeatedly linked to notions of economic growth, material wealth, and technological progress.[32] Viederman charges that "we use the words [growth and development] interchangeably, based explicitly or implicitly on the assumption that there are no limits or that they are far off and therefore largely irrelevant."[33] Altogether, as Palmer notes,

> a number of developing country and environmental organizations and individuals claim that the commission's definition of development is highly contentious. They argue that analysis and recommendations are based on its particular conception of development and furthermore, on economic growth and a prescription for imposing a western standard of living on all of the world's people, irrespective of their needs and desires.[34]

For instance, consider the Brundtland Report's explanation of how needs are to be met on a sustainable basis for fisheries and tropical forestry. One reads that "sustainable yield from these stocks may well fall short of demand."[35] It will consequently be necessary to "turn to methods that produce more fish, fuelwood and forest products under controlled conditions."[36] Such a scenario, critics argue, implies that successful sustainable management is equivalent to more sophisticated manipulation and control of resources.[37] Yet it is precisely such heavy-handed efforts to command and dominate nature that have often led to the exploitation and denigration of the environment in the first place.

The commission's notion of "maximum sustainable yield" similarly signals an attitude whereby nature is subject to quantification and to evaluation in terms of maximum utility for the good of human beings only.[38] In this respect, critics argue that the call for sustainable development remains essentially anthropocentric and utilitarian. The very definition of sustainable development as meeting the needs of the present without compromising the ability of *future generations* to meet their own needs is, they argue, a challenge of environmental care based principally upon *human* concerns.[39] Again, it is this very egocentric frame of reference that has brought us to the current state of unsustainable living, and that, therefore, may need to be reevaluated.

Are these criticisms justified? The Brundtland Commission does appear to support the status quo, if that means that many assumptions remain rooted in the overriding *Weltanschauung* of the western, technological epoch. In the commission's defense, however, it requires extraordinary courage and endurance to attempt to overturn a tradition in which one remains immersed. We shall see later how even those critics who advocate such a radical upheaval often, inadvertently, continue the very metaphysical tradition they explicitly reject. In the end, though, it is hard to dispute the fact that *Our Common Future* has played a significant role in raising environmental awareness among the general populace. The book has served as a catalyst for a renewed, international commitment to the challenges of sustainable development. More importantly, more than a decade beyond its publication, the work continues to inspire dialogue on the specifics of sustainability. Such dialogue, as we shall see, must include serious phenomenological investigation of the unquestioned paradigms that continue to affect environmental policy.

The Place of Calculative Thought

While they may differ on questions of nature and degree, both the Brundtland Commission and its critics acknowledge the need of rethinking the foundations of our current belief systems. The commission itself explicitly states that "the changes in human attitudes that we call for depend on a vast campaign of education, debate, and public participation. This campaign must start now if sustainable human progress is to be achieved."[40] Taking up an even more nonconformist stand, *Our Common Future* tells us that "the time has come to break out of past patterns. Attempts to maintain social and ecological stability through old approaches to development and environmental protection will increase instability. Security must be sought through change."[41]

One guide that may start us on such a task of breaking out of past patterns is found in the work of Martin Heidegger, a phenomenological philosopher who devoted his life to moving beyond our metaphysical tradition. In his early works, Heidegger introduced a unique and thought-provoking interpretation of the meaning of history.[42] History was seen to consist of more than the recitation of a series of specific events and relics from the past. A historical tradition was, on the contrary, handed down and appropriated by human beings subtly, often without explicit reflection upon the inherited horizons of meaning and taken-for-granted paradigms. In this sense, history was seen by Heidegger to consist of more than a clearly demarcated "object of contemplation," as in a well-defined history curriculum.[43] Instead, the very essence of being human is history. One could not *be* in the absence of history and time. Human existence is understood by Heidegger as historicity itself.[44]

Heidegger hardly intended to be intentionally esoteric or obscurantist in such a statement. As we have seen, he maintained that, in the modern, technological epoch, western society had inherited assumptions and worldviews from a metaphysical tradition whose roots extended as far back as ancient Greek philosophy. This inheritance was not to be understood as an inheritance only of deliberately selected, explicit terms or concepts. Rather, it consisted of unquestioned assumptions, and taken-for-granted interpretations of what was real, or what was true. These assumptions, then, were seen as providing the context for our explicit undertakings, and the prism through which specific values and attitudes were colored.

More specifically, when Plato defined Being in terms of immutal forms, he grounded a western philosophical tradition that was to favor beings or specific, material entities over Being itself.[45] To this day, such a worldview persists, according to Heidegger. Pervasively, what is real is that which is empirically defined and capable of measurement. This description can only apply to positively existing things, but not to Being which is seen to be vague, mystical, vaporous, and ultimately meaningless.[46]

In what Heidegger described as an essentially calculative, metaphysical worldview, the modern technological era becomes predominantly one that values quantification and technical efficiency over less precise, qualitative assessments of meaning.[47] This emphasis is problematic to the degree that calculation becomes the exclusive way of thought in contemporary society. Heidegger does not suggest that quantification has no value. Rather, he denies that it is the only legitimate descriptor of meaning and truth.

He describes two kinds of thinking—the calculative and the meditative—each possessing its own merit.[48] In calculation, one studies, organizes, and computes explicitly given, empirical realities without pausing to inquire originatively about the essential meanings that sustain these investigations. Calculation seeks to order and classify objects that are clearly delimited and defined piecemeal. So, for example, I might describe the forest in terms of the clearly quantifiable market value of its lumber, or in terms of the visible parameters of the landscape or the number of animal species that it contains. I may even describe the forest as a specific resource that requires efficient management of its individual components, or as an aesthetically beautiful object of contemplation, where "the essence and reality of art dissolve into nervous states, into processes in the nerve cells" and art is reduced to a physiological state of rapture.[49]

Meditative thinking, on the other hand, does not simply seek to compute *things* but, rather, it is more oriented toward investigating the complexity of relations among things and even the sometimes mysterious, indeterminate context and interpretive horizon within which specific entities find their place and their meaning. In meditative thinking, Heidegger tells us that "we can affirm the unavoidable use of technical devices and also deny them the right to dominate us, and so to warp, confuse and lay waste our nature."[50] Rather than calculatively impose, at all costs, definitions and classifications upon the richness of the world, meditative thinking returns us to an originative contemplation of the grace of existence and the recognition that all things in the universe are not present merely for the sake of their utility and for our control. Humility accompanies such originative thinking. The ecosystem of the forest is no longer seen merely in terms of its resource potential and the number of planks that it might produce, but, perhaps, it is now seen as sacred and not capable of substitution in replanted tree farms—even if the number of trees replanted are equal to the number destroyed in lumber production.

I do not mean to suggest here, that meditative thinking inspires inaction—purely contemplative awe of existence or poetic reverie, in place of sound, environmental management practices. On the other hand, Heidegger helps us to recognize that in modern times, we have become expert specifically in one type of thinking only, and that is *techne*—so that not only things but other people come to be seen, exclusively or primarily, within the horizon of calculation. A case in point was provided to me by a social scientist at a recent environmental workshop. She argued that all aspects concerning human perceptions and values (her research area) could be quantified and statistically measured. She adamantly maintained that what was at first sight nonquantifiable could be translated into calculative terms without any loss of meaning. I wondered whether her conclusion applied, also, to the experiential depth of her love for her children.

I would argue that the full experience of being human exceeds the reductionist limits of calculative thought. While human beings can themselves be classified according to statistical measures, Heidegger is right to guide us beyond quantifiable models to a more holistic understanding of the meaning of Being.[51] In this respect, while the Brundtland Report is avowedly anthropocentric and human beings come first, this does not necessarily mean that humans have been well understood and their needs comprehensively identified. The irony of *Our Common Future* is that a foundational knowledge of the meaning of Being-human, is largely absent.

"Essential human needs" are restricted to a calculative inventory of poverty, employment, food, housing, water supply, sanitation, and health care.[52] Acknowledging that there has been a retreat from social concerns in the present decade, *Our Common Future* nonetheless denigrates genuine human concerns by its persistent references to human beings in terms of human *resources*.[53] To be a human being is to be more than a mere "resource" or even "the ultimate resource." Webster's defines "resource" as "an available means."[54] Other people are more than mere means to achieve utilitarian ends, as Martin Buber knew well. He wrote:

> When I confront a human being as my You and speak the basic word I-You to him, then he is no thing among things, nor does he consist of things. . . .

Even as a melody is not composed of tones, nor a verse of words, nor a statue of lines—one must pull and tear to turn a unity into a multiplicity—so it is with the human being to whom I say You. I can abstract from him the colour of his hair or the colour of his speech or the colour of his graciousness; I have to do this again and again; but immediately, he is no longer You.[55]

To be human is to be other than a very important object, held together by an inventory of sectoral "needs," personality traits, or physical descriptors. Paradoxically, though, it is precisely in a predominantly *subjectivistic* epoch that humans come to be denigrated to the level of *objects*, resources, or mere statistics. How is such a dualism of subjectivism and objectivism to be explained?

Subjectivism and Objective Truth

Heidegger believed that the overriding subjectivism of our times was well grounded in a famous motto, *Cogito, ergo sum*, arising from the work of the father of modern philosophy, René Descartes.[56] Descartes aimed to secure modern philosophical thinking in a firm, unshakeable foundation, just as he perceived that science was built upon such a foundation of certitude and exactitude. In reading Descartes' works, one senses the full breadth of his disillusionment with centuries of philosophical speculation that, in the end, could offer no conclusive proof of the existence of God, of the soul, or even, for that matter, of physical reality either.[57] Inspired by the accomplishments of modern-day science, Descartes was determined to ground philosophy, once and for all, in what he saw was to be a "certain and indubitable" foundation.[58] Once that foundation was secured, he reasoned, it would be possible to logically build upon it a metaphysic beyond dispute.

The problem, of course, was to determine what that indubitable foundation might be. Could it be found in the existence of the material world? Descartes reasoned that instances of optical illusions or even our dreams in sleep could trick us into believing that something existed when, in fact, it did not.[59] Often, one could be deceived by inaccurate perceptions, so, clearly, the existence of material objects (including my own body, as material entity) could not constitute an indubitable philosophical starting point. Inconclusive ontological proofs for the existence of God showed that even His existence could not be proven, once and for all, to the satisfaction of sceptics.[60] The more that Descartes sought an indubitable starting point for his new mode of philosophy, grounded in certitude, the more he was driven to recognize that the only reality that could not be doubted was the process of doubting itself. On that account, Descartes believed that he had discovered his indubitable starting point: *Cogito, ergo sum.* I think; therefore, I am.

This grounding of all philosophical truth in the human subject cannot be written off today as a mere quirk of a single philosopher. On the contrary, Descartes is known as the father of modern thought precisely on account of his subjectivist metaphysic—a metaphysic that has come to define our western way of life. No longer grounded in the ancient Greek cosmology, nor in the medieval, religious faith in the Creator, the modern worldview that comes to pervade western culture particularly, is one where humans come first. Descartes' vision is simply a paradigmatic moment that gathers together and articulates a way of being that is peculiarly definitive of modern, Western society as egocentric.

At the same time, Heidegger believes that it is no accident that Descartes described the foundational human subjectivity as "*a thing that thinks* . . . that is to say, a thing that doubts, perceives, affirms, denies, wills, does not will, that imagines also, and which feels."[61] Such statements confirm, for Heidegger, the implicit, Cartesian definition of human beings *as objects*, secured through a methodology that Descartes describes as his attempt "to be a spectator rather than an actor."[62] Eventually, Descartes argues for the objective reality of corporeal substance and the quantification of the empirically verifiable physical world.

So, as subjectivistic as this epoch appears to be, it is, strangely, also one that is objectivistic at the same time. In a predominantly subjectivist era, truth is defined primarily in terms of objective, scientific evidence.[63] This dualism of subjectivism and objectivism is, according to Heidegger, hardly coincidental. "Certainly," says Heidegger, "the modern age has, as a consequence of the liberation of man, introduced subjectivism and individualism. But it remains just as certain that no age before this one has produced a comparable objectivism. . . . Essential here is the necessary interplay between subjectivism and objectivism."[64]

Objectivity only makes sense in relation to subjectivity. The nature of a dualistic relation is such that the meaning of one requires the other. For instance, consider what it means to say that a scientific truth is *objectively real*. It signifies nothing less than to be clearly manifest within circumscribed limits—in Heidegger's words, to be grasped as picture (*Bild*) in relation to a positing subject. When we say that "we get the picture," we mean that something stands before us and is grasped as a cohesive whole.[65] "What is, in its entirety," writes Heidegger, "is now taken in such a way that it first is in being and only is in being to the extent that it is set up by man, who represents and sets forth."[66] Such a systematic re-presentation (*Vorstellung*) of the world aims at completeness. By means of such a hypostatization and reductionist manipulation, the calculative paradigm aims to secure and control, in a value-free, objective representation, what might otherwise be a far more confusing synergistic, nonlinear givenness of the lived world.

In this sense, Heidegger explains, human beings become "the relational center of that which is as such," even in the quest for objective certitude.[67] The so-called objective laws of natural science originate *within us* as hypotheses and abstractions. In this sense, what I eventually see in the world as true is dependent upon the projections of conceptual frameworks that guide my seeing.[68] Such a predominant world picture provides the frame for the implicit assumptions that color my interactions with the world.

Moreover, it is by virtue of a *correspondence* between the subjective idea and its objective correlate that calculative thinking seeks truth. The appearance of truth is restricted to the phenomenon of correctness and the "accordance" between the subject's statement or belief and empirically tangible objects.[69] Only inasmuch as the essent is objectified in a re-presenting (*Vor-stellen*) before oneself, can calculation ensure certitude and security of a particular visualization of reality. "Man contends for the position in which he can be that particular being who gives the measure and draws up the guidelines for everything that is."[70]

This is particularly evident in terms of the goals of much, modern-day technology. Heidegger suggests that the essence of such technology is a challenging (*Herausfordern*) that aims to "regulate and secure" the natural world.[71] Rather than cultivating in terms of "taking care of and maintaining," the field is now set-in-order as a resource that can produce the greatest possible return.[72] "Agriculture is now the mechanized food industry. Air is now set upon to yield nitrogen, the earth to yield ore, ore to yield uranium, for example; uranium is set upon to yield atomic energy, which can be released either for destruction or for peaceful use."[73]

In a technological era, the Rhine is dammed up into the hydroelectric plant to supply water power—or else, the river becomes an "object on call for inspection" by tour groups and the vacation industry.[74] The world becomes an object to be regulated by the human will. A bank of elevators guarantees that my wait to ascend the high rise will not be too long. Gigantic grocery stores place all my potential buying needs within a single, enclosed space for my easy access. Water and electricity are supplied without interruption, so that both appear to be endlessly available. Any shortages are rare and, when they occur, they are particularly annoying in a society that aims to secure the world as "standing-reserve" or stock, ever ready for human consumption.[75]

Heidegger's critique of technology is far reaching. On the other hand, beyond the criticism, he does admit that the contemporary technological worldview "cannot exhaust itself solely in blocking . . . all appearing of truth. Rather, precisely the essence of technology must harbor in itself the growth of the saving power."[76] Heidegger does not explore in detail the positive promises of technology as much as he leads his readers in a critical review of the dangers of modern conceptions of *techne*. He is able also to reveal what, for many of us, still continue to be hidden assumptions about the relation of humans to their environment. Heidegger's phenomenological uncovering of these assumptions on the essence of technology constitutes a vital moment in our understanding of the dangers and promises of sustainable development policies as well, particularly to the extent that these policies are grounded in the calculative worldview that Heidegger describes.

Technical Efficiency of Production

Another characteristic of calculative thinking is its reliance on an overall goal of technical efficiency. This means that calculation is goal oriented: "we can count on definite results."[77] Calculation is purposeful activity; thus any activity that produces no quantifiable outputs is deemed to be unproductive, wasteful, and contrary to reason. This adherence to calculation helps to explain why art and poetry—particularly if they are not financially lucrative pursuits—may appear to have little utility for their own sake, compared to professional and scientific endeavors. The specter of calculative thinking may also shed some light on the compulsive *busyness* of society today: the test of the good life is often measured against the number of concrete tasks accomplished rather than in terms of the overall quality of experience.

Such predominant goal orientation finds expression at many levels in society. Consider, for instance, one aspect of our everyday relationship to technology. In order to drive, I do not normally require a thorough working knowledge of my car's engine; all I demand of it is that it reliably *run*. Clearly, a simple tool—say, a pen—becomes a means directed toward an end beyond itself—in this case, the written word. With advanced technology, however, the increased complexity of the technology distances me even more from the immediate workings of such technology, so that the goal of the technology becomes central. Technology becomes magical: I do not know how something works and I never need to know, as long as it performs the functions that I expect.

With the increasing complexity of the mechanized world, we cannot individually know *how* all technologies function. We do, however, expect that they will function and that they will produce the results for which they have been designed. This is our new religion—our faith in reliable technological production. Policy analyst David Wann recalls his conversation with Princeton scientist Robert Socolow, who laments how modern society intentionally perpetuates "consumer humiliation by breeding dependence on systems we can't understand, control, diagnose, repair or modify."[78] The degree to which we depend upon the definite results of equipment only becomes evident with the breakdown of technological systems. A power failure becomes an education in our existential dependency upon complex systems, the essence of which most individuals cannot fully comprehend.

Our reliance upon efficiency of production does not extend only to machines, however. Take the example of our relation to domestic duty. In a calculative era, the goal of housework is seen in the light of quick and easy results. From advanced vaccuums to easy-care appliances to services that provide a team to clean your home in record time, the goal is minimal commitment to an arduous physical task. Who can complain? Certainly this is an accomplishment of the age rather than any kind of a drawback.

Yet, something is lost in the process. Gaston Bachelard describes an alternative vision that arises when *techne* no longer defines domestic care:

And so, when a poet rubs a piece of furniture—even vicariously—when he puts a little fragrant wax on his table with the woolen cloth that lends warmth to everything it touches, he creates a new object; he increases the object's human dignity; he registers this object officially as a member of the human household. . . . Objects that are cherished in this way really are born of an intimate light, and they attain to a higher degree of reality than indifferent objects, or those that are defined by geometric reality. . . . From one object in a room to another, housewifely care weaves the ties that unite a very ancient past to the new epoch. The housewife awakens furniture that was asleep.[79]

To some critics, this may be a mere romanticizing of thankless domestic chores. Today, who has time to polish the silver candle sticks? Dip them instead in the liquid silver cleaner and revel instantly in the shiny surface! In a goal-oriented epoch, time itself becomes a commodity to be managed efficiently in order that tasks be accomplished most productively.

Techne and Actualitas

Another characteristic of calculative thinking is that it assumes that something is true if it is *actual*. Heidegger describes how we typically distinguish true gold from false. "False gold is not actually what it appears to be. It is merely a 'semblance' and thus is not actual."[80] Inasmuch as Being comes to be interpreted in terms of *actualitas*, the real is defined as that which can be seen, felt, touched, and empirically measured. It is distinguished from the imaginary as the objective is distinguished from subjective illusion.

The seeds of such an interpretation of truth and reality were at least partly planted inadvertently by Aristotle, who in his *Metaphysics* distinguished between *ens reale*, Real Being, and *ens rationis*, Conceptual Being.[81] The reference to Real Being signified that which was actual—that which possessed real and positive existence and was empirically accessible to experience. Conceptual Being, on the other hand, referred to that which possessed existence of some sort, but primarily "within the mind." For instance, if we were to state that "Le Corbusier's Ideal City consisted of the *Ville Radieuse*," this would constitute a true proposition about something that was never built in reality. The proposition about this nonexisting thing was seen to "be" in some sense, and therefore, qualified as "Being," but it was understood to refer to something that never existed in *actual fact*.

By medieval times, the Aristotelean distinction had led to the conclusion that "conceptual entities" were restricted not only to propositions and thoughts. Also included were all privations, absences, and entities that could not be subjected to empirical measures. St. Thomas Aquinas provided the classic example. He described the physical privation of blindness by explaining how blindness itself is not real: while the eye and the cataract are real, the blindness itself, argued Aquinas, the not-seeing, "is" an entity only insofar as the proposition "the eye does not see" may be true.

In reflecting upon a similar case in the field of human settlements, we might consider an example offered by Louise Million in her fascinating account of the meaning of involuntary displacement for a group of ranching families who had to leave their land that had been flooded by the construction of a dam.[82] One might imagine a house by Alberta's Oldman River Dam; both the house and the dam are "real" entities, according to the Thomistic understanding. But then the land is expropriated and residents are displaced as the dam is flooded. The house is demolished, and so we say, "the house no longer exists there."

While originally the house and the dam both were real, positive entities, ultimately, following the demolition of the house, only the dam remains so. *The absence of the house* cannot be seen, touched, or experienced in the same way as the house itself was when it stood by the dam. Therefore, it falls into the medieval thinker's second category, *ens rationis*. Yet, the "absence of house" indicates more than mere conceptual being, more than mere propositional truth. It may well indicate the end of an entire way of life for the family who occupied the house—the destruction of a home and a center from which all other life activities emanated.

In *Being and Nothingness*, Jean-Paul Sartre refers to an example that reveals a major flaw in the Thomistic way of thinking about Being and existence.[83] He offers the case of looking for Pierre in a café. Pierre is *not there*; but Pierre's absence is quite different from the absence from the café of the unexpected person of Napolean Bonaparte, for instance. I have expected to find Pierre, and my expectation is not met. This absence of Pierre from the café will affect my life quite differently from the absence of Napoleon, whom I did not expect to see in the first place. In other words, the difference rests on *meaning* and the significance of expectation and anticipation.

Philosopher William Barrett, similarly, sees problems with Aquinas' blindness example. He asks us to conceive of the case of a man who wakes up one morning, only to find that he is blind:

> He has fallen into a great black pit, his whole life has been swallowed up in a darkness. Non-seeing, a privation, has descended on him with more crushing effect than brick from a rooftop. Roaring with anguish, he crashes and stumbles about his room. A doctor arrives, and examines his eyes. If the doctor philosophizes in the manner of Aristotle, St. Thomas or Carnap, he will observe: the eyes are real, and the growth over the eyes is a real substance, but

the non-seeing of the eye is itself not an object, and therefore, not an *ens reale*, a real entity. And if doctors still know Latin or if this one has a slight touch of Molière, he may even pompously and soothingly quote St. Thomas: 'Caecitas non habet esse in rebus' (Blindness has no being in things.)[84]

The doctor, Barrett muses, deserves to be prevented from leaving the room, so that he might be subjected firsthand to the blind man's wrath. This doctor's language, "for all its Latin gravity, is humanly frivolous; and what is humanly frivolous ought to be somehow and somewhere philosophically wrong too."[85] For the blind man, his blindness could very well be the *non-esse realissimum* of his entire life.

What these examples show is that, when a tradition locates real Being exclusively in the positively existing object and material entities, the tradition becomes detached from complexities of meanings associated with the very essence of being human. The calculative way of thought, which locates truth and reality only in positively existing, measurable objects, threatens to obscure a fundamental ontological significance of the phenomenon of absence, of the fundamentally incalculable, of the fluidity, dynamism, and unpredictability of *relations among* entities.

For instance, one reads in the Brundtland Report that the world produces more food per head of population today than ever before in human history. Yet 730 million people did not eat enough to lead fully productive working lives.[86] We tend to locate the fact of insufficiency of food—and sometimes its sheer absence—to the level of an abstract proposition or a statistical number. Instead, we might consider the existential meaning of hunger: we might recognize that 730 million people's entire lives were handicapped under the shadow of famine and the depression, outrage, and indignity of unsatisfied human needs. An ethical challenge begins to emerge here, of moving beyond calculation to comprehend the full human significance of the absence of food. Hunger may not be an *ens reale*, an *actual* material entity. However, entire lives continue to be defined by lack and need, far beyond propositional truth claims.

Causality and Linear Thinking

It is significant that our western Christian inheritance teaches us that God is *actus purus*—pure actuality perpetually fulfilled. In fact, God is not only the highest reality but the *supreme cause* of all existents. By virtue of our metaphysical tradition in modern calculative thinking, we similarly continue to seek explanations of phenomena by way of an identification of their cause. The result is that in our search for understanding in terms of cause and effect, we inquire in a linear fashion. B. F. Skinner's reductionist explanation of human behavior in terms of stimulus-response mechanisms is a case in point. Similarly, Freud sought to explain symptoms of neurosis or personality disorders by virtue of their direct causes in the past.[87]

In such a scenario, the *openness of the future* as sheer possibility cannot truly be accommodated. By way of example, consider the following passage from Dostoevsky's *Notes from Underground*. The author muses, in cynical fashion,

> I am a sick man. . . . I am a spiteful man. I am an unattractive man. I believe my liver is diseased. However, I know nothing at all about my disease, and do not know for certain what ails me. . . . I refuse to consult a doctor from spite. . . . I used to be in the government service but am no longer. I was a spiteful official. . . . I was lying when I said just now that I was a spiteful official. I was lying from spite.[88]

Dostoevsky's hero is not willing to be defined by preset categories. His spite is testimony to the impossibility of reducing the complexity of being human to linear cause-effect models.[89] We read that "spite, of course, might overcome everything, all my doubts, and so might serve quite successfully in place of a primary cause, precisely because it is not a cause."[90] The hero's stand is in the name of freedom and in a refusal to be defined by any psychologist's naive presumptions and simplistic categories. Is this stand ultimately not common to each and every one of us?

The linearity inherent in causal explanations closes us off to the essence of freedom and individuality no less than to the truth of art, the revelations of chaos theory in mathematics, or Einsteinian relativity theory. In reflecting upon the meaning of sustainability, we must remember, too, that ecology teaches that environmental relations are diverse, synergistic formations—more complex than we can know in a simplistic linear mode of causal analysis.

Calculative thinking, according to Heidegger, is also inherently manipulative, and seeks to control. In such a mode of thinking, I may attempt to understand a human being by identifying prior conditions that may have influenced specific impulses. So, for instance, I may analyze dreams, or slips of the tongue, or similar behavioral errors to control *future* forms of behavior.[91] I may explain human actions in terms of a hypostatized Human Nature—a static, predetermined given to be understood, categorized, and ultimately managed through controlled therapy or drug treatments. All in all, the other is seen as an object whose predestined behavior is predictable and, ultimately, subject to manipulation.

It is not only other people whom we seek to control within the calculative paradigm. Nature itself becomes something that we feel we can "tame and direct."[92] Heidegger reminds us that in a technical relation of human beings to their environment, "nature becomes a gigantic gasoline station."[93] The world becomes a standing reserve, a resource for the manipulation and efficient calculation of humans for their own use.

Truth as Correspondence of Entities

Calculation, then, is the central mark of our technological epoch, according to Heidegger. To comprehend how and why this is the case, Heidegger describes the history of our western metaphysical tradition as a gradual forgetting of the question of the meaning of Being *in favor of an emphasis on beings*, and a parallel interpretation of truth as the correspondence between discreet entities.[94] In the Greek roots of our tradition, the cosmological origins of Platonic metaphysics reify Being, in The World of Ideas. By the middle ages, the theological vision of ultimate truth is found in another entity, the highest being of God. In modern times, the human *subjectum* becomes the ultimate entity and ground of truth (*hypokeimenon*), in an era where, Nietzsche tells us, God is now dead.[95] The subject, as foundational entity, is now defined by Descartes as a thinking *thing*.

Criticism of the "materialism" of western, consumerist society is common, but, as we have seen, Heidegger would argue that such materialism is, itself, grounded in a more fundamental worldview that implicitly assigns value to positively existing entities only. The search for truth, then, becomes a quest for certainty in the discovery (*entdecken*) of objective things, and in the conformity between mind, as one entity, and essents, as another. Our metaphysical tradition proceeds, from the start, with this conception of truth as a correspondence between disparate entities—between concrete statements and empirical facts, or between the clear and distinct perception and the object in reality. "Aristotle says that . . . the soul's 'Experiences'. . . are likenings of Things. . . . Thomas Aquinas . . . also uses for 'adaequatio' (likening) the terms '*correspondentia*' (correspondence) and '*convenientia*' (coming together.)"[96] We come to equate the meaning of truth with correctness, and, in the process, we conclude that this is the final word on the issue.

Why is there a problem, according to the Heideggerean phenomenology, in restricting the understanding of truth merely to the notion of correctness? For one thing, in such a scenario, it becomes meaningless to speak of the truth of a piece of poetry or of a sculpture. Does an artwork reveal truth inasmuch as it is an accurate depiction of facts? Why is it that we typically do not speak of the "correctness" of a work of art or of a poem? Does this not indicate that on a prereflective level, we are aware that truth may mean something more? We may sense that poetry reveals truth, but in another way than that which is revealed by way of the conformity theory of truth.

Whether it is in the form of a proposition or an idea, such relationships with the world can only occur in an area of overtness, a revealedness, that opens up the possibility of understanding. In short, the condition of the possibility of the calculative equation of truth with correctness, is an originary projection in the world that implicitly defines a horizon of interpretation, against which such an equation makes sense. This is what Heidegger means when he says that "Being-true means unveiling. . . . Truth is the presupposition for our being able to presuppose anything at all."[97]

To deny this position is to restrict oneself, once again, merely to the adequation of tangible, material entities, forgetting thereby that such entities appear within the context of a prior, taken-for-granted horizon of understanding. Heidegger urges us to listen to the ancient Greeks, who knew well that the condition of adequation between intellect and thing was a presence (*aletheia*) and originary unveiledness (*Un-verborgenheit*) that open up a world of meaning and a ground of interpretation in the first place.

The Greeks also knew that calculation "remains indispensable" as a way of thought.[98] Heidegger's aim is never to dispense with calculation but simply to recall that it is not the exclusive or even the primary mode of thinking. Mathematical calculation is hardly peculiar to the contemporary epoch only. While modern science rests on a mathematical foundation, one cannot conclude that ancient thinkers did not measure or engage in some calculation as well.[99] Heidegger notes how Plato placed over the entrance to the Academy, the words: "Let no one who has not grasped the mathematical enter here!"[100] In what sense was the ancient Greeks' understanding of mathematics fundamentally different from modern-day conceptions of measurement and calculative thinking? Might our understanding of this difference help us to recognize some of the limitations of calculative thought as it has come to have prominence today?

It is enlightening to note that the contemporary Webster's Dictionary definition of mathematics is "*the study . . . of numbers* and operational symbols."[101] Heidegger reiterates that for the current epoch, it is numbers that commonly define the mathematical.[102] Mathematics comes to be equated with that which can be counted, measured, and ordered.

Yet, the essence of mathematics encompassed much more in ancient times. For the Greeks, *Mathesis* meant genuine learning; *mathemata*, that which is learnable.[103] According to Heidegger, the greatest challenge of such learning is making explicit that which we already know.[104] Consequently, the Greek roots of the mathematical were not defined by numbered entities. Rather, *mathesis* as learning signified the condition of understanding of the world around us. In Heidegger's words, "we do not first get [the mathematical] out of things, but, in a certain way, we bring it already with us."[105]

How is this so? In what sense is the essence of mathematical thinking with us rather than rooted in the empirical objects that we measure and count? In a particularly revealing example, Heidegger asks us to consider the example of counting three chairs:

> We see three chairs, and say that there are three. What 'three' is, the three chairs do not tell us, nor three apples, three cats, nor any other three things. Rather, we can count three things only if we already know 'three'. In thus

grasping the number three as such, we only expressly recognize something which, in some way, we already have. This recognition is genuine learning.[106]

The number "three" is the condition of the possibility of counting "three chairs," but it is not equivalent to the visible reality of the three chairs themselves. Today, we tend to assign priority to "facts"—to empirical realities that themselves can be measured, quantified, and objectified as if truth resided therein only. In the process, we tend to forget the implicit context without which explicit material entities remain meaningless.

Unless we can learn how to expand our understanding of the meaning of thinking beyond mere quantification, unless we can begin to comprehend both the implicit context as well as the explicit text, the genuine possibilities of sustainable development will be missed. Needless to say, it is naive to argue for the elimination of calculation. On the contrary, calculation is essential to human thought. It is also necessary, however, to acknowledge that there is more to human thought and imagination than the cumulative assembly of discreet entities in a simplistic, linear order. To forget this means that policies and programs aiming to achieve global sustainability may risk remaining at the level of mere busywork.

In a recent progress report, the Canadian National Round Table on the Environment and the Economy reports that "the overarching goal of reporting on sustainable development is to improve the way we make decisions."[107] In order to move toward such an improvement, the Heideggerean phenomenology offers us an important lesson. By supplementing calculation with originative thinking, new insights may well evolve regarding the meaning of sustainability itself. Originative thinking may be better understood as the condition of interpreting central themes of sustainability in a more holistic and foundational manner. Before we explore such a possibility, however, let us consider in the following chapter how the very theme of sustainable development comes to be affected by calculative paradigms of the contemporary epoch.

3

Calculation and Sustainability

[W]e have great difficulty in representing the world of experience to ourselves
without the spectacles of the old established interpretation.
—Albert Einstein

Despite the limits of calculative thought that are increasingly recognized from philosophical to scientific circles, a dependency upon *techne* relentlessly continues to exercise a grip on our society. The western metaphysical interpretation of reality rests on a positivist vision where *things* become more central than relations, or hidden grounds, or phenomena that are in some ways beyond the bounds of empirical measurement.

"Positive" meaning is, thereby, assigned primarily to those entities that are deemed to be objective, quantifiable, and capable of being publicly and definitively verified. Phenomena that lack these characteristics are, typically, deemed to be less valuable inasmuch as they lack the concreteness and delimitability of material entities or empirically quantifiable concepts. Positivism—like calculative thinking described in the previous chapter—seeks causal explanations and analytic truth. As fundamentally calculative, positivist theories argue that knowledge is restricted to self-evident, logical truths (those tautologies or propositions evident by definition) or to concrete, empirical evidence. In the end, such a calculative vision profoundly affects our interpretation of self and others, of urban and environmental issues, and, ultimately, of sustainability itself. Let us consider each of these themes in turn.

Calculating Others

In the previous chapter, I showed, in a preliminary way, how the predominance of the calculative mode of thought affects the foundation of interpersonal relations.

The topic deserves more attention here, particularly as it impacts upon the discussion of sustainability. Too often, we tend to forget that human beings are neither mere objects nor resources to be defined in positivist terms of a sectoral inventory of needs. In this respect, we might benefit from the reflections of Thomist philosopher Jacques Maritain, who distinguished between *individuals* and *persons*.[1] As individuals, each of us are parts of a wider whole—of a family, a community, "a single dot in the immense network of forces and influences, cosmic, ethnic, historic, whose laws we obey."[2] In so far as we are persons, however, every human being is a unique whole, "a principle of creative unity, of independence and of freedom."[3] The mystery of personality is the essence of the living subject and is confined by no material boundaries. It finds some expression in the poetic imagination—in emotional, artistic, intuitive, and profound intellectual sensibilities.

In our highly rational, calculative era, we must learn to guard against the tendency to devalue Maritain's notion of personhood in favor of individuality, by transforming unique human beings into statistics or into mere units of a collectivity. Margaret Catley-Carlson, president of the Canadian International Development Agency, echoes this sentiment when she describes the difficulties in discovering just and affordable means of enforcing environmental controls, precisely on the level of the human *person*. She writes:

> Consider a taxi driver in Calcutta, whose dilapidated old heap belches black smoke. If you fine him for polluting the air, or demand he get his car tuned, where will he find the money? He's just barely making enough each day to feed himself and his family. And if you impound his vehicle, how would he and his children eat?[4]

Catley-Carlson asks us to multiply this dilemma by 5 million cars, in order to begin to comprehend the huge challenges facing Calcutta in battling air pollution. At the same time, a genuine understanding of the problem requires a fuller awareness of the human implications than such an easy calculation may suggest. The solution to a serious pollution problem in this case would involve intervening in an *entire way of life* that, presently, has its just returns on the level of the human person. This realization does not mean, of course, that we must consequently abstain from environmental intervention. It compels us to do so fully aware, however, of the human dimension and fully prepared to cope with the personal, as well as social, costs of such intervention.

Calculative thinking grounds many of our ways of being with one another. For example, to recite abstract statistics about the state of world hunger similarly risks distancing us from the full meaning of human suffering. Recall that the Brundtland Report tells us that, in 1985, despite the objective abundance of food production, "more than 730 million people did not eat enough to lead fully productive working lives."[5] Others tell us that ten thousand people starve to death daily and

460 million are permanently hungry.[6] These figures are significant, but as numerical abstractions, they also, insidiously, allow us to disassociate ourselves from the full breadth of meaning underlying the numbers.

Other, less calculative perspectives may inform us in a way that is closer to heart. One shudders to read that "hunger is a child with shrivelled limbs and a swollen belly. It is the grief of parents or a person gone blind for lack of vitamin A."[7] Even bringing the numbers down to the level of the everyday has its merits. Philosopher Louis Pojman asks us to consider the following analogy:

> Imagine ten children eating at a table. The three healthiest eat the best food and throw much of it away or give it to their pets. Two other children get just enough to get by on. The other five do not get enough food. Three of them who are weak manage to stave off hunger pangs by eating bread and rice, but the other two are unable to do even that and die of hunger-related diseases, such as peneumonia and dysentery.[8]

The example implicitly reminds us that, while we may remain disengaged from the misery of world poverty through our recital—or ignorance—of statistical compilations that reach into the millions, at the personal level of each child, a fundamental injustice prevails in such easy, calculative abstractions. Free-floating numerical concepts, while informative at some level, also risk collapsing the essence of hunger into the comfortable domain of what Heidegger called "das Man"—the impersonal, neutral, and ultimately, inauthentic distantiality (*Abständigkeit*) of "the they."[9] In such a domain of "publicness," Heidegger explains that "overnight, everything that is primordial gets glossed over as something that has long been well known. Everything gained by a struggle becomes just something to be manipulated. Every secret loses its force" in an overall "levelling down" of authentic possibilities.[10] By transforming the concrete, lived reality of a child's hunger into the "averageness" of an empty statistic, it is a simple task to take the next step and disengage oneself from any responsibility or feeling of authentic care.

Positivist interpretations of human relations subtly infect our policy discussions of sustainable development at various levels. Consider another example that relates to the current debate about "future generations" in the field of environmental ethics. The World Commission on Environment and Development explains that their own message of hope is "based on the premise that every human being—those here and those who are to come—has the right to life, and to a decent life."[11] But to what extent can we speak consistently of the "rights" of unborn generations? How rational is it to speak of the *existence of rights* for *nonexistent* rightholders?

Some philosophers maintain that it is meaningless to do so. While one may feel that it is unethical to ask future generations to pay for our mistakes (for example, in the disposal of nuclear waste) others question whether it is proper to deprive the poor of our own generation for the sake of nonexistent future generations. In this respect, some ethicists go so far as to suggest that since we do not know *who* or *what* they will be, or even wherein their convictions will lie, it is meaningless to specify obligations to nonexistent people—to nonentities.[12]

A related argument suggests that there *is no single* future generation to whom we can be said to owe anything or whom we harm by our present-day actions.[13] If we say that future people would be "better off" if we pursued more sustainable environmental policies today, we assume that a *particular* group of people would be affected by these policies. Yet different policies lead to different outcomes that themselves lead to alternative contingent events—and these events, in turn, may result in the birth of different people. We are asked to imagine how many events might have prevented our own parents or grandparents from meeting. Had events happened in some alternate sequence, we ourselves would not exist.[14] Similarly, a single, specific "future generation" not only does not exist now, but we have no obligations to our descendants, since the composition of any one generation itself may be affected by our own actions or even by circumstances beyond our control. In fact, a future generation that does not yet exist, can possess no rights. It follows that I cannot have a duty to a nonexistent entity.

I find these kinds of logistical acrobatics to be ethically misdirected. To maintain that I owe nothing to future generations because I cannot touch, feel, or empirically experience them or describe them exactly—is intuitively offensive. To suggest that rights of future generations are nonexistent because those same generations are nonexistent follows the narrow rules of logic but not of rationality in a broader sense: the implication seems to be that if future people have no rights, neither do they really matter.

This conclusion goes against the grain of what it means to exist as a member of humanity and of a broader social world. Such philosophical machinations deny the significance of human compassion and of care beyond the confines of one's own self-grounded concerns. This kind of denial can only happen when human beings are interpreted in a reductionist model, as discreet "things" that either do exist now in the present or else remain but a futural fiction of one's imagination. Later, I will say more about the need of a holistic vision of human being, one that incorporates notions of conscience and care in a nonpositivist, phenomenological vision. At this point, however, I wish only to flag some of the dangers that arise in our philosophical reflections on the meaning of right and wrong, when human beings—and their rights and duties—are defined by way of a positivist reduction to empirically accessible realities only.[15]

We turn, finally, to one last example of the hazards of interpreting human beings as mere material entities. The Brundtland Report points out how "women farmers, though they play a critical role in food production, are often ignored by programmes meant to improve production."[16] Others have similarly noted how women's contributions to informal sector activities have been left out of abstract stereotype models of the developing world, because these contributions have been difficult, if not impossible, to *measure* and record.[17] None of this is unusual, in an epoch that seeks to present a neatly defined, conclusive picture of the human ideal. Ecofeminists argue against androcentric models of humanity, because these very models present an image of the perfect human being as male, rational, and in control. Characteristics such as compassion, care, and emotional sensitivity are typically interpreted on this model as being inferior and, often, feminine qualities.[18]

Not only do ecofeminists question such an androgenic, reified conception of the human being, but some go even further to criticize essentializing tendencies of some ecofeminists themselves. Critics suggest that those who purport to speak of a woman's way of knowing as if there is a single woman's voice (usually with an implicit classist and racist bias) are themselves falling into the trap of objectifying Woman as if she can be defined as a neatly circumscribed, hypostatized entity.[19] The single-minded notion of a simple, unified feminine experience, separate from the masculine experience, has been questioned persuasively.[20] While ecofeminists are in general agreement that there is a significant relation between the exploitation of women and the exploitation of nature, one realizes in surveying the ecofeminist literature that its strength lies precisely in the *lack* of a solidifed consensus on the meaning of Being Woman.[21] The attempt to delimit the feminine experience within neatly circumscribed limits is just another expression of the current tendency to compartmentalize the human experience within rigid, ahistorical definitions—definitions that ultimately deny to that experience its richness and ontological breadth of significance.

It has been said that inasmuch as something exists, it exists to a certain degree and in that sense is subject to measurement.[22] Certainly that claim applies to empirical entities like tables and chairs. It cannot, however, apply in the same way to human beings, whose social, cultural, and historical experiences transcend the boundaries of material entities in their essence.

Significantly, Canada's submission to the Fifth Session of the United Nations Commission on Sustainable Development in 1997 addresses the theme of "Strengthening Our Social Fabric" by collapsing that issue into two categories of discussion on "human capital" and "social capital."[23] As an update of Canadian progress in this field, the document testifies to the fact that we still tend to reduce human affairs to quantitative, economic terms. Of course, social networks and civic institutions can be viewed from the economic perspective. The full depth of human experience, however, consists of understanding, imagination, intuition, sensibility, and complex nuances of meaning that are revealed in the temporal unfolding of each human life. To collapse the richness of that experience within a simplistic, calculative framework is, at best, naive. At worst, it threatens genuine progress toward a sustainable and a more humane society.

The Environment as More Than Some Thing

Moving beyond a calculative framework requires a similar reassessment of our current understanding of *environment*. In *Our Common Future,* Charles Caccia suggests that we tend to see ourselves as "managers of an entity out there called 'the environment,' extraneous to us, an alternative to the economy, too expensive a value to protect in difficult economic times."[24] Such an attitude distances us emotionally and intellectually from the recognition that the environment is hardly an object separate from human beings but is the condition of the possibility of life itself.

We must keep in mind that the etymological roots of environment relate to that which *surrounds (environs)*—not merely in a geographical or geometrical sense but, rather, in terms of a meaningful *milieu*.[25] The environment is neither an abstraction in the form of a mere "cause" for environmentalism, nor is it something to which we can either choose or not choose to pay attention. Inasmuch as we exist as human beings, we are in-the-world.[26] This notion of being-in-the-world signifies an essential belonging between human beings and the environment within which they are situated. This belonging may consist of an emotional attachment to specific places, but ontologically it signifies more than mere sentiment. I cannot *be* in the absence of place.[27] In this sense, the environment as *milieu* immediately involves me in my essence as a human being.

Landscape architect Michael Hough points to a revealing example of how we typically view nature as a static object "out there" to be manipulated for the human good.[28] He describes how a conference was convened in 1964 by the American Falls International Board, because a talus had broken off on the American side of Niagara Falls, causing a huge agglomeration of rock at its base. A large amount of publicity had been generated and detailed landscape studies had been commissioned to decide what should be done with the rocks to reconstitute a more aesthetically appealing environment. Hough rightly maintains that one of the reasons that tourists visit the falls in the first place is precisely because of the awe generated by a natural feature of such power and immensity. Yet the International Joint Commission and others were intent upon regarding this natural occurrence in terms of "some gigantic engineering toy that has somehow gone wrong and must, within the limits of technological wizardry and irrelevant aesthetic standards, be put right."[29]

In the end, Hough's recommendation was to let the falls be. Rather than view the event in terms of a static phenomenon "frozen in time," he called for a recognition of nature "seen as a continuum."[30] After all, this environment has preceded our existence by tens of thousands of years and it can only be expected to continue to evolve through time. Hough's notion of natural phenomena in terms of *process* is instructive: it stands as a warning of our tendency to hypostatize nature, particularly in terms of an aesthetically appealing picture to be manipulated according to our current tastes.

This notion of environment as a domain unto itself is increasingly pervasive in contemporary thought. The concept emerges in the anthropocentric paradigms of management and control: consider for example, Repetto's definition of sustainable development as "a development strategy that manages all assets, natural resources, and human resources as well as financial and physical assets for increasing long-term wealth and well-being."[31] The environment becomes a collection of "assets" to be successfully managed by way of new sustainable development strategies. The idea seems to be that we can continue to tinker with an assemblage of discreet entities—all of which added up make up "the environment."

Such an attitude translates itself into a broader, popular conception that the environment is one among many other priorities. The National Round Table on the Environment and Economy Review reports that "in the 1988 election campaign, the environment ranked second only to the issue of free trade. But in the lead up to the 1993 federal election, the media and polls have told us that the environment is way down the list of priorities. Canadians are concerned about jobs and the economy."[32] We are naive if we assume that the environment is one choice among others. Instead, it is time that we paid heed to the fact that the environment constitutes the very sustenance of all life. "The environment" is the inescapable condition of the possibility of the emergence of other sectoral priorities.

Ironically, a similar disengagement between human beings and environment presents itself even in the radical, ecocentric philosophies that hope to overturn traditional paradigms. Ecocentric thinkers argue that the reason for the current environmental crisis lies in the self-centered, anthropocentric worldview that elevates human reason above the natural world. Such a paradigm, ecocentric philosophers argue, supports the attitude that nature can be manipulated and controlled and that its value is defined only in relation to human needs. Objecting to such attitudes, these thinkers argue that nature has more than instrumental value, namely, that it has intrinsic value, in and of itself, apart from its utility for human beings.[33] For instance, while "shallow ecology" may assume that nature has little or no value apart from the good it provides for human beings, such paradigms are overturned by "deep ecologists" who argue instead that the value of nonhuman life-forms is quite independent of their usefulness for narrow human needs.[34]

I would counter that to speak of the environment in such terms, however, often runs the risk of grandiose abstraction.[35] To choose to center intrinsic value within the world "in itself," independent of the human subject, is to remain within the very metaphysical dualism of subjectivity and objectivity that grounds the "shallow" calculative worldview in the first place. My reverence for "the environment," which shelters value somehow in and of itself, to the exclusion of the human valuer, implicitly involves a choice to assign value to the external world, rather than to the human subject.

By choosing "Earth first, humankind second," ecocentric philosophers continue to operate within the bifurcation of reality that results in a dualism between subject and object, between value and fact, between mind and body.[36] Leave aside the linguistic impossibility of assigning value to a supposedly independent, non-human environment by way of human moral categories.[37] The fact remains that ecocentric philosophies that assign intrinsic value to the environment independent of human understanding are themselves trapped in a positivist reification of the world in and of itself, namely, of a valued *object*.

Philosopher David Cooper clarifies this last point in a recent paper on "The Idea of Environment."[38] He cites an imaginary incantation of a new eco-ethic, where the author might contend that such an ethic

> will promote attitudes of reverence, awe and respect towards living things and systems, the whole environment in fact. For these have their own sanctity and intrinsic value. Underlying these attitudes will be the appreciation that our world is a seamless whole, an eco-sphere.[39]

Cooper argues that such sweeping conclusions—where my reverence is to extend across huge geographical and cultural differences—are misplaced. "I do not revere or hold sacred the Amazonian rain forest, not because I am irreverent or profane, but because, never having been remotely engaged with that forest, such a vocabulary is inappropriate coming from my lips."[40] Large-scale abstractions lead to a vision of the environment that is, in Cooper's words,

> something much too *big*. The environment for which we are supposed to feel reverence is nothing less than nature itself. . . . Each person's environmental concern is supposed to extend everywhere. . . . The expression 'the global environment' makes this largeness of scope explicit. . . . The definite article and singular noun indicate that there is just one big environment. . . . From now on, I refer to the environment so conceived with suitably large letters—'The Environment.'[41]

In both the anthropocentric and ecocentric paradigms, nature risks becoming an entity separate from the human understanding—in one case to be managed and controlled, in the other to be revered. Philosopher Jim Cheney points out how "the lovers of the earth and the destroyers of the earth often have one thing in common: the attempt to handle ambivalence without resolving it, using the defective tools of identification or dichotomization respectively."[42] In both scenarios, nature is reified as something external to ourselves.

Such an abstraction denies the originary, mutual interdependence of the human-environment relation that is the condition of the possibility of any abstraction in the first place. The environment and human beings are not two separate entities that are somehow brought together conceptually for the sake of "environmentalism" in the abstract. On the contrary, there is an originary belonging of humans to their world. Heidegger describes human Being as in-the-world.[43] This indicates that prior to assigning primary value to either human subjectivity or, on the other hand, to the external, objective world, human beings are pretheoretically, spontaneously and immediately interpreting all meanings on the foundation of an originary belonging to the world. The environment is the incarnation of my very existence.

The City and Urban Planning

As nature is hypostatized, it becomes for us some thing to which we travel on weekends or on holidays. Similarly, "The City" becomes something else: a concrete jungle, or a suburb with artificial urban design incentives of green belts. Contrasting images of nature versus city abound in the modern worldview. Thoreau wrote of the "indescribable innocence and beneficence of Nature."[44] Other romantics similarly suggested that nature, untouched by the human presence, was thereby ideally preserved in its ideal, unspoiled state.[45] On the other hand, the very origins of our contemporary cities are clouded in images of contamination and blight: Toronto (formerly York) was poignantly described as consisting of "stagnant pools of water, green as leek, and emitting deadly exhalations . . . yards and cellars send forth a stench . . . sufficient almost of itself to produce a plague."[46]

More recently, a manager of New York State parks declared that open space is like virginity: once lost, it can never be regained.[47] This is certainly true. On the other hand, as Loenthal points out, it is only nonvirgins who can produce more virgins.[48] Landscapes are not unchanging entities separate from human beings and there is no reason, in principle, that human intervention cannot lead to increasingly diverse and even healthy environments.

The dichotomy that develops between urban and environmental issues and concerns deserves to be rethought, if we are to learn to reintegrate environmental awareness into our human settlement design. Hough describes how perceptually, we fail to make the obvious links between city and countryside, seeing them instead as mutually exclusive places:

> We fail to see nature as an integrated connecting system that operates in one way or another regardless of locality. Water supply and disposal systems leave no indication that the water supplied to the kitchen tap had its origins in the forests and landscapes of distant watersheds; or that rain falling on rooftops and paved surfaces and disappearing without trace into catchbasins and underground sewers is part of a continuous hydrological cycle. The turf and specimen trees of the urban park and garden, its plants brought from Korea and the Himalayas, its turf maintained like a billard table, are difficult to associate with the diverse community of plants that convert sunlight

into energy, and produce food and materials necessary for survival. The frozen and heremetically sealed plastic package one finds in the meat section of the local supermarker bears not the slightest resemblance to the animal from which it came. Maintenance has usurped natural succession.[49]

Initiatives that serve to remind citizens of the linkages between natural and built environments are rare, although the work of the Urban Ecology group in Berkeley, California, is one exception. By stenciling messages on streets above culverted creeks that "creek critters" are affected when motor oil is dumped down a drain, this group reminds city dwellers that their storm drains connect to local animal habitats and, finally, to the San Francisco Bay. Signs warn of "no dumping— drains to bay," making explicit the hidden veins that bind our natural and built environments.[50]

More typically, however, as I meander through the local shopping mall, surrounded by exotic imported plants, in an environment suitably climate controlled, it is easy for me to remain oblivious to the cycle of the seasons.[51] By virtue of the perceptual lack of contiguity between nature and urban form, it is easy for me to slip into a mind-frame that separates city from countryside as if they were indeed distinct entities—independent geographical containers of either urban or natural environment experiences.

The next logical step is to seek to manipulate and control this urban entity as if it were a static phenomenon. Just as Niagara Falls was viewed as a nonchanging picture, frozen in time, so too there has been a tendency in urban design to analyze the built environment as if it were a static model. Geographical maps, no less than architectural blueprints, take a bird's-eye view as their conceptual starting-point for planning and design. Such perspectives typically seek to encapsulate the complexity of the actual conditions on the ground within an abstract portrayal that remains disassociated from unseen social, cultural, and historical forces that ultimately determine the actual use of the spaces that are designed and built.

The example from the Environmental Simulation Laboratory in Berkeley, California, is instructive: the director of the lab built three-dimensional models of architectural students' blueprints that represented the buildings "from above." Then he "walked" these same students through the designs at eye level through the models, with the aid of a periscope camera. Not a single student was able to recognize the buildings that they themselves had designed.[52] It may be more straightforward to simplify the synergism of the lived world within a static representation but, ultimately, it distances one from the very reality that one is seeking to understand.

Certainly it is time to recognize that built environments are more than material entities—buildings, roads, sewers, and people—to be calculatively ordered through the imposition of grand master plans. Gaston Bachelard reminds us that "space that has been seized upon by the imagination cannot remain indifferent space subject to the measures and estimates of the surveyor."[53] This is so because "inhabited space transcends geometrical space."[54]

It is naive to assume that any single, premeditated utopian solution can be succesfully imposed, top-down, upon a community: the unsustainability of the model Garden City is a case in point. Statistical summaries of human behavior and aerial maps of geometric spatial designs certainly provide necessary data in the accomplishment of urban planning. I would argue, however, that such data insufficiently captures the synergism of human settlements—a synergism linked to the relations between the data under study and to the hidden ontological significance of human attitudes, values, and paradigms, all of which ultimately exceed the scrutiny of methods of study of empirically measurable entities.

Rethinking Sustainability

How we interpret other human beings, as well as our built and natural environments, ultimately affects how we understand sustainability itself. The popular view seems to be that "the pursuit of economic growth has environmental costs, and a clean environment has economic costs. The challenge is to find compatible and sustainable combinations of the two."[55]

Yet I would argue that the challenge of sustainability involves much more than a juggling act of individual entities, such as natural resources and economic concerns. It is encouraging that ecologists have promoted an understanding not only of individual organisms, but of whole ecosystems in terms of the interactions and interdependencies of living and nonliving entities. English ecologist, Arthur G. Tansley, who coined the term "ecosystem" in 1935, reminds us that organisms "act upon one another, modify one another's actions and produce new actions which are jointly dependent on two or more components."[56] Environmental philosopher Neil Evernden builds upon this premise of interconnectedness in ecology, wisely concluding that "environmentalism, in the deepest sense, is *not* about environment. It is not about things but relationships, not about beings but Being, not about world but the inseparability of self and circumstance."[57]

A holistic, ecological perspective has, to some degree, informed the work of the World Conservation Strategy on resource conservation for sustainable development.[58] The authors symbolize different approaches to preserving genetic diversity in terms of a conceptual image of an iceberg. The "tip of the iceberg" appears above water and, in this respect, portrays the solution that is most clearly and empirically accessible. As one moves deeper below the surface toward the foundations of the iceberg, there is increasing complexity and less capability of manipulation of ecological connections.

The World Conservation Strategy advances the claim that the aim of programs to preserve biodiversity must be to understand the iceberg as a whole. In a more recent document, however, the IUCN, UNEP, and WWF recognize that such a task is never simple. "There can be no long-term guarantee of sustainability, because many factors remain unknown or unpredictable. The moral we draw from this is: be conservative in actions that could affect the environment, study the effects of such actions carefully, and learn from your mistakes quickly."[59]

In the forests of the Northwest Pacific, the example of the spotted owl provides a revealing case study.[60] For some time, debate has raged over the number of forestry jobs to be lost, "merely" for the sake of preserving the spotted owl. In 1993, President Clinton led the Forest Summit, where a Forest Ecosystem Management Assessment Team was assembled to consider the feasibility of various forest management options and their effects beyond the owl, on a broad range of species to be preserved in old-growth forest ecosystems.

One report states that "in carrying out its charge, the team found that owls were just the smallest tip of the forest-ecosystem iceberg."[61] Beyond the spotted owl, the Forest Ecosystem Management Assessment Team recognized the need to assess the impact of forestry management options on 524 species of mushroom and fungi; 106 of mosses; 142 species of lichens; 127 of vascular plants; 102 of slugs, snails, and other mollusks; 18 of amphibians; 38 of birds; 27 of mammals; and more than 7,000 species of insects and other invertebrates.[62]

It began to be evident that preserving each one of these species presented a formidable challenge to the team and to the government behind them. Critics conceded that it would be financially prohibitive for the government to acquire and preserve habitat for every one of these rare species. They recommended instead, off-site genetic conservation in germplasm banks and cultivated populations.[63]

Beyond such recommendations, however, the Forest Ecosystem Management Assessment Team recognized the need of preserving the ecosystem as a whole. More important than the individual species themselves are the operational relations between them. As particle physicists have discovered that subatomic particles are themselves not simply smaller, discreet particles themselves but rather are defined in terms of their interrelations, the same may be said to apply to ecosystems themselves. As Dunstan and his colleagues conclude:

> While it may be possible to conserve species in zoos or conserve their genetic materials frozen in test tubes, this misses the essence of their existence. What's important is not the species themselves, but their interrelationships. As physicist Fritjof Capra put it, "It's not the dancers, but the dance." When we degrade the environment, it's not the loss of species that is of ultimate importance, but rather the loss of connections and dynamic interrelationships.[64]

A more holistic approach to illumining the meaning of sustainability addresses particular issues in their relation to one another. This conclusion is true beyond our example of species preservation, extending to the preservation and creation of overall quality of life and sense of place. In this regard, I quote the moving comments made to the Brundtland Commission by a Krenak Indian:

> When the government took our land in the valley of Rio Doce, they wanted to give us another place somewhere else. But the State, the government, will never understand that we do not have another place to go.
>
> The only possible place for the Krenak people to live and to re-establish our existence, to speak to our Gods, to speak to our nature, to weave our lives is where our God created us. It is useless for the government to put us in a very beautiful place, in a very good place with a lot of hunting and a lot of fish. The Krenak people, we continue dying and we die insisting that there is only one place for us to live. . . .
>
> We can no longer see the planet that we live upon as if it were a chess-board where people just move things around. We cannot consider the planet as something isolated from the cosmic.[65]

It is no longer a viable option to simply "move things around" in order to achieve sustainable development. Juggling economic and environmental concerns, assigning different priorities—however clever they may seem at the time—is simply not enough. The Krenak Indian bears witness to the need of a way of thought, more fundamental than that of calculation.

It is, however, easy to be critical. Simply to advocate the alternative of holistic thinking does little to explain what such holism might contribute to our understanding of sustainability. Within environmental philosophy, the benefits of eco-holism are not self-evident and the theory is not beyond criticism.[66] If reductionist modes of calculative thinking are inadequate to the challenges of sustainability and if some alternative, holistic vision is called for, the task becomes one of enlarging our understanding of this alternative. In the following part, we begin to address precisely such a task.

PART II

Foundations of Phenomenological Thought

4

The Possibilities of Originative Thinking

Generally speaking, around the world, fish stocks are in decline, notwithstanding the fact that the technology available to find fish, the technology available to kill fish, improves every year. We are putting more effort and more technology into catching less fish. That is frightening.[1]

These remarks were issued by Fisheries Minister Brian Tobin in the wake of the 1995 seizure by Canadian officials of the Spanish trawler *Estai* for its apparent overfishing of turbot just outside of Canada's 200-mile coastal limit. Tobin points to the irony of technological exploitation. Sophisticated technological advances do not necessarily promise a better world. Nor do they guarantee that our Faustian harnessing of nature can ever really be complete. Tobin's remarks provide a sense that another mode of thought may be necessary to contemplate the wider implications of calculation.

In this chapter, I propose that Heidegger's notion of meditative thinking serves as the key to understanding sustainability more comprehensively than calculative frameworks allow. Meditative thinking, as we shall see, is essentially ontological and, ultimately, phenomenological. A few words of warning are in order here, however. First, I must admit that the term "meditation" is misleading, if one assumes, as one might easily do, that meditative thinking is a passive contemplation of speculative, philosophical matters, instead of an active engagement in the concrete reality of everyday demands.[2] To avoid any misunderstandings, my preference is to refer to "originative," rather than "meditative" thinking, as distinct from calculation. "Originative" emphasizes Heidegger's own conviction that phenomenology seeks to uncover the taken-for-granted *origins* and grounds within which calculative paradigms are rooted. The term "originative" also suggests openness and creativity of thought, which are essential to philosophy proper and to that mode of comportment that flourishes "only through persistent, courageous thinking."[3]

The second word of caution relates to the popular conception that unless one is thinking in a linear, positivist, and calculative fashion, one is not thinking at all.

Note, on this account, that Heidegger describes originative thinking to be, indeed, a mode of *thinking*. While thinking originatively will invoke an "openness to the mystery," the call is not an evocation of an irrational, or emotional, or wildly intuitive mode of Being-in-the-world. To be sure, the limits of reason and what counts as reasonable will be rethought, but never at the expense of a philosophical rigor and fundamental respect for the project of thinking itself.

For Heidegger, the choice is not between rationality, on the one hand, and irrationality, on the other. Heidegger's criticism of modern society, however, is that it functions as if calculative thought were the only legitimate candidate for rationality.[4] Environmental phenomenology requires us to rethink taken-for-granted, reductionist interpretations of thought as merely calculative modes of ordering discrete entities.

My aim, in this chapter and in this book, is not to supplant proposals for rational policies, science, and technological advancement with emotivism, mysticism, and vague intuitions—as if these descriptors could substitute for sound, scientific argumentation. On the contrary, the goal is to show how thoughtfulness and good sense exceed the modern, reductionist limits of calculation. Philosophy—and specifically phenomenology—teach us that genuine reason is undervalued when it is restricted to the limitations of calculation. As Brian Tobin's fisheries example clearly shows, technological progress—no matter what apparent calculative possibilities present themselves—is bound to fail in the absence of originative, thoughtful consideration of the broader implications of sustainable development policies.

Environmental Thinking as Nonreductionist

Instead of relying upon an exclusively reductionist, mechanistic worldview, phenomenology offers the possibility of understanding environmental issues *holistically*. The notion of "holism," though, is hardly new and is certainly not a concept that is purely phenomenological. On the contrary, holistic thinking is propogated ever more frequently in the environmental literature. The Brundtland Commission itself clearly stipulates that the environment and development "cannot be treated separately by fragmented institutions and policies."[5] Instead, the common theme underlying the commission's sustainable development strategy is the need to integrate economic and ecological concerns.[6]

In Canada, the National Round Table on the Environment and the Economy agrees that "sustainable development deals with interrelationships and linkages. It means looking at decisions in a holistic way. . . . More than in anything else, the power of sustainable development lies in its bridging capability—its ability to facilitate integration, synthesis and collaborative approaches to problem solving."[7] Funding agencies of academic research increasingly emphasize the need to support innovative, interdisciplinary approaches to the study of the environment.[8] Designers advocate holistic, integrative approaches to technological innovation—approaches that look "at the big picture."[9] Altogether, definitions of sustainable development typically imply concepts of integration and interdisciplinary collaboration in an era where broad-based, ecosystem approaches to environmental decision making are favored over traditional, reductionist perspectives.

Despite this general call for a nonsectoral vision, however, it is far from clear that consensus exists regarding the meaning of apparently more-inclusive, "holistic" alternatives to the study of the human-environment relation. There are, increasingly, calls for the evolution of broader, more comprehensive "indicators" of sustainability—indicators that will do more than measure exclusively gross domestic product, literacy rate, population growth rates, or net trade balance. The World Bank, for instance, has developed a new ranking of national wealth that moves beyond the calculation of manufactured resources to include natural and human/social wealth.[10] The 1996 report of the President's Council on Sustainable Development—appointed by President Clinton in 1993 to conduct a collaborative dialogue on ways to meet the challenges raised by the Brundtland Commission—similarly advocates the creation of a variety of new economic, social, and environmental quality indicators.[11] The development of such indicators continues to be a central part of the council's ongoing activities. The recognition that narrow, sectoral measures of sustainability no longer are adequate—appears to be growing quickly.[12]

But does the mere agglomeration of a wider variety of indicators amount to attaining a holistic perspective on sustainable development? In my view, a holistic approach to sustainability cannot be reduced to accumulating discreet indicators, no matter how many we amass. The definitions of "whole" and "totality" are, as we shall see, quite different. On the other hand, describing holism credibly will be more challenging than one might expect. As policymakers continue to argue for "holistic" or integrative approaches to sustainable development and as funding agencies continue to pour dollars into "interdisciplinary" environmental research, far too little discussion is directed to critical analysis of the very meaning of these terms. Let me first consider some arguments for and against holistic approaches to environmental issues, before I turn to some remarks on the phenomenological contribution to this debate.

Some Arguments for Holistic Thinking

Although terms like "interdisciplinarity" emerged only in the everyday lexicon of the twentieth century, the concept of holistic thinking takes us back to the very origins of western philosophy. At the turn of the fifth century B.C., the pre-Socratic philosopher Parmenides wrote his "didactic poem" and captured the philosophical question of the meaning of Being as a unity. He wrote of:

> how being, without genesis, is without destruction,
> complete, alone there
> without tremor and not still requiring to be finished;
>   nor was it before, nor will it be in the future,
>   for being present it *is* entirely, unique, unifying, united,
>   gathering itself in itself from itself (cohesive,
>   full of presentness).[13]

Plato's own image of a World of Forms—of timeless ideals and eternal truths—portrayed a transcendent order that unified the diverse, multidirectional pursuits of the everyday world of becoming and flux.[14] The famous "Myth of the Cave" asks us to imagine human beings living in an underground, cavelike dwelling. The prisoners are shackled to prevent them from turning their heads. A fire burns behind them. Shadows cast by puppets behind the prisoners are assumed to be real objects, although the silhouettes are mere reproductions of the genuine artifacts. The story illustrates how we inhabit two kinds of worlds: a transitory—though most readily accessible and conspicuous—world of particular shadows, on the one hand, and a silent, unifying world of eternal and immutable forms on the other. So "the turning of a soul round from a day which is like night to a true day," writes Plato, "—this is the ascent into real being, which we shall say is true philosophy."[15]

Aristotle's description of metaphysics as "first philosophy" similarly reflected a search for a universal philosophical foundation to ground the individual sciences.[16] The senses "surely give the most authoritative knowledge of particulars."[17] On the other hand, "knowing all things must belong to him who has in the highest degree universal knowledge; for he knows in a sense all the instances that fall under the universal."[18] First philosophy, as the study of first principles and a "science which knows to what end each thing must be done" in this light becomes "the most authoritative of the sciences."[19]

Through the Middle Ages, Christian thinkers like St. Thomas Aquinas also explained that, while sense knowledge is of particular objects, the highest intellectual knowledge is of universal principles.[20] More recently, Hegel stands as the modern representative of holistic, metaphysical thinking *par excellence*: "everything rational," he tells us, "shows itself to be a threefold union."[21] The synthetic moment is the culmination of the dialectical unfolding of history itself.

Whether in a suprasensory realm or in the progression of spirit, the notion of ultimate meaning as integrative defines the centuries-old search for metaphysical truth itself. Significantly, though, holistic thinking has described more than just the philosophers' own historical quest for unity in the universe. In modern times, Gestalt psychology emphasized how, in the everyday, visual perception of complex forms, human beings do not attempt to first perceive accurately each individual detail of the structure of shapes and objects of perception—and then somehow to abstract a vision of the whole. On the contrary, we are unable to perceive

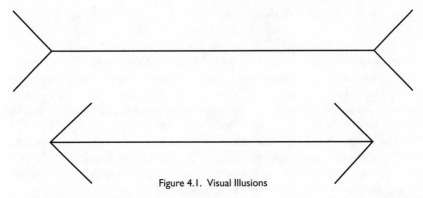

Figure 4.1. Visual Illusions

the parts of the shape independently of the whole. One famous example, figure 4.1, provides an illustration of this point. While the horizontal lines are actually identical in length, it is difficult, if not impossible, to perceive the two lines independently of the arrows that constitute a portion of the whole figure. As a result, the top line appears to be longer than the line below it. The whole, in this instance, becomes more than the sum of its parts.[22]

Similarly in the sciences, holism has emerged as significant, particularly in the development of ecology. Dissatisfied with traditional, reductionist approaches of positivist science, ecologists have recognized the need of broader study of the relationships among organisms and between organisms and their environment.[23] A primary example is found in the late-nineteenth-century work of the eminent ecologist Frederick Clements, who focused on plant succession in the prairies and grasslands of the western plains of the United States. Clements was intrigued with what he observed to be nonrandom change in the natural environment. He argued that as plant species replaced one another, an ecosystem eventually developed toward what he termed a "climax community," that is, a healthy, balanced and permanent population of biological species. In such an organic model of ecosystems, the role of the ecologist was not unlike that of the physician. A doctor diagnoses a problem, attempting to determine the normal functioning of the body. Similarly, the role of the ecologist is to study a particular habitat, and establish the proper determinants of a healthy and balanced environment as a whole.

Clements defined this climax community as a "complex organism"

> of a higher order than an individual geranium, robin or chimpanzee. . . . Like them, it is a unified mechanism in which *the whole is greater than a sum of its parts* and hence it constitutes a new kind of organic being with novel properties.[24]

This notion that the "whole is greater than the sum of its parts" is assumed by most, if not all, versions of holistic thinking. The whole is seen to be more than the simple accumulation of discrete entities. Instead, the combined action of individual parts as they relate to one another often results in a synergistic effect, greater than the mere sum of these parts. An example may be helpful here. Consider how the bacterial increases caused by dumping of organic sewage and industrial pollutants into lake water may cause illness among swimmers. At the same time, should the lake bottom be covered with metallic mercury, the overall danger increases more than twofold, since the bacteria may transform the metallic mercury into toxic methyl mercury, that itself becomes concentrated in the food chain.[25]

The fact that individual organisms interrelate within ecosystems often leads to another descriptor of holistic thinking: to use philosopher Carolyn Merchant's words—that "everything is connected to everything else."[26] In their introduction to environmental science, ecologists Nebel and Wright echo Merchant's description by explaining ecosystems in this way:

> No living organism exists or can exist as an entity unto itself. Each organism is but one member of a particular *species*. . . . But no species is an entity until itself either. Every animal species depends on various plant species for food and for various habitat conditions. . . . Plant species depend on various animal and microbial species to decompose biological waste and release nutrients so that they can be recycled. All species depend on air, water, and nutritive elements from the earth's minerals. But plants, animals and microbes also play important roles in removing pollutants from air, in purifying water and in recycling mineral elements. Therefore, we can say that plants support animals; animal activities support plants; and all organisms help to support and maintain air, water and soil quality.[27]

The authors remind us that human beings "are no less a part of and no less dependent on these interrelationships than any other species, although we frequently delude ourselves into thinking that we are."[28] It is not only the case, then, that the physical, *natural* environment is understood in terms of the interrelationship among parts, but environmentalists often argue that the relation between humans and nature is itself a synergistic one, properly explained only in terms of complex interactions that are absent in a controlled, laboratory setting that isolates one or other member of the relation.

Environmental psychologist Robert Gifford points out how the very study of human beings becomes more sound when humans are described in relation to their everyday worlds. "Every field within psychology implicitly refers to everyday environments, but only environmental psychology systematically investigates this edge within each field. To offer just one example, the study of learning ultimately relates to classrooms, yet few classic studies of learning have taken place in classrooms."[29] So the unity of humans and the environments to which they belong becomes another descriptor of environmental holism.

Ecology has had a significant impact upon the development of environmental philosophy in the past twenty years. In the late 1970s, Kenneth Goodpaster set the stage for a rethinking of moral individualism and "the single-minded mapping of morality onto 'beneficiaries' and 'communities of ends' whose relation to *their* environment is still left outside, except instrumentally."[30] Suggesting that human beings "need not be the most embracing integral units in our moral universe," Goodpaster sets the stage for a far-ranging philosophical dialogue that has extended moral considerability not only to human beings, but to plants, animals and ecosystems as a whole.[31]

English philosopher Mary Midgley argues that traditional, individualist models of ethics are drawn from seventeenth-century physics, where "the ultimate particles of matter were conceived as hard, impenetrable, homogeneous little billiard-balls, with no hooks or internal structure."[32] She is critical of the common foundation of models of morality that show human society as "a spread of social atoms, originally distinct and independent, each of which combines with others only at its own choice and in its own private interest."[33] Many traditional interpretations of rights and duties have extended to individuals—and most predominantly, individual human beings, to the exclusion of nonhumans. Such interpretations have, increasingly, come under attack by a growing number of environmental philosophers, who have sought to replace individualist ethics with holistic alternatives.

Two key examples of such holistic alternatives are found in the Land Ethic of Aldo Leopold and in the principles of Deep Ecology. Leopold argued for the value of "the Land" or biotic community for its own sake. Critical of atomistic paradigms of economic self-interest arising from traditional ethical theories, he argued for a rethinking of the meaning of humans from individual rights-holders and conquerers of the comprehensive land community—to citizens of it.[34] Consider, for example, how as an individual rights-holder in a liberal democracy, I may feel justified in doing as I wish on my own property, and so I would feel that it is my decision alone as to whether I ought to construct a shopping mall on the land that I own. Leopold would decenter such a value system to the extent that my egoistic rights would need to be rethought in terms of the impact that the clear-cutting and construction would have on the broader ecological community as a whole. The land, of course, for Leopold, is not merely soil but is, rather, a "fountain of energy flowing through a circuit of soils, plants and animals. . . . The circuit is not closed . . . but it is a sustained circuit, like a slowly augmented revolving fund of life" within which humans must find their proper place.[35]

The Deep Ecology movement similarly favors a holistic image of the human-environment bond. Arguing once again for the intrinsic value of nature, deep ecologists describe the human condition in terms of its "strong identification with the whole of nature in its diversity and interdependence of parts."[36] Deep ecology is defined as "transcend[ing] the limit of any particular science of today, including systems theory and scientific ecology."[37] The movement generally aims to move beyond reductionist paradigms in favor of what Naess calls "the relational, total-field image."[38]

All in all, then, we cannot help but recognize, first, that some versions of holistic thinking can be said to have defined the very history of western metaphysics, as far back as in the times of the ancient Greeks. Moreover, modern scientific movements, from gestalt psychology to ecology, have advanced some popular recognition of the fact that the "whole is greater than the mere sum of its parts." In environmental philosophy, arguments abound that assign moral considerability beyond atomistic individuals, to much broader contexts such as ecosystems themselves. Finally, "interdisciplinarity" is back in fashion, revived in somewhat different form from the era of systems thinking of the 1970s. As funding is extended to interdisciplinary institutes and research projects, frequently, the rationale for moving beyond the sectoral domains of individual disciplines is explained in terms of a need of "holistic," as opposed to narrowly reductionist thinking. If this is the situation, then why not embrace holism? In the following section, I consider some of the current arguments against holistic thinking.

Some Arguments against Holistic Thinking

There are have been many critiques of ecoholism.[39] While it is impossible to examine them in detail here, let me try to isolate a few of the major criticisms of holistic thinking that have emerged in environmental philosophy and to suggest that these criticisms have significant merit. Consider, first, Carolyn Merchant's concise description of holistic thinking, which I mentioned earlier, that maintains that "everything is connected to everything else."[40]

David Cooper points out that, on some level, such a claim becomes trivial, vague, and even implausible.[41] He writes: "It is without interest and moral implication that a falling tree in Australia has *some* connection with the birth rate of flies in Alaska; and it is false if it is meant that such connections must be detectable, let alone significant."[42] Certainly, ecological insights into feedback and interactions of species within ecosystems may be important, he argues, but an understanding of such interactions needs to be directed toward a study of something more specific than the relatedness of "everything to everything."

Cooper is critical of those who piously invoke "reverence" and "awe" toward all living things. Recall his comment that he cannot revere or hold sacred the Amazonian rain forest, not simply because he is irreverent or profane, but because he has never been actively engaged with that forest. Consequently, such a vocabulary of reverence is inappropriate coming from him, because it "devalues the same vocabulary when spoken by those whose home the forest is."[43] Previously, we have shown how Cooper argues against envisioning the environment as something much too *big*. When our environmental valuing extends to all of nature, everywhere, as if "there is just one big environment," then "The Environment" becomes an abstraction and ultimately, an object separate from human beings instead of the very foundation of our existence.

We are encouraged by Cooper to note that the etymological root of "environment" is that which surrounds. The French *milieu* or *environs*, or the Spanish *ambiente* are closer to the sense of "environment" that Cooper urges us to recall. More than a geographical distance that can be "measured in yards or miles," the environment as concretely experienced denotes the full breadth of meaning of place wherein a creature "knows its way about. . . . An environment, that is, is something *for* a creature, a field of meanings or significance. . . . This is why [a creature] can find itself without one, as when I am parachuted into the Sahara or a badger removed to a laboratory. Neither of us then knows the way about; nothing is familiar or has anything of home for us."[44]

Cooper suggests that it is through the formation of a complex network of meanings that a cohesion—"a certain 'wholeness'"—is conferred on an environment, "rather as the episodes in a novel belong to a coherent narrative through pointing back and forth."[45] Such a notion of wholeness is one to which we shall return, but for now, it is important to recognize that it points to a notion quite different in kind from the "big" notion of "The Environment" that inadvertently becomes the focus for incantations of many versions of ecoholism.

A related criticism of ecoholism is advanced by Kristin Shrader-Frechette, who points out the difficulty of optimizing the welfare of "different wholes" in a system where everything is related to everything else.[46] Ecologists recognize that there is no standardized level, across all communities, at which some ecological balance or stable whole exists.[47] Already, then, there becomes a need to be more specific about to which "wholes" we are choosing to refer. Indeed, since many ecosystemic explanations are neither falsifiable nor testable through some conclusive proofs, some scientists will refer to ecosystems ecology as "theological ecology."[48] Clear definitions of which "whole" is to be balanced or stabilized according to ecology seem to be elusive.

A third criticism of ecoholism argues that hypostatizing notions of ecosystem "balance" or "climax communities" have unproven scientific, let alone philosophical merit. Beyond ecologist Clements' work, environmental scientists today are less inclined to support any notion of a given ecosystemic "whole" that ultimately stabilizes in an optimal state of well-being. Shrader-Frechette puts it this way:

> There is strong biological evidence of radical changes in community composition and structure throughout history. These changes in turn suggest that there is no such thing as a stable or balanced community "type" existing through time. Rather the types only appear stable because our time frame of examination is relatively short. . . . Both spatial and temporal fluctuations undercut any universal notion of a stable or balanced community.[49]

So ecosystem "wholes," as subsisting in a healthy, balanced state are suspect within environmental science. If ecosystems are not stable wholes, but are rather both spatially and temporally synergistic and dynamic, then to what extent do they qualify, philosophically speaking, as substantive wholes in the first place?

Finally, one cannot avoid mentioning the famous attack on ecoholism advanced by Tom Regan, who maintained that ecoholism amounts to no less than "environmental fascism."[50] The argument is that by shifting moral considerability from the individual to biotic wholes, the individual can and must thereby be sacrificed—with clear ethical conscience—for the good of the larger whole. The only criterion of moral evaluation amounts to the effect that an action has on the ecosystem as a whole, rather than on individuals within the ecosystem.

When Clements refers to an ecosystem as a whole that is greater than the sum of its parts, and indeed, when such a whole is seen to "constitute a new kind of organic being"—one can begin to see the danger of a totalitarian imposition of the needs of a larger entity upon component parts. Environmental philosopher J. Baird Callicott seems to reiterate this very point and (perhaps unintentionally) support the notion of a totalitarian imposition of whole upon parts when he concludes that "ecological relationships determine the nature of organisms, rather than the other way around. . . . The whole, the system itself, thus, literally and quite straightforwardly shapes and forms its component parts."[51]

There are some who try to sidestep the charge of eco-fascism by pointing out that fascism is a political term, and therefore inappropriate within a nonpolitical setting.[52] While the term may be political, the fact is that once ecosystems are defined as organic wholes that are perhaps even more real and certainly more important in the moral hierarchy than their constituent parts, one can be led to the disturbing—if not absurd—conclusion in philosopher William Aiken's words, to "eliminate 90 percent of our numbers" for the good of our global ecosystem.[53]

In my view, any philosophy that tells us that we should sacrifice ourselves and our children for the good of the larger whole is itself morally degenerate from the start. Whether fascism is or is not, properly speaking, an exclusively political term does not change the fact that when "wholes" achieve a substantial, metaphysical reality unto themselves beyond the existence of their individual parts, and when such wholes are revered within a moral order that places them *above* their constituent parts—in such a scenario, holism begins to appear far less appealing to me.

Indeed, by now it should be clear what version of holism I am *not* willing to adopt. I am unwilling to accept a version of holism that is either positivist or modernist. Jim Cheney describes modernism as "totalizing" and immodestly "colonizing" inasmuch as it hopes to "capture everything in its abstract net, disregarding individual differences."[54] I would argue that both reductionist or atomistic versions of positivist science, no less than holistic models of ecosystems as superorganisms commit the same mistake—that is, they both inherit a metaphysical model that locates truth and Being itself in the positively existing object.

Reductionism, as well as certain versions of holism, both attempt to positively delimit and definitively categorize complex phenomena within a totalizing paradigm. As a consequence, neither is able to account adequately for implicit or hidden contexts, or for the significance of complex, synergistic relations that exceed the parameters of totalizing explanations. That which is not an entity is simply defined as a nonentity and, thereby, is excluded from the modernist paradigm.

It should be noted that it is not only some versions of ecosystem thinking that unabashedly presume that the whole is so much greater than the sum of its parts or that the parts themselves become insignificant and worth sacrificing for the good of the Superorganism. Surveying the literature from the 1970s, one is reminded of the much-lauded "systems approach" to interdisciplinary problem solving, which was seen by some to be no less than a "method of inquiry, a way of thinking which emphasizes the *Whole System* instead of component systems."[55] Systems management theory, which assumed that scientists and managers would be capable of fully capturing within any totalizing simulation all the component parts of ecosystems, for example, has rightly become increasingly suspect.

But if it is the case that interdisciplinary approaches to sustainable development aim to move beyond narrow, sectoral reductionist frameworks; and yet, if it is also the case, as I have just argued, that "holism" may easily slip into a denial of difference, a denial of the value of individual, component parts in favor of some abstract, totalitarian vision of the whole as superorganism—is there any sense at all in seeking to examine sustainability from a holistic perspective? In the following section, I will sketch out what I see to be a more favorable, general direction that might be followed with the guidance of environmental phenomenology.

Rethinking Holism: Toward a Phenomenological Inquiry

Recalling my childhood of the post–World War II era, an image comes to mind that represents the optimism of the times. As rocketships soared toward the moon; as suburban developments became the symbol of wealth and urban progress; as antibiotics cured previously fatal illnesses—my school friends speculated that some day science would find a cure for death itself and our generation would be graced, at last, with the gift of immortality that it deserved.

Mine was an immodest generation. As spectacular as many scientific developments undoubtedly were, the accompanying assumption that science and technology would make it possible for us to control nature as a whole was, in hindsight, naive and perhaps, itself, childish. Yet the supposition was that the external world was, in principle, fully knowable by the human understanding, provided that the right technology and the financial support behind research were available. Such a supposition was fueled by a deep faith, growing out of the Enlightenment, in the capacity of human reason. That faith, in itself, had its commendable sides. For one thing, it seems preferable to me that one harbor hope in human potential—even if that hope is somewhat overly idealistic—than that one drift toward nihilistic despair and self-destructive skepticism.

It is true, though, that the overriding spirit of the twentieth century—so highly optimistic about the power of human reason, as well as of science and technology—risked being blinded by its own possibilities. It is a risk not unlike that taken by the self-centered egotist who, oblivious to the world around him by virtue of his conceit, forgets to listen and thereby closes off the very possibility of learning. Assuming that human knowledge of nature can be so complete that it can be captured within any totalizing paradigm has similar consequences. In forcing the world to fit the mold of one's abstract hypotheses so that definitive theories can be constructed and neatly employed, one risks closing oneself to the rich possibilities of experience that exceed the boundaries delimited by the theory itself.

A useful example of the limits of human knowledge is provided by Dutch professor of meteorology Henk Tennekes who reflects on the unpredictability of weather and shows how the global ecosystem as a whole can never be captured within a totalizing paradigm.[56] Whereas the United States Environmental Protection Agency has developed a program whose aim is no less ambitious than to stabilize the global climate system, Tennekes describes such plans as arrogant and conceited to the point of being "suffocating."[57]

While there has been a great deal of progress made in the last thirty years in the prediction of weather patterns, the fact is, according to Tennekes, that "the true nature of the weather is more capricious and unstable than the best models we can make."[58] He traces the history of weather prediction from 1960, when it was possible to forecast the weather two days ahead of time, and when it was assumed that the so-called prediction horizon of thirty days could ultimately be achieved.

By 1974, the official aim had dropped to ten days and today, there appears to be an overall consensus that the best that scientists might achieve, even with the benefit of nearly unlimited technological resources, could be a prediction horizon of no more than seven days in advance.[59] We cannot, Tennekes concludes, manipulate the climate according to our wishes. "That is no fatalistic statement, based on a poorly thought out ideology, but a sober prognosis, based on the present knowledge of complex systems which, just like the atmosphere, exhibit chaotic behaviour."[60]

Perhaps, the limited predictability of weather ensures that the integrity of the global ecosystem may, ultimately, be protected, since it depends on something other than human manipulation to sustain it. "The integrity of the atmosphere has to be protected; it has to be kept whole," writes Tennekes. "If you want to keep something whole," he continues, "you must be careful with it. You must treat it as if it were holy."[61]

These latter words of advice deserve to be well heeded. Tennekes' point is that we might learn from recognizing the limited intelligibility of coherence in ecosystems. We might recognize that this inability may be related to the fact that we are a part of the very system that we hope to comprehend. "We cannot stand outside it and we cannot study it from a distance. . . . Coherence exists within a system, not outside it. From the moment that we try to place ourselves outside the climate system, for example, by pretending that we are capable of acting as its stewards, we can no longer contribute to the self-healing powers of the planet."[62]

Tennekes suggests that we need a new paradigm to guide us in our explorations of the planetary ecosystem—a paradigm that recognizes that the planet is not simply an object or a cumulative totality of a linear, modeling sequence, but is itself a "whole" that exceeds human calculation and manipulation, although it deserves human care nonetheless.

The fact that we now know ourselves to be incapable of predicting the weather far in advance need not mean that we should give up. On the contrary, "we will have to become creative, just like poets: tackle the impossible and acquire knowledge about things that are ultimately incomprehensible. Natural scientists should carry out research under the assumption that we understand so little of the environment, that it is almost certain that we will overlook things if we do not keep our eyes open."[63]

Our attitudes and perhaps methodologies must change, and rather than shrug off the task of understanding the planetary ecosystem as impossible, we should look for alternate strategies for the discovery of relevant meanings. On this note, Tennekes offers us some important clues to describing holistic thinking phenomenologically. First, note Tennekes' suggestion that wholeness may have something to do with *not* being able to grasp the whole as a totality. Another important moment in his work comes with the realization that wholeness may have less to do with grasping the whole as an object, and more to do, instead, with illumining a referential whole *within which we are situated.*

Finally, recall Tennekes' point that there is a fundamental difference between seeking to "manage" the global ecosystem, and contributing to the "self-healing powers of the planet." It seems that to contribute to the ecological health of the planet may have less to do with actively manipulating whole systems than with the parallel ability—such as that found in a wise physician—to stand back, and to allow nature to heal itself.

I do not mean to suggest that such a standing back means a passive and disinterested acceptance of the status quo or of a predetermined destiny. Rather, the shift in attitude may suggest a different mode of thinking—one that attends to more than simply positively existing entities. This conclusion seems to be behind Heidegger's own reflections upon the fundamental difference between *totality* and *wholeness*. In his *Basic Problems of Phenomenology*, he asks:

And the world? Is it the sum of what is within the world? By no means. . . . World is not something subsequent that we calculate as a result from the sum of all beings. The world comes not afterward but beforehand, in the strict sense of the word. Beforehand: that which is unveiled and understood already in advance. . . . The world as already unveiled in advance is such that we do not in fact specifically occupy ourselves with it or apprehend it, but instead, it is so self-evident, so much a matter of course, that we are completely oblivious to it.[64]

Why is wholeness not equivalent to totality? Perhaps wholeness belongs to that which we discover in the world prethematically, implicitly—prior to the totality that we subsequently construct by way of a summative technique. Could it be, then, that holistic thinking appeals to the full breadth of our experience, beyond the limits of calculative reason, to include our prereflective awareness of implicit, referential contexts and sensibility toward relationships that exceed the boundaries of explicitly delineated totalities?

Anyone who has ever been moved by a work of poetry will know that the work as a whole is more than the sum of the words that constitute it. The significance of the poem lies not only in the words that are spoken, but also, in what remains *unsaid*. When too much is explained in a thematic fashion, the poetry itself is placed at risk, in favor of indiscriminate chatter. Yet is it only poetry that, in this sense, relies upon such a phenomenon of absence to constitute its meaning?

Consider the phenomenon of reading a text. In reading a sentence, I do not accumulate the individual words one by one, in an additive move, so that finally, in the end, I compute all the words together to form a meaningful totality. On the contrary, the hermeneutic experience shows us that understanding the whole sentence requires more than a linear sequence whereby we "store up" what has been read until the very end. Instead, the meaning of the text is progressively revealed throughout the reading. Reading is neither simply sequential, analytical, nor summative, but is meaningful and holistic, and requires human interpretation of the interplay between both whole and parts, rather than the merely cumulative significance of individual words.

Philosopher and physicist Henri Bortoft likens hermeneutic interpretation of a text to the metaphor of the hologram.[65] Contrary to regular photographic plates, if the hologram plate is broken into fragments, a single, illuminated fragment shows the same three-dimensional optical reconstruction of the original object, rather than merely a part of that object. In other words, the whole is present in each part, although more and more dimly with increasingly smaller portions.

It is true that metaphors can be misleading. Nevertheless, in this case, it is significant that with both the hologrammatic image as well as the process of interpretation of texts, the whole is something other than the mere cumulative totality of the parts; and interestingly, the whole is in some way reflected in the parts. Bortoft feels that the hologram symbolizes a relation of whole to parts where neither is ontologically primary. When we think of moving from parts to whole in a merely summative manner, the whole "comes later than" the parts and, consequently, in such a linear sequence, the whole is seen as secondary to the parts. The alternative suggestion that the parts are determined by the whole becomes equally simplistic, however. "It puts the whole," says Bortoft, "in the position of a false transcendental. . . . This approach effectively considers the whole as if it were a part, but a 'superpart,' which controls and dominates the other, lesser parts."[66]

Once we refuse to subsume the notion of "whole" into either a superentity or as the cumulative total of entities, an alternative possibility arises. Certainly, it is most natural to be explicitly occupied primarily with *something*. If the whole is not a mere object or entity, then it is no thing among things. In this sense, it is nothing—although not merely nothing. It is deemed to be nothing, only when our awareness is focused specifically on entities only.

The alternative is to conceive of what Bortoft calls the "authentic whole," which is no individual thing—but, nevertheless, not nothing.

> This possibility is difficult for awareness, which cannot distinguish the two. Yet we have an illustration immediately on hand with the experience of reading. We do not take the meaning of a sentence to be a word. The meaning of a sentence is no-word. But evidently this is not the same as nothing, for if it were, we could never read! The whole presences within the parts, but from the standpoint of the awareness which grasps the external parts, the whole is an absence. This absence, however, is not the same as nothing. Rather, it is an *active* absence in as much as we do not try to be aware of the whole, as if we could grasp it like a part, but instead let ourselves be open to be moved by the whole.[67]

Bortoft describes how the actor is moved by the whole play. The actor does not stand away from his part as if it were an object to be fully captured by consciousness. Rather, when the actor "starts to be acted by the play," and avoids trying to act the play by imposing himself on it as if it were an object to be mastered, the role is appropriated in such a way that the play as a whole is genuinely meaningful, rather than merely a recitation of memorized lines.[68] To achieve authentic wholeness, Bortoft concludes, one must "dwell in the phenomenon instead of replacing it with a mathematical representation."[69]

Bortoft leaves us with a number of important questions. How, more specifically, does one seek to authentically "dwell in the phenomenon?" How might such a dwelling be differentiated from analytic representation of the phenomenon? What is the role of calculation in such dwelling? Finally, what might a holistic mode of thinking as "dwelling in the phenomenon" contribute to our understanding of sustainability itself? In the following chapters, I explore in further detail these questions, with specific attention to the contribution that can be made by environmental phenomenology.

5

Ontological Foundations of Environmental Thinking

When you study the mental history of the world, you see that people since times immemorial
had a general teaching or doctrine about the wholeness of the world . . .
—C.G. Jung

In this chapter, I explore the possibility that holism in environmental thinking has less to do with imposing a static, unified structure upon a diverse and variegated world than with illumining an implicit order and integrity of what Heidegger calls the *functionality contexture* of our surroundings.[1] Such environmental integrity, I will argue, cannot be reduced to subjective constructs or theoretical explanations, any more than it can be explained in terms of an objective reality that stands outside human interpretation. Since phenomenology aims to avoid the metaphysical pitfalls of either a realist or idealist stance, an alternative, ontological account of the whole will be sought.

Recall that ontology raises the question of the meaning of Being instead of remaining at the level of an ontic concern for specific beings or entities. Heidegger himself proposed that phenomenology is ontology. To explore sustainability from a phenomenological perspective means, therefore, to examine the ontological foundations of environmental thinking. In this chapter, I aim to show in what sense such thinking can be said to be "holistic" instead of reductionist. I explore the possibility that a meaningful description of holism must pay heed to the significance of the phenomenon of absence in environmental perception, primordial time, the fundamental givenness of the natural world, as well as plurality and difference. Chapter 6 will then offer some clues as to how an ethic of sustainability might emerge on the foundation of phenomenological ontology. Overall, my aim is to consider the place of phenomenology in generating a more fundamental, nonpositivist interpretation of sustainability itself.

Environmental Perception and Holism

In the 1970s, environmental psychologist William Ittelson distinguished traditional "object" perception research of psychology from the newer concept of "environmental perception."[2] In Ittelson's view, traditional "object" perception research emphasized singular stimuli (such as brightness, color, or depth) and was typically undertaken in controlled, laboratory situations. While rigorous and detailed, such an analytic approach to studying human behavior necessarily severed the human subject from the complex environmental factors with which it originally interacted. Critics charged that by controlling singular stimuli, results of traditional studies were often accurate within their prescribed limits, but their findings remained artificial and methodologically problematic because they were ultimately based on an oversimplified and incomplete research framework.

Research in environmental perception, on the other hand, was to be undertaken in the field, within the functional settings of landscapes, buildings, and cities. No longer restricting themselves to investigating singular patterns of sensations or simple stimuli, researchers of environmental perception were concerned with the complex interaction of environmental processes within the lived experience of the perceiver actively engaged in the everyday world. These processes previously had been ignored by positivist psychology, and yet they were seen to constitute the ground of our everyday behavior and deserved more in-depth study in their full complexity.

One might imagine that Heidegger would have been sympathetic to this general shift in research focus, for he had argued earlier that individual entities are always originally perceived within a broader context of surroundings—within a "functionality whole."[3] "In our natural comportment toward things," he explained, "we never think a *single* thing, and whenever we seize upon it expressly for itself, we are taking it *out* of a contexture to which it belongs in its real content."[4] Our originary encounter with the items of the world surrounding us is not a piecemeal identification of each item in isolation. On the contrary, a genuine understanding of human perception recognizes that entities are perceived and interpreted as meaningful within a web of relations in which they are primordially situated.

Critical of philosopher Fichte, who challenged an audience to "think the wall, and then think the one who thinks the wall," Heidegger recognized that in "thinking the wall," one must extricate it from its originary belonging to its environment.[5] Such a move involves an abstraction and an artificial construction of an isolated object of perception. Similarly, if one attempts to "think the one who thinks the wall," a speculative attempt is made to isolate the human subject from its originary involvement and pretheoretical understanding of the wall—and presumably the room—within which the immediate human perception is fundamentally situated.

Rather than describe the "environing world" (*Umwelt*) in terms of a compendium of abstract objects isolated from their surroundings, the phenomenologist is concerned with illumining the original belonging of a functional, environmental whole that is "*pre*-understood"—that is, comprehended prior to an intellectualized analysis of discrete entities.[6] Heidegger's famous example of the hammer is instructive. He maintains that when we use this tool for hammering, our relationship to the hammer becomes all the more "primordial" in terms of what Heidegger refers to as its "readiness-to-hand" (*Zuhandenheit*).[7] When a piece of equipment is actually put to use, I appropriate this tool in a manner fitting its originary purpose or reference—or as Heidegger puts it, according to its "specific 'manipulability' (*Handlichkeit*)."[8] The hammer as a solitary object withdraws (*zurückzuziehen*) in favor of the broader context and referential whole within which the hammer's primordial meaning itself emerges.[9]

It is a very different matter when I look at this same object as "present-at-hand" (*vorhanden*). As I attempt to thematically grasp the hammer as a hammer-thing, or to theoretically circumscribe it in isolation from its context, I no longer view it in terms of its immediate belonging to its environment but, rather, as an artificially manifest object, extracted from the web of relations that help ontologically to reveal its originary meaning as a hammer. Clearly delineated properties of the tool can now be analyzed and cataloged. In the process of compiling such an inventory of properties, however, the primordial belonging of the hammer to a broader context of meanings and relationships to the world is no longer of primary concern.

Ultimately, Heidegger suggests that we perceive the world not as a sum total of individual, discrete entities, but rather, "what is given to us primarily is the unity of an *equipmental whole*" and an "equipmental contexture of things."[10] The goal of phenomenology is to explicate this whole as more than the ontic accumulation of singular objects. Instead, the aim is to illumine the whole in terms of the ontological ground that sustains it.

To return to Fichte's example, Heidegger points out that in our originary, unmediated encounter with the world, "we do not in fact apprehend walls—not unless we are getting bored. Nevertheless, the walls are already present even before we think them as objects."[11] In fact, not only the walls but many other aspects of our environment appear to us, prior to our determining individual properties through intellectual analysis, "not as a jumbled heap of things but as an environs, a surroundings, which contains within itself a closed, intelligible contexture."[12]

To help to clarify these points with my students, I ask them to imagine that in flicking the switch on the wall, I am able to transform the floor upon which their desks are sitting into glass. What would their reactions be? Without exception, their descriptions evoke images of "vulnerability," "risk," and sometimes "excitement" and even "danger." One of the interesting sides to this experiment is that the students are asked to focus on the floor differently than they would have done in their everyday experience—an experience that very likely would have meant that the floor itself was never explicitly noticed throughout the entire term. In refocusing in this way, the students recognize that they were never *unaware* of the floor, but it melted into the equipmental contexture described by Heidegger. In so doing, the floor was prethematically understood: it was neither explicitly reflected upon nor ignored, but perceived in terms of the pattern and order revealed by the room as a whole.[13]

Note that the room as a "whole" is not conceived here as if it were an explicit object of a totalizing mode of awareness. There is certainly a sense that the room itself recedes into the background to provide a meaningful context within which specific entities are situated. In this sense, a phenomenology of perception points to an understanding of holism that moves beyond the present-at-hand to an ontological ground that is never fully revealed as an explicitly articulated object of understanding. I shall return to explore this point at more length shortly.

Perception and Understanding

Not only are elements such as the floor and the wall more than autonomous, ontic entities that cumulatively constitute our environment. The very process of environmental perception—ontologically interpreted—is more than one ontic moment among others that constitute our understanding of environment. For example, consider how some environmental psychologists distinguish in their textbooks between environmental perception "as the initial gathering of information"— from environmental cognition as "the further processing of the information."[14] The task for phenomenologists becomes one of describing the unity of meaning that emerges through the initial process of transcendental understanding of the world, prior to such an abstract bifurcation between perception and cognition.

While we perceive the world from specific, individual perspectives, phenomenology recognizes that one perspective implicates and anticipates another. When I perceive a table, for example, my explicit sense impression may be of only two front legs but still, I expect—without thematically reflecting upon this judgment—that the table possesses two back legs as well. I do not possess a sensation first, then further process the information to finally possess meaning. The meaning of the perceived environment reveals itself within a holistic context of understanding. Prior to the present-at-hand dissection of experience that may separate perception from cognition, the ready-to-hand immersion in the world is such that perception is accompanied by memory, imagination, emotion, and understanding.

The work of Henri Bortoft is instructive on this point.[15] The pattern in figure 5.1 appears at first glance to consist of an arbitrary accumulation of black and white fields.[16] With a more careful attending to the patchwork, an image of a giraffe head and upper neck begins to reveal itself.

Figure 5.1. The Power of Organizing Ideas (Used by permission of Lindisfarne Books, Hudson, NY 12534.)

Bortoft points out that "the pattern registered on the retina of the eye is the same whether the giraffe is seen or not."[17] There is no change in the sensory experience of the picture, once the giraffe is noted. Rather, the image is differently interpreted, on the basis of what Bortoft calls a different "organizing idea."[18] I prefer the term "ordering idea," since it suggests a less thematic process of constituting meaning, but still, the point is that sensory perception does not happen separately from or even temporally prior to the interpretive moment.

Indeed, as Bortoft notes, the aim of some scientists to objectively and *directly observe* the world is philosophically naive, because every observation emerges within a horizon of interpretation that affects what we see in the first place: "Eliminating all concepts would not, therefore, achieve a direct encounter with the world. On the contrary, it would only achieve the end of the world."[19] The world is meaningful because it appears within an ordering horizon of understanding that accompanies sense perception and that, spontaneously and often prethematically, places distinct entities within the context of a referential whole. To begin to comprehend environmental perception in this way as more than the sensation of discrete, present-at-hand elements is to move closer to the ontological ground that Heidegger himself is intent on exploring.

Temporality and Environmental Awareness

While it is true for Heidegger that environments are encountered "holistically" in the sense that connections and relationships among objects are prethematically understood, the question remains: Does Heidegger's interpretation of the ready-to-hand say anything more than that our tools are situated within a context where "everything is connected to everything else?" If not, can Heidegger avoid the criticisms of this notion of holism that were pointed out in chapter 4?

Indeed, Heidegger describes psychology as an "ontic" science rather than an ontological endeavor. In what way—if at all—is his ontological description of the ready-to-hand significantly different from the psychologist's (presumably ontic) environmental perception research that purports to study holistic, everyday behavioral settings rather than contrived laboratory conditions? In advocating environmental perception research over traditional "object" perception research, were environmental psychologists like Ittelson not in fact enlarging upon Heidegger's inquiry? Or is it that they were inadvertently still locked within the paradigms of positivist, ontic endeavors after all? A concomitant question can be raised regarding the degree to which ecologists concerned with the holistic study of ecosystems are also still operating within the traditional scientific paradigms that they explicitly criticize.

To understand how phenomenology moves us beyond such paradigms is to see how ontology is to be differentiated from ontic inquiries. Let us return for a moment to Heidegger's example of the hammer. We recall that when it is put to use, it is not theoretically analyzed. Heidegger tells us that the hammer itself must "withdraw in order to be ready-to-hand quite authentically."[20] What is the essence of such "withdrawal?"

In hammering, I am not primarily concerned with the tool itself, but rather, with the work to be produced—in other words, the "towards-which" of the hammer. While the hammer does not physically disappear, its very meaning as a hammer is secured by virtue of the fact that its existence as a present-at-hand object withdraws in favor of the task at hand. This means that the ontological meaning of the hammer is, in some sense, traced back to the work process and to the one who executes the work.

When Heidegger speaks of the meaning of the hammer in terms of the "towards-which," he indicates that it finds its meaning within a basic, anticipatory stance that carpenters employ in completing their task. Such an anticipatory stance is present because in perceiving our environment, we do not simply *see*, but we also *look for*. Instead of simply *hearing*, we also *listen for*. Human beings encounter their world by being, in some sense, always *attuned to it* and open to possibilities that may announce themselves in the future.

In describing the essence of human understanding, Heidegger tells us that "the being that we ourselves are is not *also* present in the lecture hall here, say, like the seats, desks and blackboards."[21] Being human means that we do not simply exist as tangible, clearly delimited objects but are ontologically defined as being-ahead-of-ourselves. It is for this reason that the early Heidegger refers to human beings as *Dasein*—that is, as Being-*there*, rather than simply predefined as static entities here and now. More than being simply *present*, as are tables and chairs, human beings appropriate their *past* histories through memory and imagination and project themselves in their hopes and in their expectations toward a *future* that is yet to be delineated. In this sense, time—as an ecstatical unity of past, present, and future—defines us in our very essence.[22]

Time, though, is more than the clock on the wall or calendar entries. We do not exist simply *in time*, but our understanding of the world is temporal through and through. In Heidegger's special wording, "ecstatical temporality clears the 'there' primordially. It is what primarily regulates the possible unity of all Dasein's existential structures."[23] Inasmuch as we are temporal and all understanding requires temporality as the horizon within which beings appear, time will be seen to constitute the fundamental, ontological clearing within which specific, ontic entities and events find their meaning in the first place.

On such an interpretation of time, it is evident that temporality is more than the ontic measure of the clock. The condition of the possibility of the quantification of time is primordial temporality, ontologically understood as more than one entity among entities. As the original horizon of meaning within which ontic moments of clock time are measured, temporality is fundamentally constitutive of human interpretation of the world and provides the clearing within which items within that world are understood. Time is neither a present-at-hand entity, nor ready-to-hand but rather, it *temporalizes* itself, making possible and indeed unifying the multiplicity of human modes of Being.[24]

What would it be like to try to conceive of anything in the absence of time? Even the eternal—as being beyond time—can only be comprehended against the backdrop of temporality.[25] Indeed, our very language expresses concepts temporally in tenses and is historically situated.[26] For this reason, Heidegger refers to "primordial time" as ontologically constitutive of all human understanding.[27] Inasmuch as primordial time is not an entity, it is not some Thing. As the condition of the possibility of the emergence of entities, it is no-thing.[28] Such an interpretation of primordial temporality places a lack and a nullity at the very core of our Being. How do we understand such a lack? Might it have something to do with the "withdrawal" of the hammer that we began to investigate earlier?

According to Heidegger, "the being we call Dasein is as such open for . . . Openness belongs to its being."[29] Rather than being, in our essence, closed and homogeneous entities, we are projecting possibilities toward a future that is-not-yet, in a world that constitutes our very meaning as Being-there. We are not entities that exist independently of the world within which we are thrown. On the contrary, as being-in-the-world, we are always transcending: "transcendence is precisely what essentially characterizes its being. . . . The selfhood of the Dasein is founded on its transcendence."[30]

The father of phenomenology, Edmund Husserl, taught that pure consciousness never persists in and of itself in a vacuum but, as intentional, is always *consciousness of.*[31] Similarly, Heidegger builds on this notion of intentionality, suggesting that human existence is defined in terms of a fundamental, ontological projection and interpretive stance that are in-the-world. Such a stance, however, is not simply a relationship between two entities—subjective consciousness and objective world. On the contrary, transcendental understanding constitutes the condition of the possibility of our differentiating between entities—and subjects and objects—in the first place.

To understand the phenomenon of being human in terms of a fundamental *lack* is to recognize that we are defined in our essence as incomplete—open to the ever-more of a world that I did not create but that I am always aiming to comprehend in my fundamental, transcendental comportment toward the world.[32] If the essence of my being-in-the-world is constituted temporally so that an open-ended future of possibilities defines my interpretive stance, then it follows that I am more than a neat, hypostatized bundle of sense impressions. Our very being-a-whole consists in the fact that we are underway—developing, changing, and interpreting the world from diverse horizons of expectation.

Heidegger tells us that in being-ahead-of-ourselves, there is always something "still outstanding" for us: "It is essential to the basic constitution of Dasein that there is *constantly something still to be settled [eine ständige Unabgeschlossenheit]*. Such a lack of totality signifies that there is something still outstanding in one's potentiality-for-Being."[33] The unifying structure of temporality is not a structure that definitively bounds our being, but on the contrary, the temporality of understanding points to an interpretation of human beings as other than ontic entities—as on the way, as finite, and as fundamentally defined by unrealized, future possibilities.

The Withdrawal of the World

The "withdrawal" of the hammer, then, occurs within a horizon of understanding that reveals the world at different levels of thematic and prethematic discernment. Human awareness, as temporal, is more than a container of explicitly delineated objects and definitively bounded events. The hammer recedes as a direct object of contemplation because the carpenter is not simply a human subjectivity whose attention is directed to the appropriation of the totality of present-at-hand objects. For the carpenter, the hammer is situated within a horizon of possibilities that are themselves defined by the work at hand and the holistic, temporal process of production.

One begins to see how Being-a-whole, in Heidegger's terminology, is differentiated from being constituted as a totality of ontic moments. Human interpretation of the world amounts to more than the accumulation of discrete entities—whether those entities are objects, ideas or states. Grounded in a nullity, the holistic interpretive moment involves an ontological, transcendental projection of understanding that is, in essence, capable of doing much more than amassing discrete entities.

Indeed, to say that such entities are always perceived holistically as figures against a "ground" is insufficient, because that ground is more than another, larger contextual entity. On the contrary, the ground is, in Heidegger's thought, an "*Ab-grund*," or a ground-without-ground. One recognizes, for instance, that the hammer is more than a brute, physical object but always appears within a temporal horizon of interpretation. There might be as many interpretations of the hammer as there are human beings now and in the future. In this sense, the hammer is more than a mere physical entity, because it always exceeds my current perspective of it. No single interpretation can ever capture even the simple instrument of the hammer conclusively and definitively, because every interpretation is finite and essentially perspectival and could, in principle, be redefined indefinitely into the future.

Recognizing the significance of the interpretive moment does not mean, however, that we are compelled to admit that the hammer collapses into the domain of merely subjective judgment calls. I do not *create* the hammer by virtue of the fact that I perceive it in my own unique and perhaps even creative manner. Indeed, to recognize this fact is to see that the world always exceeds my interpretive grasp of it. Any Faustian illusions of grandeur become tempered once one recognizes that my existential comportment is directed toward a world that exceeds my control because, in some sense, it will always surpass my limited, temporal understanding of it. In this sense, I become humbled and even beholden to the fundamental, existential *givenness* of a world that I did not create.[34]

Even time itself—previously described as more than a container but as the condition of understanding—is misconstrued if it is viewed simply as a horizon that collapses within the domain of subjectivity. For the later Heidegger, true time is even more than the ecstatic unity of past, present, and future, but is four-dimensional: "Time-space now is the name for the openness which opens up in the mutual self-extending of futural approach, past and present. . . . The unity of time's three-dimensions consists in the interplay of each toward each. This interplay proves to be the true extending, playing in the very heart of time, the fourth dimension, so to speak."[35]

Ultimately for Heidegger, "time *is* not. There is, It gives time."[36] Being and time are fundamentally offered through a giving, a grace of presence in its epochal transmutations and a primordial opening up of existence itself. We have seen how human understanding of the world is more than a totalizing activity of accumulating discrete entities. More than this, though, an exploration of human awareness leads us to the fundamental mystery of the givenness of Being and Time wherein historical events and moments of understanding find their place.

Heidegger steers clear of any religious or spiritual accounts of the grace of Being. He carefully avoids collapsing his ontological reflections into theological abstraction. Perhaps his notion of the givenness of the world is best understood not in a pastor's fabricated sermon but in the moment when one stands in the majesty of an old growth forest, fully recognizing that such a wonder cannot be recreated by human ingenuity in the absence of time and nature's own unfolding.

Consider, for instance, the case that arose in 1993, when almost three hundred men, women, and children were apprehended by the Royal Canadian Mounted Police for protesting clearcut logging in British Columbia's Clayoquot Sound. This event constituted the largest mass arrest in the history of the province.[37] I suspect that such considerable commitment was not simply deduced by way of a scientific inventory of present-at-hand effects of logging, although those effects would have been a large part of the problem. To risk a criminal record in defense of an ecosystem suggests to me a fundamental respect of the natural environment that is worth exploring further.

What emerges as I make my way through an old growth forest, such as in B.C.'s Clayoquot Sound? Certainly, nature *can* be viewed as present-at-hand and often is, by scientists and researchers who set out to examine its properties and to explain its causal relations. But when this happens, Heidegger writes, "the Nature which 'stirs and strives,' which assails us and enthralls us as landscape, remains hidden. The botanist's plants are not the flowers of the hedgerow; the 'source' which the geographer establishes for a river is not the 'springhead in the dale.'"[38]

Heidegger begins to echo the refrains of a Romantic, but he is engaging in much more than an empty sentimentalizing. Drawing from before the dawn of a metaphysical age to the insights of the pre-Socratic Greek philosophers, Heidegger aims to describe an originary understanding of nature, ontologically prior to our own positivist interpretations. He urges us to rethink the emergence of nature as *physis*, that is, as "self-blossoming emergence . . . opening up, unfolding, that which manifests itself in such unfolding and perseveres and endures in it; in short, the realm of things that emerge and linger on."[39]

Heidegger argues that *physis* denoted for the Greeks much more than merely "physics" or even the physical existence of entities. Instead, "*physis* is Being itself" and refers to the process of self-emergence that arises and endures, that shows itself while at the same time being rooted in concealment and self-withdrawal.[40] As I make my way through the old growth forest, I need not explicitly focus on or generalize from every piece of individual wildlife in my path to comprehend that here, nature as *physis* is a primordial unfolding that emerges from its own accord, beyond my whim or my aesthetic or academic interests.

The enduring presence of nature as it appears here in the old growth forest is more than that of a perfect specimen or a reified picture of the environment as a whole. The richness and diversity of the forest environment is experienced as a revelation of the very *essence* of nature as *physis*. To speak of the "essence" of nature, however, is to recognize that essence for Heidegger—though not a metaphysical absolute—does indicate a historical congealing of meaning and a "holding sway"of the self-extending presence of Being, whereby the belonging together of discrete events within the natural environment is made manifest. While never spared from the effects of time, "essence" for Heidegger is a moment within the temporal unfolding of Being itself. Essence is a preserving whereby that which comes later could not be without that preserving moment.

It is significant that, in speaking of notions such as "holism" or "essence," we tend to hypostatize these concepts and definitively bound them to secure their

meaning. But holism in Heidegger's phenomenology is not a reference to any totalizing entity any more than the notion of "essence" is understood as a substantive, reified quality of Being. We may use "essence" and "nature" interchangeably,
such as when we describe the nature or essence of a piece of artwork, or of a
piece of poetry. Heidegger points out, however, that the root of the Latin *natura*
can be traced back to the metaphysical reification of nature as present-at-hand
and is indicative of the search for the "whatness" (*quidditas*) of things.

The notion of "essence" is fundamentally distinguished from such a substantive, unchanging ontic understanding of *quidditas*. To contemplate the essence of
the natural environment is, in the words of philosopher Bruce Foltz, to see that
the "fertility of the earth and . . . the sweet fragrance of blossoms . . . are neither the
immutable populace of a supersensuous realm nor the configurations of trend
and fancy. They endure not forever, nor as absolutely self-identical, yet prevail-
ingly; they show themselves to be such as they are and *are* precisely in that self-
showing. We count on them, as we should and, indeed, must."[41]

To contemplate the essence of nature is not to speculate on an abstract, enduring quality of the environment. Heidegger's notion of essence is more truthfully
revealed to me in less philosophically dramatic moments. For instance, the essence
of nature may be more meaningful when I retreat to my garden in autumn and
wonder at the height of the trees and the splendor of the colors of the leaves;
when my imagination roams and in the background, I revel at the song of the dis-
appearing bluejay; when I am subsumed in the full presence of the sunlit landscape in a unique moment of silent reverie. Fixed categories and descriptions
never can do justice to the awareness that nature as *physis* points to an emerging,
living process and a breaking forth that is never entirely secured but is treasured,
nevertheless, in a lingering moment that "holds sway."

The Grace of Nature

Yet that to which I bear witness is nature as presencing, emerging, and abiding—
as well as in terms of its opacity and withdrawal. When Heidegger speaks of the
earth, he is describing not the substance from which things are constituted, but
rather, "whence" the self-extending presence of Being arises and "unto which" it
returns.[42] Earth is the "serving bearer, blossoming and fruiting, spreading out in
rock and water, rising up into plant and animal."[43]

Many scientists say that the old growth forest cannot be replaced by replanting,
because the ecosystem as a whole needs time to evolve in its fullness and its complexity. To recognize this fact is to recognize that nature unfolds beyond my control. It is to acknowledge that the grace of life extends beyond the mechanism of
"self-regulating systems" or "cybernetic models" and embraces the mystery of
self-concealment as the very source of the possibility of the emergence of nature.[44]

What happens when the old growth forest is destroyed by a clearcut? I suspect that the three hundred protesters at Clayquot Sound were not there simply to defend individual trees. The passion that drives such loyalty is likely directed to something deeper. Perhaps they were overtaken by this rupture of a landscape, particularly in terms of the lack of humility that drives such an intrusion. Human engineering may have seemed to lay wholescale claim to an environment, as if this setting were simply a collection of replaceable items instead of a hallowed moment of life's unfolding and the grace of emergent nature.

My own feeling when I stand in the midst of such destruction is a sense of guilt that is more than a merely psychological state of mind. To deny one's beholdenness to nature through large-scale environmental destruction threatens to deny a relation between human beings and their world that should include care and respect for the mystery—understood not as something yet to be conquered through knowledge, but as the ever-more of the source of existence itself. To bear witness to the self-emergence of the natural world is to acknowledge that I belong to this world, not as conquerer but as protector and even servant.[45]

The humility elicited by such a stance toward the world is not a moral imperative in the form of rules as to how one *ought* to act but, rather, an illumination of the fundamental ontological relation between human beings and the world in which they are thrown. It is naive to assume that my own being is separate from the mysterious givenness of Being and the unfolding of nature as *physis*.

It is equally naive to think that our predominant understanding of social, economic and environmental issues in light of this realization remains unchanged. Consider the example of the 1997 closing of Japan's Ministry of Education's Geodesy Council—one of the last remaining earthquake-prediction programs in the world. In the 1960s, geophysicists believed that their rapidly increasing knowledge of the movement of the earth's rocky plates would allow them to predict when and where earthquakes would occur. The closing of Japan's Geodesy Council signals the end of an era of technological optimism in this field. Mistaken predictions climaxed in the failure of the council to anticipate the Kobe earthquake in 1995 that killed sixty-four hundred people in an apparently seismically inactive area.

The example of such programs indicate the practical economic and social consequences of a pervasive faith in human technological prowess, and a forgetting of the mysterious relation between human beings and the grace of Being itself. To elicit humility in such cases does not mean that we must philosophically reflect on some abstract concepts of the givenness of nature. What Heidegger's reflections do suggest is that, rather than expending our energy in programs that seek definitively to predict and control nature, it might be wiser to direct our concerns toward properly responding to nature as it offers itself in the fullness of its mystery.

Some might understand this latter statement to mean that we should just passively sit back and let nature take its course, but I do not mean to suggest any policy of resignation at all. On the contrary, having spent 160 billion Yen over the last thirty years, the council is wisely encouraging the government to redirect future resources from earthquake prediction programs to the design of safer buildings and better strategies for dealing with disasters after they occur.[46] To me, this example clearly shows the difference between a policy whereby one naively assumes that one has the ability to capture nature within a holistic umbrella of rational control and a policy open to the possibility of a holistic thinking that pays heed to the grace of Being and the givenness of a natural world within which we must learn to seek our rightful place.

One final point. It is not easy to make such a shift in thinking, without assuming that the choices are simply between, on the one hand, proactive environmental management or on the other hand, passive resignation in the face of uncontrollable forces. The phenomenological approach supports neither of these two options but argues instead for a realistic interpretation of environmental issues in light of the fundamental ontological belonging of human beings to their world. The task is not as esoteric as it may seem. Polls show that fully half of the Japanese population still expect to be given proper warning by the government of future earthquakes, despite the widespread recognition among experts of the futility of such a task.[47] Humility is sometimes a difficult lesson to learn.

Holism and Environmental Health

Is holistic thinking important to environmentalism? I have advanced the phenomenological position that an alternative to reductionist thinking is needed, and this conclusion is fairly prevalent among environmentalists themselves who speak about ecosystems "as a whole" and who argue for a broadened scientific vision of ecological health.

The word "holistic," however, is not without its problems. It is too easy to slip into a mindset that views "the whole" as a larger, more significant superentity. When holistic thinking is described as an integrative activity, too often the process of "synthesis" that is thereby implicated leads to a situation where the parts are subsumed and superseded by the whole—again, as a superentity. Phenomenological thinking is primarily directed toward offering an alternative, both to artificial, piecemeal analysis as well as to reifying notions of the whole as transcending the parts that constitute it.

If we are to speak of holistic thinking at all, the phenomenological description is certainly of an ordering activity and a meaningful interpretation of events. At the same time, the unifying order of meaning, as ontological, emerges in respect of the temporality and "no-thingness" that lies at the core of our own being and the mystery of the givenness of nature that is evident to us in our finite, perspectival grasp of the world. The unity of holistic thinking must also embrace difference, and the fundamental, ontological significance of nullity and absence as well.[48]

Let me consider an example that shows how such phenomenological thinking may throw new light on our interpretation of environmental problems. The World Commission on Environment and Development maintains that "good health is the foundation of human welfare and productivity. Hence, a broad-based health policy is essential for sustainable development."[49] Similarly, the Rio Declaration, approved by the United Nations Conference on Environment and Development in 1992 endorsed the principle that "states shall cooperate in a spirit of global partnership to conserve, protect and restore the health and integrity of the Earth's ecosystem."[50]

The International Society for Ecosystem Health suggests that the idea of health "provides an immediate and powerful approach" to the daunting task of overcoming the earth's environmental crisis.[51] There seems to be overriding consensus that promoting environmental health is a priority in the development of sustainability.

There is far less consensus on what the term "ecosystem health" might mean. Despite its call for a "broad-based health policy," it is striking that the World Commission on Environment and Development persistently refers to health almost exclusively in terms of *human* health.[52] Others define ecosystem health as "a new approach to environmental management."[53] What might the phenomenological contribution be, in coming to an understanding of the meaning of environmental health? How might the ontological possibilities of absence and the withdrawal of Being inform this discussion?

In *The Enigma of Health: The Art of Healing in a Scientific Age*, hermeneutic phenomenologist Hans-Georg Gadamer argues that health is enigmatic, to the extent that when it is present, it is absent from our explicit attention.[54] When we are in good health, we take it for granted and it becomes the hidden condition for our paying heed to other events around us: "Health is not something that is revealed through investigation, but rather something that manifests itself precisely by virtue of escaping our attention. . . . It is not something which invites or demands permanent attention. Rather, it belongs to that miraculous capacity we have to forget ourselves."[55]

"Good health" becomes difficult to define, not only because it relies on many different and complex factors but because the ontological significance of absence is difficult to capture in ontic categories. If Gadamer is right, then an approach to medicine that relies on empirical description and quantification of positively existing entities may be limited from the start in its ability to comprehend the full meaning of good health. Indeed, Gadamer argues that when modern medicine seeks to *master* illness, such an approach may easily forget that restoring health is less a matter of constructing something new than of restoring a previously taken-for-granted state of affairs.

Health practitioners are urged to recognize that the art of healing involves more than the "projective construction" of generalized rules or universally applicable facts; it also demands that one learns "when to stand back."[56] Medicine as an art, rather than a mere craft, "is from the beginning a particular kind of doing and making which produces nothing of its own and has no material of its own to produce something from."[57] The expert practice of this art requires that it instill itself within the process of nature to return this process to a balanced state of health when it is under duress. The art of healing also, paradoxically, must allow itself to disappear, once the natural equilibrium of health has been restored.

The state of being healthy, Gadamer argues, possesses ontological primacy inasmuch as it is the condition of our "being ready for and open to everything."[58] Just as Being cannot be reduced to a being or entity, so too the ontological primacy of health suggests that any reduction to simplistic, ontic categories is doomed to failure. For this reason, those who hope to delimit the concept of health in narrow, disciplinary terms—for instance in terms of chemistry, biology, or even economic definitions—will find that the concept of well-being always exceeds such reductionist descriptions. Similarly, doctors who interpret medicine as merely the technical application of discrete, ontic bits of data to human lives debilitated by illness lose sight of the fact that the art of healing requires a genuine listening and discriminating regard for the patient as a whole.

Gadamer points out that "in Greek, the whole of being is *hole ousia*. Anyone knowing this phrase in Greek will also hear, alongside the expression 'the whole of being,' the suggestion of 'hale and healthy being.' The being whole of the whole and the being healthy of the whole, the healthiness of well-being, seem to be most intimately related."[59] Wholeness, like good health, is understood to exceed our thematic grasp. Neither phenomenon is the result of a projective construction. Rather, each invites a phenomenological description of an ontological ground that is taken for granted and only implicitly acknowledged through its very withdrawal from the totalizing grip of ontic categories.

While Gadamer addresses human health in his book, his conclusions are equally illumining of the meaning of ecosystem health. Many agree that the concept of environmental health arises principally when the well-being of the ecosystem is disrupted. David J. Rapport, who holds the position of chair in Ecosystem Health at the University of Guelph, suggests that "in a holistic manner, [ecosystem health] focusses attention on problems of dysfunction, emphasizes preventive approaches and provides guidance for the rehabilitation of damaged ecosystems."[60] Rapport himself recognizes that it is easier to identify dysfunctional ecosystems than to conclusively define a well-functioning sustainable system.[61] When health is lacking, it becomes readily apparent. Yet, as Gadamer has shown, well-being and good health are often most fully present when taken-for-granted and hidden from view as categories unto themselves.[62]

In summary then, phenomenology, as a mode of holistic rather than reductionist thinking, can be described as follows:

- Phenomenology seeks to illumine an implicit ordering of a functionality contexture whereby specific entities are meaningfully, rather than arbitrarily located. However, phenomenology avoids the tendency to impose a preordained order that reifies the world or that synthesizes the whole as a superpart.

- The ordering activity of the transcendental understanding is, in some sense, a unifying act, to the extent that patterns and relations *between* entities are implicitly recognized. Such unity, however, cannot be described at the expense of difference and absence, if one is to think unity ontologically rather than ontically.

- The linguistic belonging of wholeness to health is not incidental but points to an essential ontological significance of both.

How does such a holistic approach impact upon concrete issues regarding the relationship between human beings and their lived environments? Let me close with an illustration that takes me back two decades, when I was director of research in a human settlements consulting firm. I was involved in some preliminary work relating to what the World Bank and other funding agencies at the time called "squatter settlement upgrading." In surveying some of the studies that had been prepared by other consulting firms, I was appalled to see some of the recommendations that had been put forth for the provision of municipal services and infrastructure for the community of Arusha, Tanzania. Because of the exact requirements of sewers and road systems, the settlement had been redesigned according to a grid-iron plan that accommodated the underground pipelines and linear roadways. As they appeared to have been constructed haphazardly, entire neighborhoods were to be disrupted and realigned along a linear pattern.

Critical of the narrow parameters of these plans, our firm's proposal called for a broader understanding of the needs of the human settlement as a whole. This part of Arusha might look haphazardly designed when surveyed from above, but for the people who inhabited it, there was an order and a meaning that the consultants were obliged to reveal, prior to making their recommendations for "upgrading." To understand how the inhabitants' worlds were meaningfully constituted, more than an inventory of material or even social needs was required. Instead, it seemed to me that a phenomenological reading of taken-for-granted value systems and expectations would help to ensure a more discerning intervention into this whole way of life. Something as simple as the location of the windows that ensured easy and spontaneous conversations between housewives allowed for a gathering of meaning that exceeded obvious positivist measures of design.

As this example shows, an ethic begins to announce itself on the basis of such an ontological reading. Ontology illumines taken-for-granted relations and inspires an originative rethinking of environmental issues. At the same time, such a re-thinking must affect how we decide that we *ought* to act in certain circumstances. In the following chapter, I consider the relation between ethics and ontology. What is the relation between raising anew the question of the meaning of Being as Heidegger has done, and a genuine preserving of the significance of entities and things? How is environmental decision making affected by the kind of ontological considerations that we have raised so far? Let us consider how a new ethic of sustainability might be implied on the basis of a holistic, phenomenological approach to environmental thinking.

6

Ontology and Ethics

Perhaps the most important task facing those who are engaged in philosophical thought today
is to search for an ethics that can provide a measure for responsible action to even those
people who either can no longer find such a measure in the teachings of their religions,
or who are no longer convinced by the metaphysical foundations of ethics.
—Werner Marx, *Towards a Phenomenological Ethics*

Martin Heidegger invites us to raise anew the question of the meaning of Being. For many readers, this task may appear to be daunting. Nonphilosophers may consider the question too esoteric and purely the domain of metaphysicians. Philosophers themselves may interpret such quasi-metaphysical questions as too abstract and irrelevant to the concrete demands of ethics or political thought. Policymakers may be particularly disturbed by invocations of "Being," when it comes to the specific and challenging demands of environmental decision making.

To some extent, I sympathize with the critics. When we try to designate Being by defining the notion and delimiting it within some kind of stipulated parameters, we are accused by Heideggereans of the metaphysical move of reducing Being to a being and confusing ontology with the ontic sciences. Sometimes it seems as if, to be true to the Heideggeran ontology, we can do no better than poetically invoke Being as a "general form, vague as the Plotinian One, as indefinite as the Platonic Good, a kind of Great Light which spreads its illumination over the things that are and, while being none of them, while being no-thing, while, properly speaking, not being at all, brings all to be."[1]

French phenomenologist Emmanuel Levinas condemns Heidegger for his "ontological imperialism" and contends that the meaning of Being calls for "not the ontology of the understanding of that extraordinary verb, but the ethics of its justice."[2] One could argue, with some justification, that rather than philosophize in general terms about an apparently empty concept like Being, philosophy today should focus its attention on more concrete and immediate tasks of resolving specific ethical disputes.

Indeed, that seems to be exactly Werner Marx's point in the opening quotation of this chapter. Rather than being subordinate to or merely an appendage of ontology, perhaps ethical demands are more pressing and deserve broader investigation by phenomenologists. Certainly, the growing popularity of the field of environmental ethics testifies to the increasing awareness among environmentalists of the significance of peoples' values, beliefs, and perceptions.

Heidegger, however, appeared to favor ontology over ethics, and this emphasis is seen by some critics to be other than a merely incidental oversight. Perhaps Heidegger the Romantic was so engrossed in abstract musings on the question of the meaning of Being that his erudite pondering explains his political naïveté in failing to address the concrete, ethical realities of National Socialism. Philosopher Joanna Hodge makes just such a claim by arguing that Heidegger's Nazi association can be seen as a direct result of his neglect of ethical questioning.[3]

Does Heidegger's claim of ontological primacy justify such remarks? The previous chapter has shown that, as obtuse as the question of the meaning of Being might sound, Heidegger's task was to illumine ontological thinking as concretely relevant to problems of perception and such everyday encounters as our ready-to-hand relationship with specific tools. To be sure, my own philosophy students have expressed frustration in their attempts to come to terms with Heidegger's "raising anew" of the ontological question—a question that often seems so elusive and perhaps little more than linguistic affectation. Perhaps the reader similarly may have felt that the question of the meaning of Being is, at best, a question for philosophical speculation and not, properly speaking, relevant to environmental concerns.

It is the case, nevertheless, that for Heidegger, Being constituted much more than an abstract concept for speculative study.[4] That each of us can say to ourselves that we *are*, means that Being is hardly a vapor or mere abstraction. Rather, Being defines us in our very existential structure and, in this sense, is the closest and most concrete of realities. By raising anew the ontological question, Heidegger hoped to encourage a new way of originative thinking about all aspects of our lives—including, I will argue, ethical and environmental concerns.

Before we consider ethics, however, let me address a more basic issue. Ethical demands, as well as environmental decision making, require us to make specific choices. More than engaging us in an obvious way in large, ontological questions, ethical questions demand that we come to terms with particular ontic events. We ask, for instance, "should this dam be built?" Such a question entails that we consider a very specific entity—"this dam"—as well as particular events and processes that are requisite components of the decision-making process. How, in concrete terms, do we decide whether the dam should be built? If we decide to build it, what are the specific, ontic moments that will define the process of construction?

Such questions are hardly "inauthentic," simply because they do not, on first glance, engage us in an authentic questioning of the meaning of Being. On the contrary, they define ontic needs that must be met in the process of environmental decision-making. Certainly, Heidegger was critical of the metaphysical, positivist tendency to collapse the question of the meaning of Being into present-at-hand, ontic representations and reductionist concepts. Was he, however, naive to assume that specific, ontic entities—ideas, events, or things—were unimportant to the phenomenological enterprise?

In this chapter, I wish to show that Heidegger did not conceive of the question of the meaning of Being as a vague, general "Great Light." On the contrary, originary thinking opens up the possibility of approaching things and other ontic events in a more meaningful manner than positivism has been able to accomplish. As we shall see, such thinking also allows for a more thoughtful appropriation of the meaning of environmental ethics and, ultimately, of the task of attaining to sustainability as well.

The Ontic Event

While critics charge that it is concrete *things* that ultimately escape Heidegger in his philosophical endeavor, there is a certain irony in the complaint.[5] After all, it is no accident that Heidegger began his ontological investigations with an inquiry into the structure of a specific entity, namely, the human being who raises the question of the meaning of Being in the first place. "Being is always the Being of an entity," writes Heidegger and, therefore, "the meaning of Being can never be contrasted with entities."[6] Even phenomenology itself was described as "nothing else" than the famous maxim: "To the things themselves!"[7]

To be sure, Heidegger teaches us to beware of the tendency to reify Being as simply another larger, or more significant entity and, in this sense, ontology is to be distinguished from the ontic sciences that investigate beings specifically and, typically, as present-at-hand objects. Nevertheless, as Joanna Hodge points out, fundamental ontology also "invokes the experience of actually existing finite beings" and, in this sense, it is at once "both ontological, concerned with the general conditions of possibility for existence, and ontical, concerned with the actual existence of human beings."[8]

Heidegger himself makes this matter clear at many points throughout his career. In *The Basic Problems of Phenomenology*, he explains that "ontology has for its fundamental discipline the analytic of Dasein. This implies at the same time that ontology cannot be established in a purely ontological manner. Its possibility is referred back to a being, that is, to something ontical—the Dasein. Ontology has an ontical foundation."[9] Later in the same text, Heidegger reiterates his position: "There exists no comportment to beings that would not understand Being. No understanding of Being is possible that would not root in a comportment toward beings."[10]

In another volume, Heidegger similarly explains that "not only does Being ground beings as their ground, but beings in their turn, ground, cause Being in their way. Beings can do so only insofar as they 'are' the fullness of Being: they are what *is* most of all."[11] Even the later Heidegger, writing in his more mystical phase, still does not relinquish the significance of specific entities in favor of any monastic gazing upon Being. It is the artwork specifically that "opens up in its own way the Being of beings."[12] It is the jug *as thing* that appropriates the four-fold.[13] Heidegger concludes that "in the strict sense of the German word *bedingt*, we are the be-thinged, the conditioned ones. We have left behind us the presumption of all unconditionedness."[14]

It is clear, therefore, that Heidegger never intended to relinquish the world by describing Being as separate from ontic entities and that fundamental ontology cannot exclude the ontic domain. It is equally clear, however, that ontic entities for Heidegger are not merely present-at-hand objects. An originative, phenomenological thinking about things calls for an approach that is distinct from any calculative representation of entities.

Heidegger tells us that positivist science is expert at manipulating things as objects, but he doubts that science has a thorough understanding of things *as things*. Science "already had annihilated things as things long before the atom bomb exploded. The bomb's explosion is only the grossest of all gross confirmations of the long-since-accomplished annihilation of the thing: the confirmation that the thing as a thing remains nil. The thingness of the thing remains concealed, forgotten."[15]

How is Heidegger's notion of a "thing" different from the reified representative status of an object as *res*? How is an ontic entity or event to be understood ontologically? Heidegger invokes some of his most mystical language to describe "the thing" in his later thinking. "The thing things world," he proclaims.[16] As unusual as some of his writings may sound, it is important to recognize that he hopes to radically disrupt all complacency and appeal for a questioning of our most basic assumptions. Inasmuch as language clears a space for the interpretation of our world, Heidegger feels that a rethinking of fundamental notions of thingness calls for nothing less than a radical interruption of our common modes of expression as well.

These common modes of expression often collapse the essence of specific entities into nothing more than objects that stand apart from human subjects. In a reductionist, technological era, it is so simple to engage things as objects that are manipulated and technically ordered by human subjects. Heidegger argues that a metaphysical tradition, historically entrenched in a forgetting of the meaning of Being, entails a view of entities as objects for our express use and control. Objects are *standing in reserve* expressly for our utilization.

Philosopher Robert Mugerauer, provides this simple but insightful example: "Think of an elevator. We go into a building and walk to the bank of elevators.

There may be six or eight of them. We push a button indicating that we wish to go up. The one button operates all the elevators, bringing the closest one to our floor. We wait a bit. We push the button again. We are annoyed if a door does not open quickly so we can be on our way."[17] The fact that we are presented with a reserve of identical items indicates how no elevator in particular is significant for us. Any one will do, as long as one appears in an efficient space of time to satisfy our needs.

Mugerauer points out how things in our technological world appear always as "part of a system, or systems of production, storage, ordering, payment, distribution and so on."[18] In a world driven by logistics, things become interchangeable and, ultimately, disposable objects in a large-scale system of organization. To be sure, in our huge urban areas, an efficient ordering of such a system appears to be an obvious necessity.

But as we willfully order up our reserves of trees from the Brazilian forests to be processed into pulp and paper, cellulose, and even plastics and textiles, perhaps we are obliged to stop and think more carefully about where such a worldview of things as objects inevitably leads. Mugerauer reminds us that a society built around a view of replaceable, disposable entities means that "the same concept governs our understanding of human beings. Each laborer is disposable and replaceable by others in the labor pool. . . . Certainly, our very bodies are seen this way as we embark on replacing—transplanting—our original parts with parts from eye banks and kidney donors. . . . Genetic research already is opening the reservoir of genes so that we can engineer with them, creating new forms of life."[19]

Even urban renewal of cities can be understood in terms of replaceable components.[20] Buildings and people can be moved around, as long as the end result is apparently all for the greater good. The recent experience of a Canadian urban planner in China is revealing. Providing consulting advice on the land management strategy for Shanghai's central core, he was informed by officials that the plan would impact upon the area of Pudong across the river. However, since this area consisted mainly of rice paddies, the area was understood to be uninhabited.

The planner insisted, however, upon seeing Pudong for himself. From the top floor of a twenty-story apartment building, he was able to survey the area and was aghast to see a city of 700,000 people settled in Pudong. Representatives of the Shanghai municipal government reassured him that they had not meant to be anything less than forthright, but in their view, displacing this population (many of whom were squatters) when one was dealing with a total number of 1.2 billion people was simply not significant. From the Canadian perspective, however, the number of people to be uprooted was hardly inconsequential: the National Capital Region of Ottawa, Canada, boasts a comparable population to that of Pudong.

The example from China helps us to see where some of the current thinking on things as disposable objects can lead us. While we may sympathize with the management problems of such areas as Pudong, many of us will at least feel disquieted by the prospect that human beings become merely manipulable objects

and components of a logistical system of land planning. In this light, the phenomenological task of rethinking things as mere objects appears to be all the more
pressing.

The Thing in Heidegger's Ontology

How, then, does Heidegger understand specific entities, when they are situated
within his fundamental ontology and when they are approached from an originative, rather than calculative, foundation? What does a rethinking of things suggest
for the relation between ontological and ontic inquiries?

At the very least, a new way *of seeing* things seems to be called for. I am reminded of my first experiences in photography, when I lived in a particularly
beautiful section of Victoria, British Columbia some years ago. The spectacular
houses and gardens of Oak Bay had been part of my everyday world for only a
few months when I resolved one weekend to meander through my neighborhood,
capturing images through the lens of my new camera. For the first time, I took
note of details of leaded windows, garden fountains and pools, and flowers that
were, miraculously, already blooming in February.

The experience led me to realize that, while the camera focused my attention
on specific aspects of my neighborhood, what made these images special was that
they constituted more than an isolated, atomistic parceling up of the neighborhood through the camera lens. Instead, each image was significant inasmuch as it
captured and articulated in a distinctive way, the sense of place of the neighborhood as a whole. On the one hand, I was drawn to notice particular details that I
had missed, when I had not sought them out through the lens of my camera. On
the other hand, each individual photograph was all the more meaningful to the degree that the broader sense of the place as a whole was reflected and even in some
sense enriched in each photographic image.

This resonance of the whole sense of place within the unique perspective of
each, individual photograph reminded me of Heidegger's own discussion of
eventful, ontologically revealing events. In *Identity and Difference*, he tells us that
"Being grounds beings. And beings, as what *is* most of all, account for Being. One
comes over the other, one arrives in the other. Overwhelming and arrival appear in
each other in reciprocal relation."[21]

This reciprocity is described, furthermore, as a "circling of Being and beings
around each other."[22] Clearly, Heidegger is not indicating here any physical or geometric circling. At the very least, what is suggested by this notion of circling is that
the relation between ontology and ontic things is, however, more than a linear, logistical relation.[23]

Consider, for instance, how my photographs of Victoria constituted singular,
ontic visions of distinctive entities within my neighborhood. In this sense, the

images prompted me to attend to specific entities differently than I had done, before I framed an ontic picture through the camera lens. Yet, the only reason that the ontic images became significant was because they gathered together and were able to congeal the broader, ontological meaning of Oak Bay as a whole. The essence of ontic things does not point to a notion of fixed boundaries or reified constraints. On the contrary, to paraphrase Heidegger, there appears a "remarkable 'relatedness backward or forward'" between the ontic emergence of entities and their ontological *Ab-grund.*[24]

Indeed, it is in his reflections on art and poetry that the reverberations between ontic things and ontological ground are most profoundly articulated. Art, Heidegger writes, "lets truth originate."[25] How is this so? We read that "the establishing of truth in the work is the bringing forth of a being such as never was before and will never come to be again."[26] Each work of art, as uniquely creative, is more than merely a hypostatizing apprehension of an elusive realm or transcendent domain of Being. Rather, the work articulates a dynamic conflict between a need for openness and expression, on the one hand, and the impossibility of ever fully capturing a grace of Being that hides itself as it is revealed.

Heidegger describes this establishing of truth in the work of art as a conflict between world and earth. "The dawning world brings out what is as yet undecided and measureless, and thus discloses the hidden necessity of measure and decisiveness."[27] On the one hand, then, the work of art as thing gathers together and reveals Being. "But as a world opens itself, the earth comes to rise up. It stands forth as that which bears all, as that which is sheltered in its own law and always wrapped up in itself."[28] The work of art, as historically rooted, can never be a totalizing disclosure but pays heed to the "undecided and measureless" origin of existence as well.[29]

Preserving the rift between world as revelatory and earth as "striving to keep itself closed," the work of art is an articulation of thingness that pays heed to the mystery of Being, as well as to the human need to gather together and meaningfully order our world. Heidegger concludes that in determining the thing's thingness, we must do more than merely describe the entity as an object that bears particular properties or that is constituted as a manifold of sense data—or even as an Aristotelean matter-form structure. Instead, "anticipating a meaningful and weighty interpretation of the thingly character of things, we must aim at the things's belonging to the earth. The nature of the earth, in its free and unhurried bearing and self-closure, reveals itself, however, only in the earth's jutting into a world, in the opposition of the two. This conflict is fixed in place in the figure of the work and becomes manifest by it."[30]

Heidegger's deliberations on the work of art lead us to discover things as more than mere representations or as items that stand isolated from their ontological ground. When a television commercial advertises, as it did recently, a huge, warehouse art sale where the main selling feature is a limited quantity of giant, "sofa-sized" pictures at $40 each, we know not to expect to be in the presence of great art. Instinctively, we recognize that stocking up a large quantity of meaningless re-productions is contrary to the meaning of genuine art. Even if an original Van Gogh piece were to be found at such an exhibition, the fact is that the articulation of art as a large quantity of replaceable items is intuitively offensive, because Heidegger notwithstanding, we know that art must mean more.

Similarly, an investigation of poetry and language reveals, once again, a reverberation between gathering revelation and closure. "Mortal speech is a calling that names, a bidding which . . . bids thing and world to come."[31] Certainly, a poem is a linguistic expression and an articulation that seeks to gather together and express certain insights meaningfully. But a poem is more than a mere object of investigation or even cumulative inventory of apparently significant words and phrases. "Every authentic hearing holds back with its own saying," Heidegger tells us.[32] We know that a poem falls short of its aim when it collapses into endless chatter and simply says too much. Once again, the poem as thing seeks to preserve the rift between creative articulation and the withdrawal of Being. "Language," Heidegger concludes, also "speaks as the peal of stillness."[33]

The thing, then, in Heidegger's ontology is understood to be more than a merely reproducable object or fixed entity. In rethinking the essence of things, Heidegger's work guides us toward an understanding of an ontic entity as a gathering presence—a "single stay"—that reveals as well as preserves the rift between full disclosure of the present-at-hand and the historical granting of an origin that never can be completely captured by human inventions.[34] Certainly, we are drawn to recognize that Heidegger never wishes to relinquish the world and concrete things, despite his often mystical reflections on Being. At the same time, we are also led to the need of a rethinking of the ontic sciences. Just as things are more than inauthentic, ontic entities, might ethical, political, and environmental concerns be more than delimiting, reductionist inquiries, once they proceed from an ontological foundation of thought? In the next section, we consider precisely this possibility, specifically from the perspective of a need for a new environmental ethic of sustainability.

Heidegger and the Possibility of Ethical Reflection

In *Being and Time,* Heidegger suggests that the project of ontological questioning is one that is particular to human beings. Even so, the understanding of Being "develops or decays," so that there are many ways in which the question of the meaning of Being has been interpreted—and misinterpreted.[35] Human ways of behavior have been studied to various degrees by philosophical psychology, anthropology, ethics, and other ontic disciplines.[36] Nevertheless, as Heidegger notes, "the question remains whether these interpretations have been carried through with a primordial existentiality."[37] Indeed, Heidegger is openly critical of these disciplines, to the extent that they fail to come to terms with or even raise the ontological question that he feels to be essential to all ontic endeavors.

The ontic sciences have come to concern themselves primarily with things— political institutions, psychological states, economic quantifiers—without giving adequate thought to the ontological foundations that sustain positivist inquiries. The field of ethics is similarly suspect in Heidegger's writings. "Thinking in values," he tells us, "is the greatest blasphemy imaginable against Being."[38] One is led easily to conclude that there is no role at all in Heidegger's ontology for ethical questioning. He warns against the "artificial and dogmatic" temptation to simply round out "on the practical side," the supposed "theoretical," ontological endeavor, by "tacking on" an ethic.[39] Finally, the very definition of phenomenology as descriptive, rather than prescriptive, is inherited from Husserl by Heidegger and explicitly articulated.[40]

To be sure, Heidegger was an ardent critic of a certain *way* of examining ethical issues. Not only was the history of metaphysics forgetful of ontology, but the discipline of philosophy proper came to define itself in terms of a positivist division between its various, ontic domains. Metaphysics addressed the nature of reality. Epistemology focused on theories of knowledge. Ethics was charged with examining questions of moral values.

To this day, the danger of such a segregation is that ethics risks becoming a theoretical discussion of abstract moral principles, disengaged from questions of truth or even from the concrete demands of the lived world within which we find ourselves. A related hazard is that ethics becomes a domain for experts only. Environmental ethics and bioethics become fields for specialized, philosophical speculation—as if the concerns of ecological and human health did not touch each and every human being.

Centuries ago, Plato knew that ethics signified more than a matter of speculation on moral rules by only a select audience. "The matter is no chance trifle," he wrote, "but how we ought to live."[41] Ethical deliberation hardly constitutes a subsidiary aspect of our lives but is central inasmuch as it reflects what *matters* to us in life. Everyday decisions arise from within a horizon of interpretation that impels us to act in anticipation of what we understand to be right or wrong. Questions of how we ought to act are hardly trivial and merely occasional excursions into ethical deliberation, but they define us as inquiring human beings.

Heidegger himself sensed that ethics could be interpreted, not merely as one secondary, ontic domain among others but as primordial and extending to all aspects of our lives. Reflecting on the choice of the title for his *magnum opus, Being and Time*, he warned against any tendency to interpret the word "Being" in the title in terms of its customary, reductionist juxtapositions of Being and Becoming, or Being and Ought. "For in all these cases, Being is limited, as if Becoming, Seeming,

Thinking and Ought did not belong to Being."[42] Here, Heidegger seems to be suggesting that the rift between ethics and ontology need not be substantive, as long as the meaning of ethics itself is rethought in a more primordial sense.

Indeed, exploring the Greek roots of the word, he recognizes that, originally, the term "*ēthos*" referred to the fundamental comportment or bearing (*Haltung*) of human beings.[43] Philosopher Bruce Foltz explains that, for Heidegger and the ancient Greeks, "ethics is the understanding of what it means to dwell within the midst of beings as a whole, and thus it concerns our bearing and comportment, *as a whole*, toward beings."[44]

Heidegger draws on Heraclitus, who knew that "*ēthos* means abode, dwelling place. The word names the open region in which man dwells. The open region of his abode allows what pertains to man's essence, and what in thus arriving, resides in nearness to him, to appear."[45] Our contemporary views on the nature of moral obligation commonly refer to only specific kinds of illicit activities or sanctions— or even occasional rights or obligations. The problem with such a view is that ethics no longer speaks to the wider plethora of human experience, beyond such narrow confines of moral prohibitions. In an age where pornography passes for art or technological tinkering passes for environmental activism, ethics is reduced to a narrow discussion among specialists and the remainder of existence, apparently outside the domain of ethics proper, falls prey to arbitrariness.

Though Heidegger says comparatively little about ethics specifically, it is clear that his criticism of the field extended primarily to such a restricted, and ultimately inauthentic, ontic moral sphere. It is also evident that a genuine ethic was not unthinkable to him within his ontological deliberations. "Before we attempt to determine more precisely the relationship between 'ontology' and 'ethics,'" he mused, "we must ask what 'ontology' and 'ethics' themselves are."[46]

For Heidegger, the alternative to a reductionist understanding of moral theory was to be uncovered in an originative rethinking of the Greek origins. Such origins revealed that such thinking that "thinks the truth of Being as the primordial element of man, as one who eksists, *is in itself the original ethics*."[47] It is no wonder that philosopher Joanna Hodge is able to identify a "repressed ethical dimension in Heidegger's inquiries."[48] While Heidegger was never willing to explore ethics in its positivist manifestations, as one ontic domain among others, he was willing to acknowledge the possibility of *original ethics*—of an *ēthos* that ponders the human "abode"—in an essential dialogue with ontology.

In the following chapters, we will consider the relation between ethics and dwelling to which Heidegger alluded. I will propose that a genuine environmental ethic, rooted in an ontological reading of dwelling and place, is possible and, indeed, necessary for a rethinking of the meaning of sustainability. In the meantime, if we are to hope to move beyond Heidegger to uncover the possibility of such an ethic, it will be helpful to review what a phenomenological ethic must avoid.

Moving beyond Objectivism

When Heidegger described human beings as *Dasein*, his aim was to highlight how human beings are always transcending the immediate demands of the present, appropriating a past toward a future of undefined possibilities. As *Being-there*, we are always ahead-of-ourselves, actively immersed in and belonging to the world within which we are thrown. In such an interpretation of human being-in-the-world, human beings cannot be understood in abstraction from their surrounding environment any more than the reality of the world can be disengaged from the human interpretive moment.

As a result, any reductionist metaphysic that claims either a subjectivist, idealist foundation, or an objectivist, starkly realist ground, is no longer possible. But just as it is the case that Heidegger's ontology rethinks such a subject-object dualism, so too an ethic that enlarges upon such an ontological foundation clearly must seek to avoid collapsing into either a subjectivistic or objectivistic domain as well.

To be sure, it is not uncommon to think of the role of ethics in terms of formulating a set of objective rules or principles that we follow in order to act morally. The notion of the Ten Commandments that we obey in order to live the moral life is a case in point. The history of philosophy, however, shows that formulating ethical guidelines as strict, universal principles has been more difficult to accomplish than one might assume.

Sometimes, these principles have been so general as to be ultimately vacuous. In other cases, achieving consensus as to how to resolve conflicting principles has been difficult to achieve. Objective, universal ethical rules falter, for instance, when differing customs and moral imperatives emerge among diverse cultures. Formal, codified rules and principles, in such cases, can appear, not as ethically illumining but as the totalitarian imposition of one society's version of the right thing to do, on that of another.

Timeless ethical truths have been as difficult to articulate as timeless metaphysical truths. Heidegger's ontology helps us to understand that seeking universal, objective ethical rules is not only demanding but also, perhaps, indicative of a closure of genuine ethical discourse. Rather than opening up the possibility of genuine dialogue in an effort to resolve ethical dilemmas, imposing easy and rigid rules often eludes authentic listening in moral decision-making and resolves little.

Existentialist Jean-Paul Sartre provides a useful illustration of the inadequacy of applying traditional moral principles to the challenges of ethical dilemmas.[49] He refers to the case of a student who wished to avenge the death of his older brother, who had been killed in the German offensive of 1940. He was living alone with his mother, whose only consolation in life lay in the love and support provided by her only remaining son. The student was faced with the decision whether to go to England to join the Free French Forces or to remain by his mother and help her to live and to cope with her loss.

Sartre explains that the student realized that staying with his mother meant that a concrete good would result, because he would be aiding her to live on a day-to-day basis. On the other hand, offering to fight for France could result in ambiguous consequences. By setting out for England, he could be assigned to wait indefinitely for a concrete assignment or he could be appointed to nothing more rewarding than a desk job, filling out forms. To be sure, the student might also genuinely avenge his brother's death by providing a significant contribution to the resistance effort at the expense, however, of deserting his mother in her time of need.

As a result, the student found himself confronted by two, very different possibilities: the one concrete with the promise of immediate benefit but directed toward only a single individual; and the other, an act aimed at a larger, national collectivity but, nevertheless, ambiguous, since genuine contributions to the cause could easily be frustrated along the way.[50]

Sartre asks the reader to consider how the student could be helped to make his choice. Could Christian doctrine or another formalized ethic direct him? "No. Christian doctrine says: Act with charity, love your neighbour, deny yourself for others, choose the way that is hardest and so forth. But which is the harder road? To whom does one owe the more brotherly love, the patriot or the mother? Which is the more useful aim, the general one of fighting in and for the whole community, or the precise aim of helping one particular person to live? Who can give an answer to that *a priori*? No one. Nor is it given in any ethical scripture."[51]

But it is not only Christian doctrine that appears to hold no definite answers. The Kantian ethic suggests that we must always regard others as an end, rather than as a means. If the student were to remain with his mother, she would be regarded as an end and not as a means. But by the same reasoning, by staying by his mothers's side, he would risk treating as means those who are fighting on his behalf. The opposite, Sartre tells us, is also true, that if he aids the combatants, the student would be treating them as the end and risk treating his mother merely as a means.[52]

The example illustrates how generalized principles—while noble and apparently just—often are able to offer little assistance when it comes to dealing with concrete, ethical dilemmas. We may subscribe to the theory that individual animals should not be killed, since each living being possesses intrinsic value in and of itself. Yet is the preservation of the individual deer always justified when its existence threatens the health of the very ecosystem that sustained the deer and other diverse life-forms within it?

Moreoever, we show, on a daily basis, that subscribing to generalized principles does not guarantee ethical action. For various reasons, we are torn to decide among competing "goods." The single mother wishes to preserve the natural environment for the sake of the health of her children. She is torn, however, in organizing her demanding schedule, between walking them to after-school activities and losing a half hour of her time in each direction, and driving them in her polluting car, but arriving home in time to prepare an alternative to microwaved fast food. Rules may sound legitimate "in the abstract," but the demands of everyday living not only make living up to theoretical demands difficult but, often, those theoretical demands remain too divorced from the complexity of everyday needs and particular circumstances that cannot be accommodated within the neatly compartmentalized, grandiose ethical theories in the first place.

Heidegger himself was aware that we are naturally tempted to develop rules and principles to follow, in order that we act ethically. He recalls how "soon after *Being and Time* appeared, a young friend asked me, 'When are you going to write an ethics?' Where the essence of man is thought so essentially, i.e. solely from the question concerning the truth of Being, . . . a longing necessarily awakens for a peremptory directive and for rules that say how man, experienced from eksistence toward Being, ought to live in a fitting manner."[53]

Despite such a longing for codified directives, however, Heidegger urges that we proceed with "the greatest care." In an age characterized by the ordering of all plans and activities according to technical efficiency, an imposition of formalized, so-called objective and universally applicable codified rules runs the risk of being nothing less than tyrannical. The horrors of the Nazi experiment, not to mention the perverse ideals of ethnic cleansing in the former Yugoslavia, attest to the danger of viewing ethics in terms of any totalizing vision that delimits and hypostatizes moral considerability, excluding some members of society from the edges of a rigidly circumscribed moral domain.

Even the comparatively simple code of "Earth first, humankind second" advanced by environmental radicals such as the EarthFirsters! seem to me to be dangerous invitations of totalitarian—and, ultimately, unethical—environmental activity. The fact that I choose to save a newborn child first in a burning home, before I venture to salvage the hamster or the endangered plant, should give us some pause before we blindly follow such a code of EarthFirsters!, simple and straightforward as this code may be.

When we act ethically, it is not typically the case that we do so because we have followed a set of codified objective rules as given objects of truth. Even if we seek some guidance from principles, we cannot escape *interpreting* these principles. With that act of interpretation, no longer can ethics be reduced to an objectively determined set of given truths. Does it mean, then, that ethics—if it is not objectively grounded—lapses into subjectivism instead?

Moving beyond Subjectivism

To reject ethics as an objectifying discipline or as the generation of universal, codified objective principles does not necessarily require that we opt for a subjectivistic starting point for ethics. To be sure, it may seem that if moral values are never objectively and eternally true, then the only alternative is that they must be changing and relative to each individual human subject, or contingent upon evolving historical traditions and customs.

Needless to say, such a vision of ethics arguably means the very disappearance of ethics. If morality is judged simply according to personal preferences or even is defined purely in terms of relativism, then anything goes and all measures are abandoned. As my neighbor pours old engine oil into the sewer, am I truly justified in concluding that we are each entitled to live by our own, individual codes? Does the criminal have any right to argue that his own ethic that justifies murder is simply "different" than my own?

Clearly, if ethics is to mean anything at all, the answer to both questions must be no, despite the fact that most readers probably can recall having heard a friend proclaim, in a gesture of tolerance and respect of individual liberty, that we all have our "own" value systems. Perhaps, in some sense, such a claim is true but it is hardly unproblematic.

There are other more subtle ways, however, that we may reduce ethics to subjectivism. When we describe ethics as a field that investigates *values* rather than scientific *facts*, such a description often implies an understanding of the moral domain as subjective instead of objective, as "real" science should be. The implication seems to be that "values" are a matter of opinion, whereas facts evolve from the way things "really" are.

The reader will recall from chapter 1 how problems arise in areas like risk assessment when facts are believed to be independent of human values.[54] Yet values as a specialized and separate domain of inquiry are acquiring renewed status in environmentalism: A conference on managing for ecological health seeks to "integrate science, values and resources in decision making"—as if science and values were always independent domains.[55] The Federation of Canadian Municipalities' report on Canada's overview of "The Ecological City" reports not only on land use and transportation trends, air quality and waste management, but also on "Values and Beliefs."[56]

The study of values is achieving renewed appreciation in environmental literature and, in some sense, philosophers should feel grateful that moral issues appear to be more broadly recognized in fields like environmental science. We recall that Heidegger, on the other hand, has said that such a study of values is "the greatest blasphemy."[57] Despite this claim, Heidegger does not object to the study of ethics. Rather, he is critical of the very term "values," because he feels that it harbors an insidious subjectivism that hinders the progress of genuine ethics.

Heidegger tells us that "every valuing, even where it values positively, is a subjectivizing" because in assessing something as a value, "what is valued is admitted only as an object for man's estimation. . . .[Valuing] does not let beings be. Rather, valuing lets beings be valid—solely as the objects of its doing."[58] Neither stones nor animals nor ecocsystems engage in the valuing process themselves because, by definition, that process is restricted to human subjects who are seen by Heidegger to be projecting their own systems of values on only those objects that they deem to be worthy of moral considerability.

In such an anthropocentric view, the danger is that objects are valued only to the extent that they satisfy our own subjective interests and instrumental demands. Is the forest valuable as nothing more than a resource for lumber or an object of aesthetic representation? Many philosophers have seen the limits of such a worldview, arguing that any genuine environmental ethic must recognize also intrinsic value in and of itself to the forest ecosystem and its inhabitants.[59]

It begins to be evident, however, that the subject-object dualism that Heidegger investigated in the contemporary metaphysical worldview continues to hold sway in the field of ethics as well. Certainly, ethics may collapse into mere subjectivism in those instances where personal preferences define all values. Subjectivism, however, also hides behind even those moral theories that aim to achieve a certitude and objectivism, apparently independently of subjectivist whims. Two dominant paradigms of contemporary moral theory testify to such dualism: utilitarianism, on the one hand, and rights-based rulings on the other.

Consider, for instance, the utilitarian reasoning that continues to have a strong influence over economics, regulatory functions, and public policy generally. According to utilitarian philosopher John Stuart Mill, this theory "holds that actions are right in proportion as they tend to promote happiness, wrong as they tend to produce the reverse of happiness. By happiness is intended pleasure and the absence of pain."[60]

Although different versions of utilitarianism may question the pleasure principle, these versions, nevertheless, are united by their common understanding of moral good in terms of the wider well-being of the human community.[61] The good is arrived at, not by intuition or divine decree but, rather, by means of agreement among the human collective. One problem with such a theory is that there is little provision for guarding against tyranny of the majority. When a moral theory is grounded in the human subjectivity, that theory is hard-pressed to explain why majority rule does not always explain or guarantee the rightness or wrongness of an action. A cannibalistic society may feel justified in its moral creed and while I may be outnumbered in my objections to its creed, an ethic that is grounded in the agreement of the human collective offers me no avenues for justifying my objections.

Paradoxically, utilitarianism aims at objectivism as well, and this is where it becomes evident that a tradition of metaphysical dualism between subject and object conditions contemporary ethics. How does one evolve moral rules that satisfy the human collective? Utilitarianism aims to quantify values objectively in a mathematical calculus of costs and benefits. Once those goods are quantified, our expectation is that they will be properly institutionalized within a bureaucratic and regulatory structure that will guarantee those goods to the community.

This need to quantify and legitimize through a rational ordering and institutionalization of moral rules helps to explain the tendency that I have perceived among nonphilosophers to assign ethical issues to the philosophical expert, who can lay claim to have studied the objective moral domain, just as the chemist is perceived to be expert in his or her own field. "Environmental ethics" has achieved in the last few decades a status of its own, with its own collection of specialists. The same applies to the fields of business ethics and biomedical ethics. When moral deliberation becomes an objectively defined exercise and the property of experts, it is no wonder that ethics recedes into the background of our everyday lives in a prevailing attitude that Werner Marx describes as nothing less than "imprisonment constituted by the *indifference* towards his fellow-man and the community."[62]

A second popular paradigm currently permeates rights-based ethical theories that some philosophers trace back to the thought of Immanuel Kant. The Nietzschean proclamation of the death of God did not mean, for Kant, the death of the source of ethical directives but, rather, a new grounding of ethics in the power of human reason. Rational principles were seen as categorical and universal. Kant's categorical imperative that required that persons be treated, not merely as means to an end but as ends in themselves, is reflected in some of our central, contemporary assumptions of democracy and civil liberties. Significantly, however, at the same time that such imperatives are grounded in the human *subjectivity* through the power of reason, they aim to order and enshrine ethical principles in universally applicable, *objective* moral rules.

No longer a "way of living" as it was proclaimed to be by Plato, ethics remains trapped in the very subject-object dualism that Heidegger maintained was characteristic of the metaphysical foundations of the modern epoch. Such a bifurcation of subjects and objects is more than a mere philosophical nuisance. When ethics becomes nothing else than an exercise in subjective, human "values," these values are easily denigrated as the vague or arbitrary opinions of philosophers, of secondary importance to the objective validity of science. On the other hand, when ethics seeks to attain the finality of an objective, universally applicable set of rules to be applied top-down to individual circumstances, ethics risks collapsing into mere abstractions, irrelevant to the intricacies of particular, local needs.

If Heidegger was right and the metaphysical dualism between subjects and objects required rethinking, the same is true no less in the field of ethics. As we seek, in Plato's words, to *live* ethically rather than to deliberate and speculate in an abstract sense on moral dilemmas, might we seek to evolve a more genuine ethic that *precedes* the subject-object split? In part III, I consider the possibilities for a rethinking of sustainability that emerges through a genuine ethic that will remain consistent with the insights of the Heideggerean ontology.

PART III

Phenomenological Guidelines for Sustainability

7

The Emergence of Place

It is popular to refer to the "impact of human settlements on the environment," as though the environment were some independent entity, separate from human beings and their way of life. The fact is that human beings live in human settlements which are the greatest part of the environment, and the real question to be faced is how the environment can support human settlements productively and sustainably.
—A. Ramachandran, Executive Director,
United Nations Center for Human Settlements

The field of environmental ethics typically argues for a rethinking of our relationship to the natural world.[1] Less central to the literature is an appreciation of the significance of the built environment. Ramachandran reminds us that to reflect upon the value of nature in abstraction from human places is, however, philosophically naive and, in practical terms, jeopardizes any genuine quest for sustainability.

Years ago, anthropologist Margaret Mead pointed out that the process of building settlements is no less "natural" for human beings than is the creation of nests for birds or dams for beavers.[2] This fact is often forgotten by environmentalists who align themselves with a long-standing tradition of romanticizing the virtue of wilderness and admonishing the evils of cities. In 1898, Sierra Club founder John Muir described the "delightful" tendency of growing numbers of "thousands of tired, nerve-shaken, over-civilized people" to wander in wilderness and to be awakened "from the stupefying effects of the vice of over-industry . . . and to get rid of rust and disease."[3] For many people, to this day, "nature serves to call us home, to remind us of what we 'really' are and to critique culture."[4]

Philosopher Edward Casey feels that it is not surprising to find homelessness to be prevalent in cities that he describes as "in many respects the antipodes of homes. Cities certainly contain homes," he continues, "but in their capacity to demand and distract, they are continually luring us into the streets. They take us out of our homes and into a more precarious and sometimes hostile extra-domestic world."[5]

To my mind, a city and even a megalopolis can be and often is a home to its residents. Theologian Harvey Cox reports on the experiences of a woman who, after the war, found the encounter with the wholesale destruction and leveling of her town by Germans to be as traumatic as facing the loss of her family.[6] Home can and does often extend beyond our own front doors and to various scales. For that matter, environmentalists might hope that we might consider the very planet itself as our home.[7]

Claims, such as those cited above, that our settlements are nothing more than evil enclaves of "vice . . . rust and disease" with streets that "lure" us into a "precarious" and "hostile" world do not explain the staggering rate of urbanization worldwide. The World Commission on Environment and Development contends that we live in "the century of the 'urban revolution.' In the 35 years since 1950, the number of people living in cities almost tripled."[8] Why would increasing numbers of people be so attracted to places that, apparently, are inherently evil?

Statistics aside, it is worth remembering that romantic notions of nature and wilderness are themselves mediated by culture and language. Even Thoreau, who sought refuge from civilization on the shores of Walden Pond, carried with him assumptions and language structures that arose within civilized society and colored his interpretation of the natural order. Moreover, those environmentalists who denigrate cities seem to forget that wilderness, as existing *somewhere* and as *named*, is, in these senses, place-based.[9] Even when we are lost in the wild and apparently "nowhere," this very notion is only comprehensible because, as we shall see, human beings themselves are ontologically implaced.

In this chapter, I argue for the ontological primacy of the phenomenon of *place*. That primacy will then be shown to be the condition of the possibility for evolving a more genuine, place-based ethic as alluded to by Heidegger. The final chapters of the book will suggest how the notion of sustainability may be better informed through phenomenological ethics and ontology.

The Phenomenon of Implacement

From the early 1970s, Ted Relph's work *Place and Placelessness* rightly has been credited as the pioneering work in the phenomenology of place.[10] More recently, beyond Relph, many geographers, architects, planners, and philosophers, from Bob Mugerauer to Edward Casey, have continued to explore and reflect upon the notion of place.[11] Journals have come to be devoted to the study of place research, and conferences are convened to report upon as well as to advance such research.[12]

On the other hand, the term has been the subject of some criticism. Some authors have argued that place is little more than a passing academic fad.[13] Others, such as architect and environmental designer, Amos Rapoport, contend that "place is never clearly defined and hence vague; when definitions are found, they are illogical."[14] Rapoport has a point. Place is difficult to define. Perhaps, it is ulti-mately not capable of a conclusive definition.

It may be, however, that this very difficulty in defining the notion of place is, paradoxically, essential to our understanding of it. St. Augustine reflects that when no one asks him, he knows very well what time is. It is only when asked to define time that he finds himself incapable of explicating it in a determinative way. Simi-larly, when we aim to definitively delimit place, we find ourselves in a situation where it is difficult, if not impossible, to demarcate the notion in universally ac-ceptable parameters.

While we find it difficult to categorically delimit, the notion of place is hardly devoid of meaning. Indeed, one reason why place is difficult to define is precisely because it is more than a fixed container and therefore exceeds reductionist cate-gories. We have seen in previous chapters that we are more than mere objects in the world. By the same token, place, phenomenologically interpreted, becomes more than a mere physical container of objects but reflects instead the ontological primacy of dwelling.

When place is appropriated within one's lived experience, it recedes as an ob-jective, present-at-hand entity in and of itself, and in so doing, constitutes the less obvious, taken-for-granted context within which we say that events and activities "take place." When a place is appropriated as "one's own," as a place where one feels that one belongs, that place as a geometric object recedes or withdraws, opening up a clearing within which a sense of community is situated.

Human beings have sensed throughout history that place indicates a primordial phenomenon of human existence. Edward Casey points out how the medieval dictum: *ex nihilo nihil fit* (from nothing, nothing can emerge) indicates that there can be no creation without place.[15] The Hebrew word for God, *Makom*, means place. God, encompassed by nothing, encompasses all things and it is only fitting that "if God is a place, the act of creation undertaken by any such deity will also be place-bound."[16]

To be sure, Heidegger's ontology will not interpret place or dwelling in theo-logical terms but, rather, in terms of being-in-the-world. As we have seen, we are not free-floating subjectivities that occasionally engage in relationships with ob-jects. Inasmuch as *we are*, we are *in-the-world*, which means that we are always im-placed.[17] Although for many readers the notion of "place" may indicate geograph-ical location, such a notion is only meaningful to human beings who are already ontologically defined through dwelling. In the words of Edward Casey, "to exist at all . . . is to have a place—*to be implaced*. . . . The point is that place, by virtue of its unencompassability by anything other than itself, is at once the limit and the con-dition of all that exists."[18] To exist is to exist *somewhere*, in some place.

The above statement may seem self-evident until one recalls Heidegger's state-ment that only human beings can be said to *exist*. "Rocks are, but they do not exist. Trees are, but they do not exist . . . Angels are, but they do not exist. God is, but He does not exist."[19] Human existential understanding, as transcendental, is constituted by a primary, ontological projection that is temporalizing but also always implaced.[20]

The poet Noël Arnaud writes: "Je suis l'espace où je suis" [I am the space where I am].[21] Arnaud's pronouncement attains special significance when one recalls that for Heidegger, to be is to be-in-the-world, temporally and always as implaced. Dwelling is hardly an incidental feature of human existence but is the very "manner in which mortals are on the earth."[22] Only insofar as human beings dwell in-the-world can place be delineated subsequently, either in terms of a subjective "sense of place" or the objective boundaries of geometric spaces.

If place, however, is neither grounded in the human subject nor in objective, geographic location, could the notion of place arise in the very interplay between self and world? Wherein do we seek the philosophical space of place? Let us turn again for guidance to Heidegger, particularly to his reflections on what it means to build and dwell.

Building, Dwelling, and the Fourfold

Today, building is often interpreted as little more than construction of physical, architectural structures.[23] Ideally, these structures are aesthetically pleasing.[24] Architects and planners with greater sensibility may acknowledge that built form consists of more than beautiful material objects but accommodates and molds human subjects as well. "I am firmly convinced," writes environmental psychologist Kiyo Izumi, "that architecture . . . can be considered an art only when it reflects an understanding of the perceptions of the consumers of the designed environment."[25]

Broadening the picture even more, some theorists may recognize that good architectural design will include elements of the "natural environment" as well.[26] Economic and technological components of design also may enter the picture, as might regulatory and cultural factors.[27] Finally, we cannot forget how architecture can have deep theological significance. Of the glory of Renaissance space, Palladio reflected "how we cannot doubt, but that the little temples we make, ought to resemble this very great one, which, by His immense goodness, was perfectly compleated with one word of His."[28]

As far-ranging as these descriptions may be, what is absent from such a catalog of diverse meanings of building? For Heidegger, building cannot be reduced to a mere physical form, where "social," environmental, theological, or other components are simple afterthoughts. When buildings are interpreted as material *objects* that also invite *subjective* projections of meaning, the phenomenon of building is implicitly represented as mere "picture" and is subsumed within the metaphysical, subject-object dualism that Heidegger has already criticized.

Proust remarked once how "the literature that is satisfied merely to 'describe things,' to furnish a miserable listing of their lines and surfaces is, notwithstanding its pretensions to realism, the farthest removed from reality, the one that most impoverishes and saddens us."[29] Might building—interpreted in a more originary manner—signify something more fundamental than an arbitrary, piecemeal inventory of discrete characteristics?

Heidegger will no more feel that a building is a physical structure that also *refers* to supplementary symbolic structures of meaning than he feels that language is mere symbolic representation. "Language speaks," we are told.[30] Language does not simply mediate between mental thoughts and physical texts; rather, it serves as the occasion for the granting of a world.[31] Similarly, buildings are not mere physical symbols, but the sites of dwelling wherein, Heidegger tells us, the ontological event of the fourfold—earth, sky, divinities, and mortals—is spared and preserved.[32]

What sense can we make of such outrageous language? Is Heidegger merely lapsing into mysticism or poetic musings, thereby abandoning all practical sense? Let me reassure even the most vehement practitioners of programs for sustainable development that Heidegger's reflections here promise to return us to the most concrete, lived experience of building and dwelling. We must recall architect Christian Norberg-Schulz's reminder that "to dwell in the qualitative sense is a basic condition of humanity. When we identify with a place, we dedicate ourselves to a way of being in the world."[33]

Heidegger tells us that, inasmuch as we exist, we exist as mortals, for a certain finite "stay" on the earth. "On the earth," however, also means that we dwell "under the sky" and, if we are fortunate, before the increasingly elusive divinities. The earth is seen by Heidegger to be "the serving bearer, blossoming and fruiting, spreading out in rock and water, rising up into plant and animal."[34] When one experiences the expanse and grandeur of the open sea or the spring awakens what Bachelard calls the "immediate immensity" of the forest, infusing the senses with the advent of new life, perhaps then one might begin to sense how "earth," for Heidegger, captures the wonder of the originary grace of creation as it emerges from within the immeasurable and impenetrable source of the natural world.[35]

For the early Greeks, this originary arising and emerging in all things was referred to as *physis*. The earth is that wherein *physis* arises and to which it withdraws.[36] Earth, for Heidegger, is more than mere "mass of matter deposited somewhere" or the "merely astronomical idea of a planet."[37] On the contrary, the nourishing earth is that "whence the arising brings back and shelters everything that arises without violation. In the things that arise, earth is present as the sheltering agent."[38]

Poet Jay Macpherson captures an essential moment of Heidegger's understanding of earth when she writes how "the stone's unordered rigor stands/ Remote and heavy as a star."[39] To disregard the earth as serving bearer in the design of our built environment is to do more than neglect to plant flowers and trees.

Such disregard disrupts the primal oneness of the fourfold and threatens the very essence of human dwelling in the world by denying the originary, inviolable ground of existence itself.

As we are on the earth, we are also "under the sky." Geographer Yi-Fu Tuan traces the development of dwelling forms from Neolithic times, when the basic structure for shelter was a round, semisubterranean hut—a "womblike enclosure"—that only later emerged above ground.[40] The differentiation between interior and exterior came to be marked by the "aggressive rectilinearity" of walls and rectangular design of courtyard domiciles. "It is noteworthy," says Tuan, "that these steps in the evolution of the house were followed in all the areas where Neolithic culture made the transition to urban life."[41]

Projecting beyond the grace of the earth, building opens up a world and articulates previously undisclosed possibilities and structures of human expression. Once again, the poet informs us: Rudyard Kipling reflects how "Out of the spent and unconsidered Earth/ The Cities rise again."[42] As a work of art is "truth setting itself to work," so too building means "to bring to a stand."[43] To bring to a stand is to fashion a world under the broad expanse of the sky.

Heidegger tells us that "the temple's firm towering makes visible the invisible space of air."[44] Under the sky, the steadfastness of the built environment secures its place while, at the same time, disclosing the natural world to which it integrally belongs. "Standing there," we are told, "the building holds its ground against the storm raging above it and so first makes the storm itself manifest in its violence."[45]

To be sure, our technological wizardry makes it possible for us to build our shelters, oblivious to the sky—to "the vaulting path of the sun, the course of the changing moon, the wandering glitter of the stars, the year's seasons and their changes, the light and dusk of day, the gloom and glow of night, the clemency and inclemency of the weather, the drifting clouds and the blue depth of the ether."[46]

That such building constitutes a displacement of the primary function of inhabiting, however, becomes clear at many levels. A simple example emerges from a study by environmental psychologist Robert Gifford, who asked children from windowless classrooms, as well as from classrooms with windows, to draw pictures of their schools. Significantly, students from the windowless classrooms included many more windows in their drawings than those in schools with windows.[47] Gifford draws the tentative conclusion that students will compensate for being deprived of windows by creating mental images of classrooms to include what their real school lacks.[48] Other studies have found that decorations in windowless office settings were typically dominated by nature and landscape paintings, as if to bring the outside closer.[49] Recently, an increasing number of local American governments have begun to regulate lighting to "bring back starry skies" at night in overlit urban settings.[50] The need of exposure to the expanse of the outside world and the changes of weather, seasons, daylight, and even night-sky patterns is more profound than we may think.

Moreover, we have come to realize how orienting buildings in response to environmental constraints—wind currents, exposure to the sun, flood and drought patterns—assures a more successful architectural intervention than one that remains oblivious to the landscape within which the building is situated. Heidegger's invoking of "the sky" signals such an awareness and more: the need of giving serious thought to these kinds of design considerations is not simply one of emotional preferences of users or technical efficiency of construction but signals a broad range of essential moments of dwelling in humane and meaningful environments.

The fourfold also invokes the divinities—"the beckoning messengers of the godhead. Out of the holy sway of the godhead, the god appears in his presence or withdraws into his concealment."[51] The reverberation of the hidden and the revealed is fundamental to the phenomenon of implacement. The door left ajar; the threshold that welcomes, but selectively; corners that are never empty refuge but, as Bachelard notes, "are haunted, if not inhabited"—resonate with the interplay of presence and absence that defines human existence. Buildings that deny the mystery also deny an essential moment of dwelling as a preservation of the fourfold.[52]

Finally, "the mortals are the human beings. They are called mortals because they can die. To die means to be capable of death *as* death. Only man dies, and indeed continually, as long as he remains on earth, under the sky, before the divinities."[53] Mortals dwell in the way that they spare and preserve the fourfold. To dwell is to care for—not merely as one emotional state among others but as definitive of the existential structure of human comportment. To contemplate the meaning of building and dwelling, we are compelled to engage the question of human beings as mortal, as finite, and certainly as temporal.

Time and Place

Recall that for Heidegger, the originary, transcendental projection of human understanding of the world is temporal through and through. Each human being has a history from the moment of birth toward the last moments of death. This history is not something that we own but, rather, that which we *are*. Time infuses existence, not simply as a container of activities but as the horizon within which all meaning arises in the first place.

Our everyday expression tells us that historical events *take place*. Time and place seem inextricably linked. Is that link spurious? Edward Casey raises an interesting point when he questions the modern philosopher's emphasis on time, pursued at the expense of profound reflection on place. Casey suggests that we live in an era, stretching from Galileo to Heidegger, when "Time came into its own. . . . 'Time on the Mind': this phrase . . . epitomizes the occasion of the modern."[54]

It is no wonder, he argues, that, in such an epoch, we are harassed perpetually by apparent lack of time: "Scheduled and overscheduled, we look to the clock or the calendar for guidance and solace, even judgment! But such time-telling offers precious little guidance, no solace whatsoever."[55] The central position of the problem of time in modern philosophy is hardly coincidental, for it reflects a broader, epochal organization around temporal coordinates. The result is that we often feel harassed by the passing of time, the lack of time. "Had we but world enough and time," writes Casey, "but we don't, and we don't precisely because we have come to conceive the world itself as a predominantly temporal ordering of events."[56]

The modern propensity to measure linear time and to order space geometrically arises, according to Casey, on the foundation of a forgetting of the original significance of place. Time, he argues, is only meaningful as grounded in the more primordial phenomenon of implacement. "My conviction," writes Casey, "is that time is an extension of the extensiveness of place. . . . Place situates time by giving it a local habitation."[57] He concludes that the same holds for the relation between place and space, since space and time have been seen by scientists and philosophers alike to belong together.[58]

Altogether, "the *gigantomachia* between Time and Space—a contest of giants orchestrated by Newton and Leibniz, Descartes and Kant, Galileo and Gassendi—is a struggle that overlooks Place."[59] Reaching back into medieval roots, Casey deconstructs Augustine's famous reflections on time, uncovering in the process that these descriptions themselves signal a prior, implicit recognition of the primacy of place. When Augustine refers to a "long time" or a "short time," for example, these phrases indicate a placial understanding of "long" and "short" that precedes the description of temporal duration.[60] Then, as today, place should be seen, Casey concludes, as ontologically prior to time.

In my view, Casey has every right to be critical of the modern fascination with clock time and with ontic representations of linear duration. Certainly, a tacit understanding of temporality as clock time translates into built environments that organize and manage people, principally for the purposes of efficiency, in artificial and, ultimately, dehumanizing places.[61] Ellen Eve Frank eloquently reminds us that "space is where time is."[62] Geographers Don Parkes and Nigel Thrift agree that "it is the timing component which gives structure to space and thus evokes the notion of place."[63] In an epoch that defines time as an efficient, linear ordering of present-at-hand now-points, it is no wonder that subways, high rises and other aspects of our fast-paced cities are designed to discourage lingering in favor of a functional processing of human traffic.[64]

Heidegger's understanding of *primordial time*, however, deserves to be distinguished from everyday concepts of time as a collection of present-at-hand now-points that rigidly order our lives. As interesting and thought provoking as Casey's argument may be, I would suggest that his comments apply principally to positivist interpretations of time and space. Heidegger's phenomenological discussion of temporality and even the spatializing activity of human understanding only serve to enlarge upon the notion of place.

Casey writes that "we need to get back into place so as to get out of . . . space and time."[65] I would propose, alternatively, that time, space, and place are hardly separate coordinates, each vying for the position of primordiality over the other. Instead, they interweave with one another to constitute the meaning of dwelling indicated, originally, by Heidegger in his own works.

Just as we are mistaken to forget place in favor of time, there is also a danger in viewing time as a place. When Casey writes of "the place of time," there is a risk that time may be represented as a container, within which we spend our existence.[66] One must remember, however, Heidegger's early lessons about primordial time. If we pay heed to these lessons, we will know that time is more than a mere ontic entity but indicates, instead, the transcendental horizon of human understanding and being-in-the-world.[67]

Scientist René Dubos acknowledged that "we progressively become what we are at any given moment because we can use both conscious and unconscious memory to incorporate the past into present conditions."[68] He might have added that such an appropriation of the past through the present happens within a horizon of understanding that is also always futurally projecting. In Heidegger's words, temporality "is the primordial 'outside-of-itself' in and for itself."[69] Futurally projecting, my very existence as Being-toward-death is defined by my finitude.

As finite, my interpretation of the world is never complete or all inclusive. On the contrary, my comprehension is necessarily *perspectival*. Certainly, such perspectival situatedness means that placial descriptions of *nearness* and *farness* are immediately invoked as I orient myself within the world. In my walks along the shores of Lake Ontario, it is clear that the geese floating by are closer than the oil barge making its way to the loading docks several miles to the west. My orientation along this lakeside, therefore, is made possible, only because placial images of direction, dimension, and proximity are invoked.

At the same time, however, such implacement is hardly atemporal or ahistorical. On the contrary, my historical situatedness locates me within a western tradition that, in this case, naturally projects a vision of the lake as an industrial port— a vision clearly inaccessible to natives centuries ago. My historical tradition infuses my interpretation of place, just as much as the temporal foundation of transcendental understanding makes it possible for me to experience the movement and change of the moving barge or the shift in weather.[70] As Casey himself writes, "there is nothing like a completely static place."[71]

Time, then, is integral to place as even Casey acknowledges in the final chapter of his book, appropriately entitled "Moving between Places: Homeward Bound." The Hopi people know that, "if it does not happen 'at this place,' it does not happen 'at this time.'"[72] Time and place are "inseparable."[73]

The Space of Embodiment

As time interweaves with place, space can also be seen to be integral to the notion of implacement. Once again, however, it is not the ontic notion of space but, rather, the ontological notion of spatiality that will be seen to be central. The dictionary definition of space is of "a three-dimensional extent in which objects and events occur" and terms such as "distance, area, and volume" are implicated.[74] It is, however, only the primordial, spatializing comportment of being-in-the-world that makes such an ontic definition meaningful.

Recall Heidegger's argument that human beings are more than mere present-at-hand entities that are placed in material spaces.[75] Heidegger refers to the "spatiality of being-in-the-world," and he explores this concept in terms of the originary space within which entities find their place.[76] This notion of space no more originates in the subject than in the objective world of things, "'as if' that world were in a space."[77] Being-in-the-world, however, "if well understood ontologically, is spatial."[78] What does Heidegger mean?

Inasmuch as we are temporally transcending the present toward futural possibilities, we take up a fundamental, anticipatory stance toward a world and entities that we try to understand. In so doing, we situate entities and events and order them by "making room" for them and by interpreting them within a holistic context.[79] Heidegger suggests that in "making room" for entities, we are opening up a *region* within which entities are situated and, thereby, we "give them space."[80] When we explicitly orient ourselves in terms of the placement and proximity of entities to one another, "the kind of place which is constituted by direction and remoteness . . . is already oriented towards a region and oriented within it."[81]

The fundamental, interpretive stance that seeks to order the world in some meaningful manner is one that opens up a space within which entities find their place. In this sense, place and spatiality are intertwined. Implacement happens inasmuch as we are spatializing beings, opening up a region and interpretive horizon within which entities and events appear to us as significant.

In his later writings, Heidegger links the ontological notion of space with dwelling even more explicitly than he does in *Being and Time*. Reiterating that space is neither an external object nor an inner experience, he tells us that "spaces open up by the fact that they are let into the dwelling of man. To say that mortals *are* is to say that *in dwelling*, they persist through spaces by virtue of their stay among things and locations."[82]

Places only appear to us as meaningful inasmuch as our fundamental comportment in the world consists of both a temporalizing and spatializing activity of human understanding. Heidegger gives an example that helps to clarify this conclusion. He suggests that when I head toward the door of a lecture hall, "I am already there and I could not go to it at all if I were not such that I am there. I am never here only," he says, "as this encapsulated body; rather, I am there, that is, I already pervade the room and only thus can I go through it."[83]

The example is illumining: in pervading the room as a whole, I am implaced and this implacement is only possible to the extent that I am not a self-enclosed entity but am ahead-of-myself, interpreting the world and engaging myself prethematically and reflectively with entities within it. In the words of poet Pierre-Jean Jouve, "car nous sommes où nous ne sommes pas" [for we are where we are not].[84]

Some readers may feel that, in describing the lecture hall experience, Heidegger is merely describing a mental activity. After all, in physical terms, I am not at all already at the lecture hall door but am only moving *toward* it. To say, as Heidegger does, that I am not only here but am also *there* suggests a definition of implacement as nothing more than a subjective feeling and, ultimately, an activity in the mind.

I would argue, on the contrary, that the dwelling described in this example can occur, not only because we are interpretive beings but also precisely because *we are embodied*. Heidegger himself writes little about the body and when he does refer to the term, he is openly critical of reductionist tendencies to view the body as a corporeal entity, distinct from the mind.[85] While he is right, in my view, to guard against the positivist tendency to collapse embodiment into ontic categories, it seems to me that notions like implacement and the spatializing/temporalizing activity of being-in-the-world are only enlarged through an ontological discussion of embodiment.

Let me return to the example of the lecture hall door. Suppose that my intention is to exit as quickly as possible because I have an important meeting scheduled immediately at the end of class. A large group of lingering students obstructs my path. I am jostled, the space is stuffy and hot and, gradually, I feel frustrated in getting from here to there.

Note that in describing my situation, it is not *my body* that I feel is hot and suffocated. *I* am stifled. To be sure, I am stifled *as embodied*, but this conclusion simply means that "the body," as other than an abstract concept, is more than a closed container of activities. On the contrary, as essentially open to the world, responsive, and resonating of the situation within which I find myself, my embodied existence defines the place and my situatedness within it as hot, stuffy, and stifling.

Certainly, my upright posture demands that I orient myself predominantly by viewing the world straight ahead of me.[86] This originary stance of implacement conditions my prethematic orientation in specific places, in terms of basic categories of up and down, left and right, near and far.[87] Prethematically, my place is determined according to my postural condition that places the ceiling above and the floor below, or the blackboard at my back and the students ahead of me. Once again, I recognize that the lecture hall door is *over there* and I am *here*.

Such orientation, however, involves more than a merely physical, visual processing of sense data. Neither is this directionality invoked always by way of explicit reflection. My eyes face forward but it is true that places are experienced on more than a strictly visual level. We often hear references to a "sense of place" or "spirit of place." Such expressions serve as reminders that we navigate through places, responding to both visual and auditory cues but also to a fundamental *presentiment* or feel for place.

Such a feel is more than a mere emotional or psychological state but rather, as philosopher Joseph Grange explains, a "dim, throbbing backdrop that supports orientation."[88] There is a different "feel," for instance, to the shelter of an old, English Manor than to its suburban, "monster home" imitation, despite the intentional resemblance of specific details of design. By virtue of my embodiment, I am attuned to different places in different ways.

In summary, the environment that surrounds me is not simply outside of my body, any more than my body is separate from its surroundings. As essentially transparent to the world, my embodied existence is itself a spatializing and temporalizing activity of being-in-the-world and a fundamental opening up to the situation within which I find myself. Because I do more than simply occupy space but *inhabit* it, place is not a container of my inert body but echoes its incarnation within the world.[89]

This recognition of the essential belonging together of world and embodiment offers some philosophical justification for the linkages that scientists themselves are beginning to recognize between the health and well-being of human beings and the ecosystems within which they are implaced. Phenomenology reveals the naïveté of meaningful encounter with the environment as pure, objective fact, separate from human interpretation, oblivious to human activities. At the same time, the human subjectivity cannot *be,* except as implaced and as essentially belonging to the *environs* within which it is situated. No longer conceived atomistically as separate entities, human beings and the environment in which they are implaced are, in the Heideggerean phenomenology, finally recognized as inextricably related.

Rootedness in Place and Being-at-Home

If human being-in-the-world is, as Heidegger describes it, a fundamental temporalizing and spatializing activity of implacement, it is clear that places within which we find ourselves are hardly incidental backdrops of our everyday existence. Instead, they virtually define who we are by conditioning our moods, our sense of meaning, and orientation in the world. Rather than merely providing physical shelter or avenues for community development, a holistic, phenomenological description of places reveals that they are the primordial domain of our embodied existence.

Once the ontological primacy of dwelling is acknowledged, it becomes easier to understand the full force of place attachment and place identity that develops within communities. For example, an environment may appear to some as aesthetically unpleasant but, for others who dwell there, the meaning of the place extends far beyond mere aesthetics, becoming absolutely essential to their sense of well-being and belonging.

In 1947, the first redevelopment proposal in Milwaukee was defeated by residents, one of whom reported: "Slums, they call us. Why, that's a terrible word. Those are our homes, our shrines! We live there!"[90] The meaning of places is constituted by more than aesthetics or economics or physical structures—or even all of these factors cumulatively. My holistic sense of who I am is, often, intimately tied to the places within which I dwell. Sense of place inevitably exceeds reductionist categories or inventories of characteristics that can be nearly cataloged, precisely because implacement is ontologically primordial rather than merely significant on an ontic level of hierarchical ordering of preferences.[91]

Perhaps no society has understood the primordial power of place better than the aboriginals. Representing the World Council of Indigenous Peoples, Hayden Burgess writes: "Next to shooting indigenous peoples, the surest way to kill us is to separate us from our part of the Earth. Once separated, we will either perish in body, or our minds and spirits will be altered so that we end up mimicking foreign ways, adopting foreign languages, accepting foreign thoughts."[92] Rodolfo Stavenhagen agrees that "an Indian without land is a dead Indian."[93] In addressing the plight of Aborigines, Australian senator Neville Bonner dramatically declared that "my race is psychologically scarred and such condition is a direct result of the dispossession of our traditional lands."[94] Belonging to the earth has not only been a slogan for the indigenous people of the world but has defined their very mode of being. Displacement from their homes has led to the deepest disorientation possible on a personal and social level as well.

A leader of the Kayapo of Brazil, Paulinho Paiakan, hopes that an understanding of the ties of indigenous cultures to the land may educate modern, western society about the fundamental importance of caring for the earth. "I am trying to save the knowledge that the forests and this planet are alive," he reflects, "to give it back to you who have lost the understanding."[95]

It is certainly true that, to some degree, technologically driven global societies need to recall the primordial significance of rootedness to place. Dolores Hayden argues that the power of place remains essentially unexplored in American cities. She offers the possibility of a renewed awareness of urban landscape history as one avenue for reviving citizens' "public memory."[96] Unearthing a broad diversity of ethnic histories in the city of Los Angeles—a city typically cited for its apparent uniformity of place—Hayden shows how an awareness of local traditions may inspire a renewed appreciation of the significance of one's dwelling place.

It is important to learn from those cultures whose rootedness to place is so central to their existence. At the same time, I wonder if we need to look very far to contemplate the power of implacement. In North America, suburban sprawl—

"the quintessential physical achievement of the United States"—has been the target of criticism of many champions of higher density, environmentally friendly alternative settlement forms.[97] At the same time, however, these critics often realize how difficult it can be to modify peoples' perceptions and values that tie them to their dwelling places.[98]

From the reckless destruction of agricultural lands and ecosystems to the pervasive dependence on automobiles, suburbs have been criticized by advocates of sustainable planning.[99] In many cases, these advocates realize that, from the purely technical point of view of environmental benefits and costs, suburban sprawl is no longer a sustainable settlement form. Modifying human perceptions of suburbs, however, has proved to be a major challenge.

Some studies have undertaken to identify and better understand suburbanites' cultural preferences.[100] The perception that new things are always better than old often pervades the suburbanite's consciousness, as does a sense of remaining close to nature and preserving rural ideals.[101] The car symbolizes the mobility and freedom that are often perceived as basic rights afforded to citizens of a western society aiming to preserve individual liberties. Generally, the destiny of the "American Dream" seems to have been captured in the vision of the suburb.[102]

The full power of these cultural values can only be appreciated once one recognizes the primordial meaning of rootedness in place and being-at-home. Belonging to place is more than merely an emotional tie to suburbia for its citizens. That belonging is also constituted by something more than a catalog of intellectual rationalizations for remaining in suburbs. Whether remaining in suburbia "for the sake of the children" or as an "escape from the frenzy of the city," simply addressing an inventory of rationalizations alone will not reach to the heart of the attraction for place.

Instead, there is good reason, in my view, to ponder more seriously the description of suburban dwellings as "havens."[103] In his phenomenology of the imagination, Gaston Bachelard reflects how "abstract, 'world-conscious' philosophers" believe that they can "know the universe before they know the house."[104] Nevertheless, "before he is 'cast into the world,' as claimed by certain hasty metaphysics, man is laid in the cradle of his house. And always," Bachelard continues, "in our daydreams, the house is a large cradle. A concrete metaphysics cannot neglect this fact, this simple fact, all the more since this fact is a value, an important value, to which we return in our daydreaming."[105]

The value of house as haven is not merely one subjective "value" among others but instead points to the primordial, oneiric significance of home as shelter. No mere abstraction, home as haven congeals the most concrete reality of all: the need of a place that will nurture and protect its inhabitants from intrusion. That homes often do not accomplish this purpose—for example, in abusive relationships—does not undermine the fact that, on an oneiric level, home serves as "cradle" and as center.

Even the appeal of the automobile—a staple of suburban culture—can be seen as reflecting the notion of home as haven in new technologies. Some authors argue that the car may provide one of the last "free spaces" for refuge from the oppression of civilization, as "car time" comes to be one of the rare occasions for privacy.[106] Altogether, reflected in the suburban dream is an oneiric vision of the house that helps us to say: "I will be an inhabitant of the world, in spite of the world."[107]

Nearness and Remoteness

The appeal of home as center and as a place of peace suggests positive possibilities for moving toward sustainability. The places to which we are passionately tied are, clearly, those toward which our care will be most directed. David Seamon suggests that "rootedness in place promotes a more efficient use of energy, space and environment than today's place relationships, which emphasize social mobility and the frequent destruction of unique places."[108] The very roots of the NIMBY ("Not-In-My-Backyard") syndrome, often criticized as an antisocial sentiment, also reflect the positive possibilities of residents' fundamental need to protect the places wherein they dwell and to care, in a deep way, about the environment that sustains their homes.

On the other hand, as philosopher Mick Smith points out, "there is no reason to suppose, in general, that a language of *place* . . . need be environmentally friendly. . . .[T]he development of language and place hand-in-hand *may* have produced the destruction of many features of the original prehuman landscape."[109] Thoughtfulness is not necessarily an element of belonging to place—or is it?

Let me suggest that when the temporal foundations of implacement are forgotten, there is a danger that the meaning of rootedness to place can degenerate into an inauthentic and even unethical interpretation of place. If rootedness to place is interpreted in terms of closure and static permanence, there is every reason to believe that the ontological meaning of place is at risk, as is the genuine search for sustainability. Consider, for instance, how the ethnic cleansing of the former Yugoslavia invites an unhappy, often deleterious interpretation of place as closed to nonnationals and outsiders.

Paradoxically, the very notion of rootedness in place can potentially lead to the destruction of place, if place comes to be viewed as a static accomplishment or as merely geographically bounded and thereby exclusionary of difference. Some people feel that it would be comforting to define place conclusively, establish once and for all its universal characteristics on the basis of some neat, hypostatized blueprint, and then simply proceed to build good places. When we survey the quaint, comfortable, and horrifyingly sterile subdivisions that were built in the name of the suburban dream, we know that such a model of good places is elusive and even destructive of the very essence of place, ontologically understood.

Poetic theorist Gerard Manley Hopkins warned that "perfection is dangerous because it is deceptive. . . . Recovery must be by a breaking up, a violence."[110] Static conceptions of perfect places are naive at best; at worst, they threaten the ontological significance of implacement. Gaston Bachelard understood that places are more than immutable, fixed accomplishments. "The real houses of memory," he wrote, "do not readily lend themselves to description. To describe them would be like showing them to visitors. . . . The first, oneirically definitive house, must retain its shadows."[111]

Indeed, Bachelard cites Henri Bosco's novel, where a lamp waits in the window "and through it, the house, too, is waiting. The lamp is the symbol of prolonged waiting. . . . It is an eye open to night," and, one might add, to change.[112] Place, in the end, is hardly a mere finished product or accomplished state, but more a temporal process. Genuine dwelling can remain close only if it avoids the closure of totalizing visions.

Heidegger has told us that "to be a human being . . . means to dwell."[113] Just as humans are temporal and changing, so too are dwelling places. Edward Casey agrees that "human beings are . . . restless creatures; they cannot remain stationary in one room for more than twenty-four hours without going stir crazy. The problem is the stationariness, not the singleness of the room."[114] Implacement, therefore, is more than a permanent state; it is a resonating of the interplay between nearness and familiarity, on the one hand, and open possibilities on the other.

As Heidegger has suggested, if our fundamental structure of comportment toward the world is one of anticipatory projection and being-ahead-of-ourselves, that stance immediately invokes a reciprocal relation of nearness and remoteness. Entities that surround me in my environment are *not me* and yet, I try to bring them close to understand them, to appropriate them and situate them within my circle of meaningful order. Recalling the example of the lecture hall door, I could not begin to make my way to the door if I were not, in some sense, already "there" in my anticipatory stance and in terms of how I organized the room around this task of reaching the door.

Heidegger himself has clearly indicated how nearness and remoteness define our originary stance in-the-world. "There lies an essential tendency," he writes, "towards closeness. All the ways in which we speed things up, as we are more or less compelled to do today, push us on towards the conquest of remoteness."[115] Edward Casey takes up this thought by declaring that "the here and there, the near and far are the most pervasive parameters of place. Given that *parametrein* means 'to measure out,' we can say that every place we encounter (and know and remember) is measured out, given its full extent, by those four locative predicates."[116]

At the same time as we seek to conquer remoteness, we immediately invoke the phenomenon of *distance*. "Remoteness, like distance," Heidegger writes, "is a determinate categorial characteristic of entities whose nature is not that of Dasein."[117] As I attempt to appropriate the world by comprehending it and bringing it close, at the same time, I instinctively recognize that entities are also at a distance from me. The lecture hall door is present to me, precisely as an entity that is situated farther away from the desk by which I am standing. Nearness and remoteness reverberate in my implicit and meaningful ordering of place.

As Joseph Grange points out, it is our bodily posture that initiates us into such an ordering of place. By virtue of our postural setting, " 'what is' appears initially to be on the vertical-horizontal axis; at the same time, 'what is' shows itself always in the first place to be straight ahead, over there, over against us."[118] Moreoever, the distancing occasioned through such embodied implacement is the condition of forethought and reflection.[119] Sometimes I need to distance myself from an entity in order to see it better. On other occasions, my distance from entities motivates me to bring them closer by ordering them and explicitly relating them to one another reflectively. In both of these cases, one begins to see how representational, positivist thinking is, in some sense, a natural consequence of our distanced observation of the world, made possible by virtue of the postural setting of implacement.

This distanced relation of contention with the world is also the condition of building human settlements. Grange explains how the phenomenon of distance arising from posture and our ocular setting grounds our detachment from nature: "Without this sense of difference, we would be engulfed by our environment—drowned in an ever-shifting and thickening viscosity of sensations" and, moreover, "no built environment could ever be created. Engagement with nature requires a primary disengagement."[120]

The interplay beween nearness and remoteness is of primary ontological significance to the phenomenon of implacement. The reverberation between engagement and disengagement not only conditions our ordering of entities within places but similarly illumines the very meaning of place as temporal and alive. As we shall see, that reverberation will also inform a dialogical, place-based ethic that aims to guide us in our actions, not through the imposition of static principles and rules but, instead, by teaching us the meaning of being *attuned* to a balanced, *fitting relation* between human beings and their world.

8

Place-Based Ethics

The ethical space opened by environmentalists has a new vitality and, like the climbing tendrils
of the bindweed and the anastomizing rhizomes of the honey fungus, its effects move
between the flat surfaces presented by modern life, creating cracks and fissures
through which we can glimpse the existence of another possible way of life.
—Mick Smith, "Against the Enclosure of the Ethical Commons"

Ethics today is viewed less as an obscure discipline confined to the halls of academia than a prerequisite for practical wisdom and even, as Smith points out above,[1] for a new way of living. Ethical deliberation is particularly central when it comes to environmental decision-making. Often, scientific conclusions need to be balanced with economic, political, social, and regulatory concerns in policy formulation. Deciding which issues matter more than others or arguing for the *right* course of action among competing policy alternatives means that moral evaluations and prescriptions are necessarily invoked.

In some cases, scientists lack sufficient evidence to predict the consequences of environmental intrusions with certainty. Decisions must be made that rely, in a most fundamental way, upon implicit and explicit value judgments. For instance, hormone-mimicking effects of certain chemicals and their impact on environmental and human health have been documented but the scientific debate on endocrine modulators is far from conclusive.[2] Are we obliged to wait until the scientific evidence indicating probable harm to humans and the environment is well-established or should we act on the evidence that suggests only *possible* dangers? What is the right thing to do and why? These questions clearly invite ethical deliberation.

Assessing potential environmental risks when the scientific evidence is incomplete is a frequent requirement of today's society. Professor of Science, Technology and Society Studies Sheila Jasanoff points out that "when knowledge is uncertain or ambiguous, as is often the case in science bearing on policy, facts alone are inadequate to compel a choice. Any selection inevitably blends scientific with policy considerations, and policymakers accordingly are forced to look beyond science to legitimate their preferred reading of the evidence."[3] To look beyond science means, in most cases, to look toward moral questions as well.

In this chapter, I offer some preliminary thoughts on the place of phenomenological ethics in environmentalism. A number of claims will be defended. First, I want to suggest that, while we may be unable to invent quick-fix solutions to problems of environmental ethics or to propose a single, overarching system of "right" ways of valuing our natural and built worlds, we must not conclude that ethics collapses into subjectivism, relativism, or is in any way arbitrary. On the contrary, originative thinking can inform an approach to environmental ethics that is capable of offering some concrete realization and guidance in environmental decision-making.

Second, I hope to show that place-based ethics may offer some important clues in our understanding of the meaning of sustainability itself. A recent survey of *The Economist* claims that some marginal increase in security of land tenure can lead to improved environmental and living conditions among the world's poor.[4] Genuine care and sense of belonging to the places where we live may be a condition of sustainability, particularly if it is true, as geographer David Smith points out, that "sustainable" must be taken to mean "not only indefinitely prolonged but also nourishing."[5]

I will suggest that place-based ethics—essentially dialogical and grounded in what Jim Cheney and Holmes Rolston III have called "storied residence"—offer a particularly thoughtful avenue for environmental philosophy.[6] At the same time, I will argue that the phenomenological contribution to the discussion of ethics as narrative must also seek to avoid relativism, particularly in light of global demands of environmental decision-making and the growing challenges that we face in building toward sustainability.

The Place of Ethics in Environmentalism

As the need of ethical reflection comes to be recognized, many environmentalists make the obvious choice to turn to philosophers for guidance. Philosophers, after all, are recognized "experts" on questions of ethics. This fact notwithstanding, I am not alone in arguing that the concrete contributions of philosophers to environmental quandries often have been less than satisfying.

Philosopher Arran Gare maintains that, despite the growing field of environmental philosophy, his discipline still remains marginalized from the mainstream of culture. For the most part, he writes, philosophers are regarded "with a mixture of indulgent respect and contempt as clever people living in a world of their own."[7] Gare feels that, even if philosophy in its present form were to be taken seriously by environmental decision-makers, the effects might be, in all likelihood, no more far-reaching than applying a bicycle brake to an intercontinental jet, considering the complexity of environmental problems that we face.[8]

My own view is that genuine philosophical reflection on fundamental, ontological questions might, potentially, redirect the intercontinental jet by opening up new pathways. Of course, at the present time, there are at least two reasons why such philosophical guidance is not happening to the degree that it could. First, environmental philosophers could do a better job of communicating with others, beyond their disciplinary boundaries. Even the self-professed "interdisciplinary" journal of *Environmental Ethics* remains principally dedicated in style and content to a philosophical audience, although there has been some progress over the last several years to deal with issues of broader appeal.[9] University-level, environmental philosophy courses that are open to nonphilosophers are few in number, despite the fact that, once again, there has been recent progress in this area.[10]

A second reason that might explain why the impact of philosophy on environmental decision-making is less than it could be, relates to the state of philosophical discourse today. Students who seeks guidance from philosophy in environmental matters will be introduced to Utilitarian and Deontological theories. They will learn about ethical relativism, natural law and the teleological tradition. They likely will be required to learn something about more "radical" alternatives such as Deep Ecology, Social Ecology, the Land Ethic, and Ecofeminism. Consolidating widely divergent viewpoints is often felt to be impossible. Gare is, in my view, quite right when he points out that philosophy "has proliferated so many different points of view without moving toward a consensus that anyone turning to philosophy for guidance on environmental issues can only be confused."[11]

Against this bewildering background of competing views, law professor and environmental ethicist Christopher D. Stone argues the case for moral pluralism.[12] He sees the task of philosophy to be more than a matter of either-or and of grounding our decision upon a single, unified set of morally salient rules: "We simply may not be able to devise a single system of morals," he offers, "that is subject to closure and in which the laws of noncontradiction and excluded middle are in vigilant command."[13] Instead, Stone suggests that the more realistic goal of philosophy is to stimulate us "to define and come at problems from different angles" and to "advance our grasp of alternatives."[14]

There are, in my view, good reasons to reject ethical monism—an approach to ethics that maintains that the construction of a single, valid moral theory is not only required but is feasible. To be sure, many people feel that, if an ethical theory is to be useful at all, it must be *true*. For these people, the truth of ethics should be no different than a mathematical question of correctness. Recall, however, our earlier discussion about Heidegger's notion of truth. Once we recognize that the positivist conception of truth as mere correctness is called into question, then we should also realize that ethics, in any case, is not reducible to mathematical equations.

Calculative thinking expects that values and beliefs are no less quantifiable than widgets. Like individual pieces of a puzzle, the positivist would hope to be able to assemble apparently disparate values into a single, coherent totality—a conclusive, correct theory or cohesive inventory of rules and principles. I have argued earlier in this volume about the limitations of positivist conceptions of truth. The reduction of complex relations and ontological phenomena to well-defined ontic categories may bring a momentary sense of accomplishment and closure to ethical questioning, but at the risk of genuine understanding of the fundamental issues.

Still, many people continue to expect of philosophy definitive answers to moral quandries. If ethics is unable to provide such answers, these people may conclude that philosophers are unable to offer useful guidance in environmental decision-making. This conclusion, in my view, is somewhat perplexing, particularly if one recognizes that there are, in fact, few areas of our lives that match the precision of a mathematically computed science or that allow for single, clearly bounded answers. Our closest relationships to the ones we love do not come with any straightforward prescriptions for success. As we learn to balance our need for closeness to another human being with the concomitant requirement that we respect his or her own individuality and independence, we navigate often in unexpected circumstances and with few, simplistically formulated guidelines. The wisest strategy is to remain open to life's challenges, to learn from mistakes, and to commit oneself to the relationship with goodwill in the hope that we will be able to nurture an understanding of the other person, all in good faith.

Even in the field of medical sciences, it is clear that a doctor would be remiss if she were to prescribe a single solution to a health-related problem. Medications are often supplemented with suggestions for a proper diet, exercise or rest, perhaps some counseling and even nontraditional approaches to health care.[15] As Gadamer has shown us earlier in chapter 5, the wise doctor is one who can maneuver among different options and offer a balanced recommendation for overall recovery.[16]

These examples show how mathematical precision is not always the condition for decision-making. At the same time, they also show that the wise route to pursue in such instances is hardly arbitrary. Intuitively, we can all recognize that there are certain, obvious things that we must *not* do, if we are to preserve our friendships or our health. In the field of ethics, when pluralists argue for the possibility that more than one theory can be supported legitimately, they do not necessarily also maintain that just anything goes. Many moral pluralists agree that, while the chances for a single, imperialistic ethical system of answers to environmental problems is not feasible, the opposing extreme of ethical relativism—the approach that says that morals are simply "relative" to each, individual personal perspective—is also to be avoided.

Grappling with the question of *how* moral relativism is to be avoided within a pluralistic approach to ethics is, of course, challenging. Some philosophers feel that pluralism, by definition, inevitably must lead to relativism. If there is no single, right answer to a moral quandry, then, perhaps, there is no right answer at all. All that we are left with is answers that *appear* right, relative to one's own, individual situation. Moral pluralists like Christopher Stone retort that, from the perspective of moral pluralism, there certainly can be "really right" and not merely "relatively right" answers. The way to find them, however, "is by reference not to one single principle, constellation of concepts etc., but by reference to several distinct frameworks, each appropriate to its own domain of entities and/or moral activities."[17]

The phenomenological ethicist similarly would be suspicious of moral thinking that aims to develop a unified, objective system of values. Just as grand, metaphysical speculative systems engaged in a forgetting of the question of the meaning of Being and the historicity of understanding, ethical theories that aim to capture "the good" in monistic systems or principles risk covering over the intricacies of human interpretation that, as we have seen, does more than order entities.

Particularly in environmental matters, the phenomenologist might be inclined to agree with philosopher Holmes Rolston III, who points out how "we will not always be able to travel using well-charted ethical arguments," since ethics involves more than calculative thinking and also because "environmental ethics is novel . . . it lies on a frontier."[18] Furthermore, to formulate abstract, universal rules runs the risk of compromising one's awareness of the richness and mystery of life itself. Rolston captures the phenomenologist's sentiment when he writes that "if a holistic ethic is really to incorporate the whole story, it must systematically embed itself in historical eventfulness. Else it will not really . . . be appropriate, well adapted, for the way human beings actually fit into their niches."[19]

At the same time, the phenomenologist would seek to avoid collapsing ethical understanding into mere subjectivistic projection of arbitrary opinions against the backdrop of a tradition of historical relativism. Phenomenological thinking demands a rigor and discernment that the whims and caprices of such relativistic wanderings inevitably threaten. Rather than specify ethics in terms of either universal speculation, on the one hand, or the generation of multiple and arbitrary preferences on the other, phenomenology will seek to uncover the underlying suppositions that predate such a bifurcation in the first place. Let us look more closely at the phenomenological understanding of the place of ethics.

Ethics in the Lived World

There is a line of thinking in philosophical circles that argues for a logical distinction between questions of fact and questions of value. The way things *are* is not necessarily the way that things *ought* to be.[20] One commits a logical fallacy of thinking, these philosophers argue, if one defines what is good or right simply according to what is natural.[21] What *is* natural, empirically speaking, is not always what *ought* to be and, for this reason, the empirically observed and the ethical are defined by distinct categories of thinking. Accordingly, ethics comes to be perceived as a specialized domain, dedicated to the study of values.

While one may wish to agree that there is some benefit in distinguishing between what is and what ought to be, problems arise, as we already have seen in chapter 6 when ethics operates as if it were a domain unto itself. The abstractions of ethical speculation, for instance, risk indifference to the anguish and complexity that define the concrete encounter with genuine moral dilemmas. As one struggles to decide, at the bedside of a comatose friend or relative, whether to authorize the withdrawal of life-support systems, academic aloofness from the conflicting mental and emotional demands of the lived encounter with such decision-making can seem outright offensive.

Indeed, one begins to recognize that ethical reflection rarely operates as a separate sphere of activity in our primordial comportment toward the world. A number of phenomenologists have already pointed out how ethical thinking evolves as an integral moment of our ontological structure of being-in-the-world, rather than as a distinct domain of inquiry. Calvin Schrag addresses the issue within the context of his rethinking of the essence of the self. While agreeing with the postmodern assault on substance-theories and foundationalist interpretations of selfhood, Schrag argues against a postmodern jettisoning of all senses of self altogether, arguing instead for a "praxis-oriented self."[22]

He gives the example of a moderator at the opening session of the International Congress on World Population, who announces her expectation that by the year 2050, the population of the world will have doubled. The remark appears to be a straightforward prediction of a factual situation. The statement, however, carries an implicit moral message as well—one that likely suggests that a doubling of the world's population in this time frame suggests certain dangers and, therefore, is not a good thing. The context of the remark is, at once, both a a scientifically based prediction as well as an evaluation and assessment of a situation that requires some corrective action. "Within the context of our everyday communicative practices," writes Schrag, "there are no walls of separation between the descriptive, normative, prescriptive, imperative, interrogative and exclamatory functions of discourse. There is, rather, an inmixing and an overlapping. Nor is the who that is present in each of these functions—the who of description, the who of interrogation, the who of prescription—divided and multiplied, summoning an unmanageable heterogeneity of changing selves."[23]

In practice, we typically engage in normative assessments as part of the meaningful ordering of our worlds. As Aristotle well knew, ethical theory is not simply a sum total of truths concerning a specific area of study but, rather, includes from the start "praxis." Critical of Plato's idea of the Good as an empty generality, Aristotle's aim was to explore what is good in terms of concrete human action.[24]

Appropriating this insight within the context of hermeneutic phenomenology, Hans-Georg Gadamer agrees that moral being "is clearly not objective knowledge, i.e. the knower is not standing over against a situation that he merely observes, but he is directly affected by what he sees. [To act ethically] is something that he has to do."[25]

Phenomenologist Joseph Kockelmans argues that authentic moral discourse cannot afford to "separate school from life."[26] He reminds us that we are only gradually educated into a moral universe rather than immediately constructed as moral agents from birth. The process of learning occurs through an endless series of comparative experiences of success or failure and by right and wrong decisions. Explicitly formulated ethical theories are not the most prevalent guides to everyday learning but, rather, "the experiences in which ethical discourse must take its point of departure, have already occurred in the life of an individual long before they received an explicit ethical meaning in the limited sense of this term."[27] Prior to explicitly reflecting upon ethical value systems, a kind of ethical understanding begins to take shape and it is the job of the phenomenologist to lay bare such a prereflective awareness that precedes the construction of ethical systems.

Most ethical theories about the Good, natural law, the categorical imperative, ethical substance, or the need for a transvaluation of all values "begin much too late" because they fail to take into account the fullness of evolving human experience.[28] "The basic categories for moral and ethical discourse function already at a much deeper level in a not-yet ethical manner" and, consequently, "the proper meaning of the moral categories will often be misunderstood if they are not explicitly examined in light of the more basic existentials. . . .[R]eflections on the foundations of morality should begin at a level where the distinction between ontology, anthropology and ethics is not yet relevant."[29]

That moral reasoning consists of more than construction and top-down application of a neatly bounded, theoretical calculation is confirmed and enlarged upon in the work of phenomenologist Eugene Gendlin.[30] Gendlin contends that the foundations of ethical meaning extend beyond the content or conclusions of moral theories, to the actual generation of such content and the dynamics of the decision-making process itself. "Ethics," he writes, "is best cared for as distinctions between kinds of processes. After all, it is the process which determines the contents. Thoughts, feelings, desires, and other experiences are not just given things. They are generated by processes."[31]

Gendlin asks us to consider a case where a good friend has decided to marry and you approve of the choice. While marrying this person appears to be a good thing, in general, is that sufficient for you to call the decision "right"? To quote Gendlin:

> Would you not need to know more about *how* your friend decided? What if the decision was made on a drunken afternoon to get married that very day? Suppose your friend badly wants money and the intended spouse has some?

Suppose the wedding was announced and your friend wants to back out but is scared of disappointing the relatives? What if your friend talks mostly of not wanting to live alone? We commonly call these "wrong reasons." Why? They indicate something about the process of arriving at the decision.[32]

While we may agree that the foundations of ethics point to more than content but to the process of arriving at a moral decision, Gendlin and others in the phenomenological tradition want to say more. The moral process, they contend, is fundamentally different from technical process; moral process "forces us to reject the assumption that events occur only as previously existing forms and units. More order, forms, and units arise from this kind of process than existed at the start" and as a result, "we must reject the usual science model which 'explains' every event by constructing it out of the forms and pieces of earlier events."[33]

While we may recognize that fear of disappointing relatives, or deciding to marry while intoxicated are wrong reasons for marrying, the answer to the question of "why" these are wrong reasons indicates something about the process of arriving at a "right" decision. "The trouble is not exactly," writes Gendlin, "the reasons themselves. After all, one rarely marries for the 'reasons' one gives oneself. Many people spend the rest of their lives trying to discover why they married as they did. In my examples, these clearly wrong reasons indicate something more: the lack of the kind of decision-making process we respect."[34]

In trying to delineate the "right kind of process," one might ask oneself how long one's friend has thought about this marriage; or how "deeply" has the friend examined his or her decision; or we might ask for further facts, such as the characteristics of the person, his or her family, or the nature of one's envisioned future with this person. In other words, the process of deciding whether this marriage is "good" or "right" involves steps, in which what is found can also change and in which new facts can appear.

According to Gendlin, in this sort of progression, more comes out of the process than went in. Human nature, he writes, "is a different sort of 'is,' an is-for developing into what (we later say) the person really 'was'. . . . Purposes and motives develop. Persons and situations are a single interlocking system. In our kind of process, both person and facts turn out to 'have been' more than they seemed."[35]

Gendlin's example shows that the moral decision-making process may well involve some *order*, but of a special sort. Inasmuch as theories, concepts, and values are seen to do more than "merely float" on an abstract, speculative level, they are seen by Gendlin to also make possible a step of a process. Rather than predetermining the process by imposing an order from above, theories and concepts themselves may necessarily be rejected within the very process that they inspired. In short, "all we can say—but it is a lot—is that this kind of process reveals a more intricate order which can exceed and reorder existing forms. Imposed order is not the only kind of order."[36]

Hans-Georg Gadamer expands on the notion of nonimposed order by describing how moral decision-making processes involve an ordering activity that is essentially different from a technical ordering and involves an "additive" or creative function wherein "more order, forms and units arise than existed at the start."[37] Gadamer distinguishes between the *techne* of the craftsman and the *phronesis* (practical knowledge) of the judge who seeks to "apply" a specific law. The craftsman assembles an object according to certain rules of execution and design.[38] Even when the design cannot be carried out as originally intended, it is only in the service of particular, well-defined ends that the modifications can be carried out.

Moral knowledge, however, is not concerned with identifying "merely particular ends" but with "right living."[39] The judge who knows when it is appropriate to refrain from applying the full rigor of positive law is one who does so, "not because he has no alternative but because to do otherwise would not be right. In holding back on the law, he is not diminishing it but, on the contrary, finding a better law."[40] For Gadamer, moral norms are not discovered as preexisting in any unchanging, transcendent realm "so that all that would be necessary would be to perceive them."[41] Nor are moral norms merely a matter of convention. Contrary to step-by-step technical knowledge, "moral knowledge can never be knowable in advance in the manner of knowledge that can be taught."[42]

Rather, there is a fundamental moment of discernment in the moral decision-making process that distinguishes it from the idealized version of technical knowledge that we possess in a modern scientific, technological era. Moral knowing is a special kind of knowing, to be distinguished from technical knowledge to the extent that the former involves not only a manipulation of explicit facts, but a unique seeing and attunement to the moral imperative. In Gendlin's words, ethics must, consequently, involve both inclination as well as concepts.[43]

Such pretheoretical inclination, however, must consist of more than vague intuition or simple emotional preference. If ethics is to be recovered from the perils of abstraction without the risk of a loss of phenomenological rigor, then I would suggest that ethics needs to be rethought in terms of the most concrete and primordial "inclination"—the ontological, transcendental projection of human being-in-the-world. I have discussed in earlier chapters how the ontological structure of such human comportment can be interpreted in terms of the primacy of implacement. The possibility arises, then, that a genuinely concrete environmental ethic can be best informed in its relation to the phenomenon of place.

The Ethics of Place

Edward Casey does not have a great deal to say about the ethics of place, but where he does address this issue, he favors an ecocentric, rather than anthropocentric, environmental ethic.[44] His ecocentrism, however, is defined not only by the imperative to save or preserve the land; the more pressing issue, Casey suggests, is to "let the land save us."[45] He insists that "what matters is *letting the land take the lead*. . . . Taking the lead from landscape means letting its intrinsic sagacity and value become *our* sagacity and value. . . . *Its* power, not ours in relation to it, is what is at stake. And this power is none other than the power of place."[46]

Casey aligns himself with the environmental ethics of the founder of the Sierra Club, John Muir, as well as the Land Ethic of Aldo Leopold, because these philosophical positions "return ethics to its place(s) of origin."[47] Allowing the land to reposses its own rectitude is, in Casey's view, to recognize the intrinsic rights of the land and to "turn ethics in a new direction."[48] The very word "ethics" can be traced back to its Homeric Greek origins in *ēthea*—the habitats of wild animals—who have their "rightful place" and whom human beings have no right to dislodge from their habitats. Casey concludes that, for an ethic of place, "the lead is *from the Other to us*, from animality to humanity."[49]

Earlier in this book, I have taken issue with ecocentric value systems and I have suggested that phenomenology will try to avoid the dualistic confrontation between anthropocentric and ecocentric alternatives. While Casey's comments are not uninstructive, a phenomenological, place-based ethics must proceed carefully to avoid collapsing into an ecocentric philosophy where—in Casey's words—we simply "allow the earth to come first."[50] Human beings are not only passive recipients of the grace of Being. The project of living also includes an active projection and intervention of human understanding and values within the world in which they find their place.

Any linear explanation of rights and duties, emanating from a reified version of nature to human beings secondarily, risks the collapse of environmental ethics into another positivist, monistic vision of morality. To be fair, Casey explicitly argues against such a monocentric view of nature and he recognizes the role of human beings to be one of "selective husbandry" and "household management" of nature's economy.[51] He maintains that simplistic renderings of ecocentric, philosophical perspectives are best avoided if one pays heed to the "diversity of [nature's] inhabitants . . . *and of its places*."[52]

It is precisely the central significance of such richness and diversity of places that informs the postmodern, place-based environmental ethics of another thinker within the Continental tradition of philosophy, Jim Cheney.[53] Like Casey, Cheney also is critical of simplistic, monistic visions of the value of nature and of ethical systems that attempt to construct ahistorical, totalizing visions of the right and the good. He reproaches modernism for its tendency to "essentialize"—to construct a foundational and universal account of truth across borders of difference—and to colonize by abstracting theories from the settings in which they have arisen.

Beyond such totalizing, modernist discourse, Cheney proposes a postmodern alternative in the form of "contextualized discourse of place."[54] Deconstructing mythic images, Cheney hopes to articulate moral imperatives that emerge from the context of the lived reality of places within which ethical paradigms emerge. Rather than construct speculative, conceptual representations, the goal for post-modern thinking becomes one of illumining moral narratives that instruct citizens from within their concrete location and embeddedness in particular places. In this sense, truth is revealed as "bioregional," local, and specific to place.

Cheney tells us that "with language comes a taxonomy of the world, an order-ing of our cosmos, and a positioning of ourselves within this matrix. Eventually, the cosmos comes to express a moral order—it instructs us in virtue of its very manner of containing us."[55] The task for the philosopher is to illumine such a moral order that emerges through various bioregional narratives.[56] Rather than *constructing* conceptual systems that define the right and the good, the role of eth-ics becomes one of illuming implicit elements of moral instruction that emerge through the *deconstruction* of a variety of geographical, place-based narratives. "The task then," concludes Cheney, "is to tell the best stories we can. The tales we tell of our and our communities' 'storied residence' in place are tales not of universal truth, but of local truth, bioregional truth."[57]

To my mind, there are at least two important conclusions that emerge from these discussions of the new role of place-based ethics within environmentalism. The first point has to do with the meaning of ethics vis-à-vis ontology. The sec-ond point relates to the task of environmental ethics within the wider project of working toward sustainability. Let us address each point in turn.

Both Cheney and Casey recognize that, for most people, ethics is constituted by more than rational constructs and abstract, theoretical concepts. Human be-ings, ontologically implaced in a variety of different settings, are engaged daily in decision-making processes and in evaluations that imply some recognition of an implicit, moral order that is functioning within our communities. If Kockelmans is right and we are not born ethical, more realistically, we gradually become in-formed about moral expectations that implicitly instruct us through our culture, our institutions, our historical tradition, and the geographical places within which we are situated.

In that sense, ethical discernment is less a matter of intellectual construction than it is one of attunement to a particular way of being-in-place. Rather than simply consisting of a project of internalizing an inventory of rules and princi-ples, ethical awareness also unfolds prethematically and is informed by virtue of the ontological phenomenon of implacement. To be sure, appropriate moral be-havior often consists of living within the law and following certain clearly stipu-lated rules of the judicial system, but civil behavior and ethical insight are not re-stricted to such actions only. Explicit deliberation about specific cases may focus our attention on special, moral dilemmas, and in the process of resolving these dilemmas, aspects of a society's ethical expectations may need to be articulated and differently ordered, for example, through new laws. Nevertheless, ethics is more than an inventory of things that we must do. It is also an inquiry into the way that we must be.[58]

The awareness that a phenomenological ethic will not restrict itself to specifying explicitly defined, ontic expectations brings us to my second point, that asks about the goal of environmental ethics within the project of building toward sustainability. If the scope of ethics is to be understood as extending beyond ontic considerations and a hierarchical ordering of entities, then the ontological foundation of such ethics will require a discernment of a community's prethematically comprehended expectations and an evaluation of these expectations within the context of that community's implacement.

Moral texts extend beyond explicitly articulated rules and principles to include ways of organizing our built spaces, for example. The task for phenomenology, then, becomes one of deconstructing a broad gamut of expectations—not by constructing a new, ethical theory, but, rather, by opening a space for communication of values and for illumining implicit paradigms that drive a community's very sense of place. Ethics becomes a *dialogical* challenge, rather than a theoretical challenge, to discern a moral order that implicitly instructs a society through its culture, its historical tradition, and the geographical place within which it is situated.

For sustainable development policies to be realistic, it is important that we attempt to understand, from within, what constitutes a community's implicit moral texts and how they are meaningful. Such an approach to a phenomenological, place-based ethics may sound vague to some readers, particularly if the description is framed in terms of broad, ontological notions of implacement. Let us look at several examples, however, where a similar approach was found to be particularly successful in articulating implicit attitudes and promoting realistic policy decisions for sustainable development.

Some Case Studies

The global proliferation of Coca-Cola advertisements, McDonald's restaurants, and international currency of credit cards serve as reminders that the western, technological way of living is, in many ways, enveloping the world and shaping the development of local cultures and traditions. Certainly, formalized processes of colonization have come to an end, but as cultural theorists Yvonne Dion-Buffalo and John Mohawk point out, the global marketplace with its attendant intellectual and cultural imperialism "makes colonization a contemporary reality."[59] As noted earlier, the very notion of sustainable development is easily conceived in western, colonizing frameworks that imply totalizing, Eurocentric standards of morality.

Against the background of such insidious, colonizing views of right and wrong, a project in the Peruvian Andes has engaged in reimbuing the Andean people with a more traditional worldview through a process that organizers call "cultural affirmation."[60] A group of indigenous writers, academics, and former government bureaucrats have formed a nongovernmental organization called PRATEC (Proyecto Andino de Tecnologias Campesinas) dedicated to investigating and reporting on traditional Andean technologies and worldviews.[61] PRATEC has introduced a course aimed at agronomists which "presents the Andean worldview and also assesses modern, western knowledge from a native Andean point of view."[62] The importance of this work has now come to be recognized throughout the Andes.[63]

In presenting Andean worldviews, PRATEC hopes that a recognition of local customs and traditions will encourage agricultural practices that enable sufficient production of food, while preserving the environment and the overall health of each diverse community. As the unsustainability of large-scale, technologically manipulative forms of agronomy are widely recognized, alternative, more decentralized solutions become all the more important. The Andean landscape is one of the most ecologically diverse in the world.[64] For this reason, standardized agricultural solutions cannot take adequate account of this diversity, and alternate approaches are called for. Since Andean peasantry has existed for over ten thousand years, it seems sensible to conclude that peasant traditions may offer important insights into how best to regenerate these communities in sustainable ways.

There are a number of teachings of PRATEC that are noteworthy with respect to Cheney's call for a postmodern environmental ethic. Emphasizing the "situatedness of its Andean point of view," PRATEC "rejects claims to universality and absolute truth," seeing instead that the Andean worldview emerges "from the very soil and air of the Andes, inseparable from its landscape and its history."[65] A Bolivian peasant explains how "we have great faith in what nature transmits to us . . . it is the voice of nature itself which announces to us the manner in which we must plant our crops."[66] Farmers recount how the magnitude and odor of the winds speak to them about the coming weather and how the arrival of wild plant flowers signal that the land is ready for cultivation.

Reading such signals from the landscape, farmers see themselves to be in constant conversation with the world.[67] No two conversations are ever the same. For this reason, PRATEC sees its task as one of articulating the sources from which the diversity of landscapes and variety of ways of living emerge. "Rather than giving us snapshots of reality in the manner of empiricist social sciences, their efforts are aimed toward capturing something like a worldview, what they call an Andean cosmovision. It is a point of view that goes behind or beyond the happenings of everyday life with their inevitable rough spots and difficulties as well as small triumphs. It is an approach less intent on giving knowledge about a world and more akin to an invitation to enter that world."[68]

Such an invitation to enter the world of the Andean farmer suggests the need for a method of inquiry that is quite distinct from traditional modes of scientific reporting. PRATEC's position is described as a "dialogical" one—inherently pluralist and one that rejects a linear, evolutionary vision of history, entertaining the possibility "that industrial or post-industrial civilization and the global market are not the inevitable futures for everyone."[69] Such a dialogical stance opens up the possibility of new sources of understanding of sustainability, while at the same time challenging simplistic, linear notions of global development.

The dialogical stance also highlights the importance of bioregional narratives as a means for better comprehending the complex relationships between human beings and diverse environments in which they find their place. Sylvia Bowerbank reports on a set of initiatives that are emerging for the study of the area surrounding the highly polluted, steel center of Canada, Hamilton Bay. "In our society," she writes, "the stories of ordinary peoples' relationships to ordinary places remain largely a hidden and untapped resource for understanding the complicated, shifting connections between human behavior and environmental conditions. . . . Oral testimonies can be used, at the very least, to supplement the official record, which often mutes the voices of ordinary women, children and men."[70]

Bowerbank tells of an event that has been developed in Hamilton called "Our Shared Home: An Ecomusée Initiative," where a "museum without walls" is to be invented by inhabitants of the area who are invited to organize any variety of events whereby their stories can be told about particular places in the watershed that they know or love.[71] She cites artist Catherine Gibbon who remarks how "the development of a sense of place is an ongoing process. Like genetic material, it is passed on from generation to generation. . . . It requires more than an experience of sight, sound and smell. It is an inward journey of connections: between people and place, and between past and present."[72] Exploring these journeys through narratives arising from the Ecomusée initiative offers the possibility of enlarging upon our understanding of diverse environments in nonessentializing ways.

Advocating storytelling as a "cultural technology of connectivity and groundedness," Bowerbank feels that narratives open up horizons of understanding of the relation between inhabitants and their specific dwelling places that, ultimately, can better inform environmental policies. She recognizes that the task of transforming narratives into policy decisions is not an uncomplicated one: "the collective process by which a multiplicity of local narratives will eventually get transformed into good practices remains to be negotiated, in myriad ways, at the level of the bioregion."[73]

Not that storytelling is valid only at the level of the bioregion. There is no reason, in principle, why insightful narratives cannot emerge from other sources than bioregional inhabitants. In fact, there may be good reason to encourage much broader perceptions of place. Ecologists now realize that macro-ecological realities define human settlements, far beyond their physical, geographical location. Professor of Planning and Resource Ecology William Rees argues that "while we are used to thinking of cities as geographically discrete places, most of the land 'occupied' by their residents lies far beyond their borders. The total area of land required to sustain an urban region (its 'ecological footprint') is typically at least an order of magnitude greater than that contained within municipal borders or the associated built-up area."[74] Inasmuch as modern cities rely increasingly on global flows of goods from a variety of landscapes, it is naive to restrict bioregional narratives simply to small-scale, local perceptions of place.

For instance, there is no reason, in principle, why the international voyager who moves from place to place cannot recount experiences that illumine different forms and scales of place. Certainly, incidental encounters with foreign cultures do not promise meaningful testimonies. Consider, however, how some authors are able to bring the experience of international travel near to the reader's imagination, despite the broad scale of reporting. I am reminded, for instance, of Lawrence Durrell's vivid accounts of his journeys through Egypt or Greece, or Robert Kaplan's chronicles of his global journeys from Africa to China to India in what he calls a "travel book" that does much more than recite prosaic, petty facts about diverse environments but "is concrete to the extent that my ideas arise from personal experience."[75] Casual and fleeting views of places do not constitute significant additions to our understanding of environments but we must not conclude that all *non*bioregional views emerging from nonresidents are automatically inauthentic or superficial.

Similarly, nonbioregional, global visions are not necessarily facile representations of an abstract image. Don Ihde has shown how technologically mediated perspectives on our planet can offer significant and thoughtful contributions to our comprehension of our environment: "what an instrumentally embodied science gives one is precisely the opening to micro- and macro-phenomena through the mediated bodily perceptions made possible by instrumentation."[76] To suggest that moonshot or earth-as-planet or other large-scale environmental images are merely representative "pictures," in Heidegger's disparaging sense of the term, is simply naive. Greenhouse gases are not only deduced from disparate pieces of data but are "instrumentally 'perceived.' "[77] In this respect, we should avoid the tendency to romanticize narratives as if they only occurred at small, geographical scales. Inasmuch as we are human, we are storytellers and, as ancient myths no less than a traveler's chronicles or Ihde's accounts testify, there is no reason why those stories cannot extend to global and even cosmic proportions.

These narratives, of course, are more than mere fables. By invoking notions of storied residence, one is not advocating the proliferation of whimsical accounts of diverse places. Narratives, in the sense used here, are interpretive accounts of how individuals perceive the places wherein they dwell in a variety of modes, and those interpretive accounts inevitably find their way even into the most objective scientific discussions.

It is true, however, as Bowerbank points out, that "the stories we create are rarely as free and as good as we might want them to be."[78] An important lesson emerges from contemporary visions of postmodern environmental ethics that implore us to better understand the full breadth of significance of one's storied residence. On the other hand, a number of questions remain unanswered. How, for instance, do we begin to differentiate between arbitrary tales and "good" stories that embody sound environmental awareness? Assuming that we might acknowledge "positive" values that emerge from particular narratives, how do we ensure that these values are translated into effective and coherent public policy?[79] In the following section, I offer some preliminary suggestions as to how we might begin to deal with such concerns by means of a phenomenological approach to environmental ethics.

Toward a Phenomenological Environmental Ethic

In his *Basic Problems of Phenomenology*, Heidegger points out that there are three basic components of phenomenological method: reduction, construction, and destruction.[80] Through phenomenological reduction, we are led back from the apprehension of entities to their ontological ground—from being to Being.[81] That move, however, is not merely a negative methodological requirement of avoiding entities. Rather, ontological thinking demands an active, free projection—phenomenological construction—as a guide. Finally, such a construction is also a destruction—"a critical process in which the traditional concepts, which at first must necessarily be employed, are deconstructed down to the sources from which they were drawn."[82]

It seems to me that, in the postmodern turn, the moment of destruction is often highlighted at the expense of reduction and construction. For instance, Cheney's objection to the essentializing tendencies of traditional, principlist ethics finds expression in a deconstruction of these tendencies and in a call for understanding positional interpretations of place through bioregional narratives. Description and deconstruction of place-based stories are essential moments of an environmental ethic but are they sufficient in offering us guidance in decision-making?

I would argue that the goal of environmental ethics must involve more than listening to distinct, bioregional narratives as a condition of understanding place-based values. Otherwise, we are unable to begin to respond to Bowerbank's questions about *which* place-based values we are willing to appropriate and translate into policies for sustainable development. However, if reduction and, more specifically, construction constitute integral moments of the phenomenological method, how do we begin to illumine ontological foundations and provide actual guidance in environmental decision-making without falling into the trap of hypostatizing and universalizing ethical principles?

Let me suggest some preliminary guidelines for further directions for phenomenological inquiry in the field of environmental ethics. First, it seems to me that, rather than merely amassing a collection of discrete, bioregional stories, it is incumbent upon us to evaluate those stories within the broader, ontological context within which they originate. Consider an example where a westerner wishes to invest in housing for the poor in a country where, in terms of his own values, corruption runs rampant among the bureaucracy and the government. What is seen, from the westerner's perspective, as a request for a financial bribe on his part may be, from the point of view of local expectations, a fair step in a network of exchanges and a development of trust among the key role-players involved in the investment. It is probably wise, in other words, that the westerner try to do more than impose his own values, but that, instead, he attempt to comprehend the values and expectations of this foreign culture from within and in terms of its broader systems of mutual understanding.

On the other hand, unearthing these bioregional narratives may expose them as inadequate in terms of other kinds of norms and criteria, and in this respect, Cheney's directives to illumine local, mythical structures do not seem to help as much as we might hope. As careful as we might wish to be to avoid imposing apparently universal, ethical principles upon diverse cultures, perhaps it is equally true that merely listening to and describing diverse narratives does not do justice to the demands of prescriptive decision-making either. We may well feel that we are justified in concluding that the scale of corruption in the example above is unacceptable on some broader level, despite its apparent acceptability by some people on a local, bioregional scale.

In this respect, I would propose that the phenomenological direction for environmental ethics is distinct from the postmodern turn. The latter cautions us to avoid the essentializing and hypostatizing tendencies of top-down ethical directives and, in this respect, finds theoretical guidelines to be suspect in the field of ethics. While sensitive to these concerns, the phenomenologist—methodologically guided by all three moments of deconstruction, reduction, and construction—is compelled not to merely describe discrete places, but to investigate converging images that might emerge beyond the destructive moment.

It seems to me that philosopher Mick Smith is right to point out that "the absence of theoretical orthodoxy is no guarantee of human freedom. In fact, the absence of theory may actually exclude the possibility of voicing heterodoxy, of questioning the ideological assumptions incorporated in that society's world views [and] ethical values."[83] The danger is that to conceive of cultures as "isolated and essentially incommensurable" is to concede to the pitfalls of cultural relativism where "one ethic cannot be judged better than another."[84]

Instead, Smith argues for a "broader and less constrained positionality" than that advanced by Cheney.[85] Such an account would allow for the possibility of illumining similarities as well as differences between cultures at all levels. Just because distinct places frequently offer unique horizons of interpretations, one need not conclude that moral values in different societies cannot converge on the basis of similar geographical or biological conditions, cultural practices, historical traditions, or any combination of such aspects of place.[86]

Certainly human beings possess many similarities to one another on many practical levels as well as in terms of their discursive interpretations of the world. "These similarities," writes Smith, "make communication possible. Without such similarities at some level, discourse becomes impossible. In addition, communication entails a meeting of places, an expression of different perspectives."[87] To illumine converging images offers the possibility of moving one step beyond merely recounting ethical expectations to relating them to one another, to learning from them, and, finally, to eliciting moments of consensus regarding what constitutes a right course of action.

Smith concludes by calling for a "positional holism" that neither reduces human beings to a passive voice of nature nor simply catalogs diverse, place-based moral viewpoints.[88] "Such an admittedly vague form of totalizing, but, nevertheless, anti-essentialist and anti-foundationalist myth seems a more promising ground for understanding the complexities of morality than any such narrow concept as bioregionalism."[89]

Smith's article does not expand on this notion of positional holism at any great length. From the perspective of a phenomenological ethic, however, certain significant conclusions emerge. First, a place-based ethic must remain open and sensitive to moral conceptions that emerge from citizens' narratives at various scales, that indicate intimate knowledge of and meaningful relationships to the places they inhabit. Second, these narratives will often exhibit diversity, and as historically situated, they will not be conclusive, totalizing conceptions of "the good life." Nevertheless, they will imply ethical conceptions that a phenomenological deconstruction may hope to illumine. Finally, phenomenology must do more than merely amass a variety of place-based perspectives on moral goods. Beyond such an inventory, another task emerges—one that calls for thoughtful deliberation about converging ethical images, contextual references, and common, human needs.

Smith maintains that "the strength of the environmentalists' argument is that similar conclusions come from many different places."[90] Despite cultural difference, a common humanity unites people and makes communication possible. Phenomenologist Werner Marx has already shown how coming to terms with one's own mortality opens up the possibility of genuine care and solicitude toward others who share the predicaments of finitude.[91] The links that emerge in this instance are more than a series of characteristics that we can ennumerate as common to all human beings. Rather, the possibility of an openness and an attunement to the needs of other human beings emerges by way of a phenomenological description of one's shared mortality. By enlarging our understanding of one another—both in terms of our distinctness, as well as our similarities—the possibility emerges of a place-based ethic that respects the bonds that tie us to our dwelling places but one that also allows for continuing dialogue as we collectively reflect on environmental questions of right and wrong.

Even if we agree on these issues, however, many questions still remain. What other commonalities—other than one's finitude—might emerge as ontologically and ethically significant for environmental philosophy? Most pressingly, the reader may be concerned with the issue of how these deliberations on place-based ethics impact on questions of sustainability. What role does a place-based ethic play in policy development? How is the concept of sustainable development to be reconceived in light of phenomenological and ontological reflections? Can phenomenology offer some methodological considerations that are practicable in the pursuit of sustainability? The following chapter aims to address these concerns and to suggest courses for future action.

9

Phenomenology and Sustainability

> *"Would you tell me, please, which way I ought to go from here?"*
> *"That depends a good deal on where you want to get to," said the Cat.*
> *"I don't much care where—" said Alice.*
> *"Then it doesn't matter which way you go," said the Cat.*
> —Lewis Carroll, *Alice in Wonderland*

In the final pages of *Our Common Future*, the World Commission on Environment and Development highlights the importance of improved monitoring, collecting and comparing of data for the purposes of identifying key environmental issues and trends.[1] If we are to build toward sustainability, it is important to set specific goals but it is also true that the goals themselves are defined on the basis of a comprehensive understanding of existing states of affairs. To this end, the commission recommends that data collection, assessment, and state of the environment reporting functions "need to be significantly strengthened as a major priority."[2]

In this chapter, I suggest that phenomenology can play a key role in a number of areas. First, it can help to clarify the meaning and aims of sustainability. As the Cat so lucidly points out to Alice, we cannot afford to pursue policies of sustainable development in the absence of some idea as to where we are headed.

Second, phenomenology can assist in the important process of describing current conditions and expanding the information base alluded to by the Brundtland Commission. There is growing recognition of the importance of measuring sustainability in terms of "indicators." I would argue that phenomenology can contribute to the development of such indicators, particularly if they are understood in terms of qualitative as well as quantitative parameters.

Finally, in the chapter that follows, I suggest that phenomenology has much to impart to environmental education. Advancing critical thinking skills by recognizing the importance of ontological, rather than simply ontic reflection, and sensitizing students to the ethical dimensions of the places within which they live, are, in my view, central to the task of rethinking sustainability. Let us consider these issues in turn.

Rethinking Development

Recall that, according to the Brundtland Commission, "sustainable development is development that meets the needs of the present without compromising the ability of future generations to meet their own needs."[3] Sustainability is not a fixed state of affairs but is "a process of change" where the expending of resources, paths for investment, the nature of technological advancement, and institutional development "enhance both current and future potential to meet human needs and aspirations."[4]

To what extent is the phenomenologist prepared to accept the Brundtland Commission's understanding of the meaning and direction of sustainable development? A central notion to consider is that of "development." A number of critics favor a complete dismantling of the term in environmentalism while others go even further to support an alternative notion of what they call "counter-development"—a reaction to consumer monoculture and a global economy through the revival of traditional, land-based knowledge systems.[5] For these critics, "development" is an insidious term that implies western, technological and economic paradigms of growth that remain at the root of the current environmental crisis.

To be sure, the term is capable of being understood in a narrow, utilitarian sense that the phenomenologist would find troubling. The commission stipulates that "development involves a progressive transformation of economy and society" such that sustainability "cannot be secured unless development policies pay attention to such considerations as . . . the distribution of costs and benefits."[6] The phenomenologist would not be prepared to accept that development is to be understood simply in narrow terms of utility, resource distribution, and traditional paradigms of economic growth.

Nor would the phenomenologist be prepared to adopt a positivist interpretation that might suggest that contemporary, technological society is necessarily further "developed" than traditional cultures that favored a more mythological way of thinking over calculative, analytic reasoning. Development is not simply a linear process whereby knowledge becomes perfected and nothing at all is lost. Heidegger himself has shown how our own metaphysical tradition has, from the time of the pre-Socratics, engaged in a forgetting of the most fundamental question of the meaning of Being. Anthropologists also frequently point out how modern, technological societies have become disassociated from the roots of their own tradition, thereby sacrificing a measure of wisdom that often sustained only apparently more "primitive" cultures.[7]

The western, metaphysical tradition certainly has deep roots in a positivist paradigm that easily supports a vision of development as progressive and linear. Like Heidegger, philosopher Thomas Langan traces our contemporary sense of historical development back to the inception of ancient Greek philosophy, where the search for truth was conceived as a search for the absoluteness of the source of Being against the vagaries of individual *doxai* (positions or opinions).[8] Through the Middle Ages, the Church transmitted this sense of truth as universal and transcendental. It also interpreted history in terms of a searching for a particular destination—a "sense that mankind is coming from somewhere and going toward an end."[9] Within this context, it is no wonder that modern philosophical thinking became a search for universal truth and that development was easily conceived as a "generalizing science."[10]

When sustainability is located within the context of such a generalizing science of development, diverse ways of life and disparate truth claims that cannot be subsumed within such a science are threatened. Langan holds that "the imposition of the techniques, machines and mind-sets on nations of radically different cultures whose traditions are not critical in the European way, is at the origin of what we today call 'the Third World development problem.' The development crisis is not first and foremost an economic issue. It is a clash of cultures, rooted in radically different experiences of the truth."[11]

If sustainable development policies proceed on a conception of truth as universalizing, the danger is that unilaterally imposed solutions to the problems of unique and distinct cultures will remain unjust and misplaced. Langan reminds us that "we are not just possessors of the great wealth-producing machine and the saviors of mankind, but a terrible menace for every culture that commits the crime of simply being different. . . . We believe we belong to the final culture, the culture which can come to an understanding of all other cultures through a science of culture."[12]

The truth is, however, that temporal progression does not necessarily lead to progress on all fronts. Development through time may include a regression or decline in understanding. Perhaps even more realistically, finite historical understanding may proceed with an irregular, nonlinear pattern that includes moments of advancement as well as a covering over of truth in what Heidegger calls "error" (*das Irren*).[13] "The revelation of what-is-as-such" writes Heidegger, "is at the same time the concealment of what-is in totality."[14] To conceive of development as the progressive accumulation of knowledge and merely as positive progression is to forget what we have already seen in previous chapters of this book—that the temporality of human being-in-the-world reveals a finite understanding that is never absolute so that the discovery of truth will always also include some measure of forgetting and error as well.

The question remains, however, in what alternative sense might we conceive of the notion of development, if it is to be preserved at all. We tend to assume a single, definitive notion of development as "promoting the growth of" something but it is instructive in this case to note that to develop is also "to set forth or make clear . . . to make visible or manifest" such as in film processing or even in articulating rhythmic or harmonic changes in a piece of music.[15] It is to "cause to unfold gradually," such as in developing an argument.[16] To develop is "to work out the possibilities of" something and finally, it is to "go through a process of natural growth, differentiation or evolution by successive changes" such as that found in the development of bud to flower blossom or even as implied in notions of positive self-development.[17]

It seems to me that the perjorative implications of development might have overshadowed the prospects that are imbedded in the term. To develop something can also mean to actively engage oneself in uncovering that which is essential to its unfolding. To be sure, such active engagement is misplaced if it is heavy-handed or manipulative.[18] Western society can certainly be chastized for not adequately recognizing this fact. Authentic engagement, however, requires an active listening to the constraints that announce themselves in one's concernful dealings with a particular phenomenon. It is integral to the structure of being human that we transcend the present in an attempt to forge a more meaningful future, and if the positive possibilities of development can be understood to reflect such an engagement, then perhaps the term is not as problematic as it has been made out to be by its critics.

Our postmodern age has accomplished a great deal by exposing the naïveté of simplified Hegelian notions of historical progression and linear, quasi-Darwinian notions of evolution. As a result, in a postmodern epoch, it becomes almost irreverent to suggest that development and even progress might, after all, be notions worth preserving in discussions of sustainability. Alternative concepts like counter-development, however, are not unproblematic either.[19] Is our goal really to seek something *opposed* to development—particularly in Third World countries where the notion of counter-development finds its most vocal expression—or is it not, rather, a more *thoughtful* development strategy that we ought to explore, requiring an attitude of active, though discerning, engagement in the task of clarifying emerging opportunities and improving our collective living conditions?

The Brundtland Commission distinguishes between development that "tends to simplify ecosystems and to reduce their diversity of species" and sustainable development that "requires the conservation of plant and animal species."[20] The implication seems to be that there are both negative and positive possibilities of development, particularly in light of working toward sustainability.

Thomas Langan also seems to feel that, despite the disparaging interpretations of development that we have discussed, there is, equally, an opportunity to uncover an individual's or a society's "optimal rhythm of development."[21] Below such optimum, potential remains unfulfilled.[22] The objective of sustainability is linked by Langan to the recognition that different cultures are characterized by different rhythms of development to which discerning policies must respond.[23]

Moreoever, providing some "sound direction" can result in "healthy development."[24] Where do we begin to explore the positive possibilities of such healthy, as opposed to inappropriate, forms of development?

Some clues present themselves through an inquiry into the meaning of authentic self-development. Heidegger has taught us that human beings are always ahead-of-themselves, futurally transcending toward a horizon of possibilities that define us in our very structural comportment toward the world. The ontological structure of being human is understood in such a way that the self is more than a self-contained entity but, in essence, is directed toward a world that is Other. Langan reiterates Heidegger's insight when he points out how "the development of the self is a process somehow essentially related to that otherness within my person and in the situation, as I am caught up to some degree in the alien world."[25]

Authenticity indicates an essential openness to the world and, in this sense, "is the opposite of the narcissistic."[26] Healthy self-development is hardly a subjectivistic preoccupation with one's own ego but, rather, a caring engagement of being-in-the-world with others. To be sure, as temporal, we are confronted with nothingness—an abyss, a void, and a futural state of affairs that is-not-yet. Such freedom means that we are confronted with *choices*; we can and often do choose to be inauthentic and retreat from the dread and anxiety of decision-making to the comfort and security of material entities.[27] It is also true, however, that we are capable of projecting ourselves toward this futural space authentically in terms of appropriating meaningful possibilities.

Heidegger tells us that "Dasein as human life is primarily being possible."[28] Might not such possibility and the gift of freedom that it implies reflect a fundamental hope of developing a better world than the one in which I find myself? To cease from engaging oneself in the authentic development of positive possibilities—which is what I worry that the notion of "counter-development" may insidiously imply—may be, in any case, contrary to one's fundamental, existential comportment that aims to transcend the present toward an open-ended future in a search for authenticity and ontological understanding.

Langan reminds us, however, that the temporal foundations of existence are not merely futurally directed and open ended but they also demand a thoughtful appropriation of the past: "To know where we should head, we need the direction offered by the past."[29] To understand how a particular society might best "develop" sustainably, it is essential that we seek to unearth the ontological possibilities that emerge from an understanding of historical traditions, unique cultural narratives, and place-based moral orders: "Social order is not just the product of present action, but is structured by institutions which have been slowly matured over centuries and into which present action must be fitted."[30]

The World Commission on Environment and Development suggests that the satisfaction of aspirations for an improved quality of life constitutes a major objective of development.[31] Langan concurs that the global, cooperative effort of economic, social, and environmental development in which we are all engaged is "inevitably mixed with a desire to improve fundamentally the human condition and is accompanied by a strong emphasis on human rights."[32]

In an effort to improve the human condition, however, "why not go the further step and recognize that the condition for the possibility of a healthy strategy of development is some collective advance in ecumenic wisdom?"[33] As discussed in the previous chapter of this volume, the task for phenomenology becomes one of uncovering ethical narratives of specific places but also of genuine, philosophical inquiry into converging images of sustainable development. Discerning sustainable development policies, then, cannot proceed in the absence of a philosophical inquiry into the deepest, ontological roots of meaning that are handed down by specific traditions and in cross-cultural explorations of converging patterns of moral order. Such a task is no small order, but it is refreshing to see through works such as Langan's that some philosophers have begun to address precisely this goal of uncovering ways of thinking among diverse historical traditions.

The no-thingness at the root of existence means, certainly, that the future offers no guarantees for improved living conditions. At the same time, the fundamental ontological comportment of being-open-to an uncharted future suggests that anything is possible. Perhaps, even, one might see that there are grounds for hope for positive forms of development if we combine foresight and responsible commitment to the goals of sustainability at the same time that we discerningly seek to appropriate the ontological grounds of our historical traditions.

To authentically engage oneself in taking up the past in order to forge a more meaningful future and to improve the human condition—no less in the developed than in the developing world—indicates the hope and promise of a better quality of life. If the notion of development can be interpreted as indicating more than material growth at the expense of social and environmental sustainability to capture that promise, then the notion is hardly misplaced.

Sustainability and the Notion of Needs

The Brundtland Commission maintains that "the satisfaction of human needs and aspirations is the major objective of development."[34] In addition to the concept of "essential needs," the notion of sustainable development contains within it "the idea of limitations" arising from the ability of the environment to support human activities.[35] How might phenomenology contribute to our understanding of the reciprocal belonging of needs and limitations to the concept of sustainability?

Let us recognize first that to seek to satisfy "human needs and aspirations" means more than the satisfaction of an inventory of requirements of solipsistic, human subjects. To be human is to be-in-the-world and, therefore, genuine human needs will consist of more than supercilious, narcissistic demands pursued at the expense of other beings and the environment. One need not be a phenomenologist to recognize that the wilfull satisfaction of human needs, both in the developed and developing worlds, in isolation from an awareness of the impact on other people, animals, and ecosystems is ultimately self-defeating. In western society, it is precisely the desire for self-gratification at the expense of environmental costs that has brought us to the current state of unsustainability and, in the developing world, attempts to satisfy basic needs of survival are doomed in the long term if they fail to take into account their environmental future.[36]

There is certainly much merit in the Brundtland Commission's catalogue of "essential human needs" that includes such basic elements as food, employment, energy, housing, water supply, sanitation, and health care.[37] The commission probably is right to say that the satisfaction of these needs asserts a "central role in the concept of sustainable development."[38] While we may recognize these needs to be central, however, we know that they cannot be pursued at the expense of a broader context of *environmental needs and constraints*. Once we acknowledge this fact, we immediately invoke an interpretation of needs that moves far beyond the satisfaction of narrow subjectivistic demands.

Heidegger himself sees that the notion of need (the German *Not*) must be understood to extend, on a long-term basis, beyond immediate biological or even psychological human parameters. Indicating more than mere subjectivistic whims, the ontological foundations of genuine need point to a recalling of the truth of Being itself. "It is," Heidegger says, "the time of need," where the recklessness and the "needlessness" of the era of technique stands in stark contrast to the urgency of recovery of ontological thinking.[39] To raise anew the question of the meaning of Being is to pay heed to a call that remains, in essence, "mysterious" to the extent that it exceeds calculative manipulation but demands instead the "careful hearing" of originative thinking.[40]

It is no accident that Heidegger relates the notion of need to the ontological meaning of care (*Sorge*), understood as no mere sentiment but the fundamental disposition of temporal understanding and human being-in-the-world "as a structural whole."[41] In my "concernful dealing" with the world, "Being matters" since "care for Dasein has in each specific case placed Being in care."[42] At the same time, "Dasein is . . . a turning into need"—a "wandering in the need" and "thirst-for-Being of a finite *Seinsverständniss*."[43]

From the description of care as constitutive of one's temporal, structural comportment in the world, it is no longer possible to conceive of human beings as merely individual subjects, primarily engaged in a Faustian manipulation of an infinite supply of environmental resources. Instead, we are compelled to come to terms with the fundamental, ontological truth of finitude, at the same time that we acknowledge that our very being is defined by our immersion in-the-world and our concernful dealings with entities other than our own egos. For environmentalism, this ontological description of the world as finite and as the existential ground of our very implacement opens up the possibility of seeing that world differently—as more than a mere construct of technology or human will, in terms of the grace of Being itself. Through such a description, we are invited to conceive of the world, not as an object of utility but as the site of care.

For all its religious language, the description of need as a "mysterious call" similarly may throw new light on the Brundtland Commission's discussion of "essential human needs."[44] In pursuing sustainable development, we have no choice but to aim to satisfy those human needs in terms of broader environmental needs and constraints. In this respect, to genuinely begin to satisfy human needs, we may be wiser to shift the focus away from cataloging individual requirements of solipsistic human subjects to evolving a more holistic vision of *what is needed*—that is, of the *needs that announce themselves from the context of the situation as a whole*. That shift may mean that individual, human needs and means of meeting those needs are evaluated more realistically from the perspective of obligations that announce themselves in terms of the the *relation between* human requirements and the existing landscape. By way of attuning ourselves to ecosystem patterns of change and place-based opportunities and constraints, development may thereby emerge as genuinely sustainable.

Sustainability, in such a context, becomes a matter of not merely juggling costs and benefits but of authentic care for and saving of the earth. Saving, in Heidegger's sense, involves more than rescuing from ruin. It also means "to fetch something home into its essence, in order to bring the essence for the first time into its genuine appearing."[45] Technological advancement that aims to conquer or master the natural world proceeds blindly and destructively, whereas technologies that discerningly open up possibilities of nature while safeguarding the earth hold the promise of care-ful human intervention. Economic analyses that do more than quantify widgets by laying bare essential social and environmental impacts of capital investments, also move closer to originative thinking and policies that are genuinely sustainable.

In his description of a work of art, Heidegger describes it as "setting up a world" wherein "the work sets forth the earth. . . . The work moves the earth itself into the Open of a world and keeps it there. *The work lets the earth be an earth.*"[46] Heidegger's poetic invoking of the image of the artwork reminds us that any human intervention can, in principle, proceed thoughtfully, carefully, in order to safeguard the environment that sustains our very existence. The key is to remember that such a careful using "implies fitting response. Genuine use does not debase what is being used—on the contrary, use is determined and defined by leaving the used thing within its essence. . . . Only proper use brings the thing to its essence and keeps it there."[47] If we can try to ensure that our human interventions proceed with such an understanding of genuine use and care of the environment in respect of the holistic pattern of needs that announce themselves, then, and only then, can development hope to move in the direction of true sustainability.

Indicators of Sustainability

As much as we might accept the philosophical significance of sustainability, questions arise regarding the implementation of specific programs of action and how we might seek to assess our progess in making changes in the lived world of environmental decision-making. At the conclusion of *Our Common Future,* the World Commission on Environment and Development presented a recommendation to convene an international conference to review findings and to promote follow-up arrangements that would be needed "to set benchmarks and to maintain human progress" in moving toward sustainability.[48] In June 1992, representatives at the Earth Summit gathered together in Rio de Janeiro, where the adoption of Agenda 21 ensured that sustainable development became a goal of all nations across the globe. One of the outcomes of the conference was the creation of the United Nations Commission on Sustainable Development (CSD), whose mandate was to track progress of nations in implementing the objectives of Agenda 21.

At the first meeting of the commission, a common theme that emerged was the need for a set of standards—"a measuring stick"—to assess progress in achieving sustainability.[49] Such standards were clearly to be broad in scope, comprehensive, and capable of addressing the interplay between complex human and environmental activities as they related to sustainable development. Existing indicators were seen to inadequately meet these objectives and there was a call specifically for the generation of indicators of sustainable development (SDIs).[50] At its third session in 1995, the Commission on Sustainable Development adopted a five-year program that aims to have a workable set of indicators available by the year 2000.[51]

How is an indicator of sustainability to be defined? Stipulating measures of sustainability assumes some agreement on the meaning of sustainable development and a consensus on the term may be elusive. Still, most people agree that there appears to be sufficient accord to justify developing some benchmarks and, in fact, the process of evolving indicators may contribute to a better understanding of sustainability as well.[52] In this light, efforts toward developing indicators have proceeded from municipal to national scales, through international collaborations and the work is still very much in progress.[53]

To begin to understand the huge challenge involved in developing indicators of sustainability, one need only survey the range of definitions of the term. Some authors define an indicator to be a "statistical measure" and, in fact, many theorists view indicators to be intimately tied to quantifiable methods of measurement.[54] A definition adapted from the Organization for Economic Cooperation and Development (OECD) suggests that an indicator is "a statistic or parameter, tracked over time, [that] provides information on trends in the condition of a phenomenon and has significance extending beyond that associated with the properties of the statistic itself."[55] Other quantifiable indicators have been developed by the

United Nations Centre for Human Settlements (UNCHS) to include elements such as: city population; income distribution; percentage of wastewater treated; automobile ownership; house price to income ratio, and other similar data.[56] Examples of socioeconomic development indicators include data relating to child mortality, number of hospital beds, and households below the poverty line.

The United Nations Development Programme (UNDP) developed a "human development index" in 1990, similarly focusing on quantifiable information but, in this case, focusing on life expectancy, literacy, and living standards.[57] A fundamental economic and positivist framework seems to drive their report: we read that "a quantitative measure of human freedom has yet to be designed."[58] While the report purportedly is "about more than GNP growth, more than income and wealth and more than producing commodities and accumulating capital," a strong, economic paradigm seems to underly an index that explicitly defines people as the "real wealth" of a nation.[59] Indicators of sustainable development generated by the Organization for Economic Cooperation and Development similarly are reviewed "according to the criteria of policy relevance, analytical soundness and measurability."[60]

Critics argue, however, that indicators should be more than mere statistical measures: "Unlike simple statistics, indicators provide a summary indication of a condition or problem, and permit the observation of progress or change. This progress can be measured over time or against benchmarks, targets or visions for the future."[61] Others interpret indicators to be variables, parameters, or signposts: "the concept of indicator as something that points out, or stands for, something else, is clearly a particular form of the concept of sign."[62]

In general, one might conclude that indicators are "a way of seeing the 'big picture . . .' They tell us which direction we are going: up or down, forward or backward, getting better or worse or staying the same."[63] Major functions of indicators are said to be: to assess conditions and trends, particularly in relation to stipulated goals and targets; to compare existing conditions across places and situations; to anticipate future trends; and to provide early warning information on potential areas of concern so that informed policy and decision-making can occur.[64]

Certainly, many theorists maintain that one function of sustainable development indicators is to quantify existing information, but others argue that indicators can be qualitative as well.[65] In fact, experts suggest that qualitative indicators may be preferable when quantitative data is not available; when the attribute under consideration is inherently nonquantifiable; and even when cost considerations prohibit extensive quantitative analysis.[66] Some authors also believe that qualitative indicators have the advantage of being more easily communicated and understood by the general public.[67]

At a Canadian indicators workshop, some people have suggested that "subjective" indicators—"indicators which are more evaluative of an individual's satisfaction with a certain aspect of the built environment, natural environment, economy and the social domain"—should be included as one category among indicator "types."[68] In the Greater Toronto Area (GTA), a public opinion survey is planned to consider residents' attitudes toward their quality of life. This survey specifically is expected to provide a methodology to collect "subjective" indicators as part of a broader assessment of quality of life in the GTA.[69]

In another area of environmental concern, the Canadian "steel town" of Hamilton Harbour has initiated a large-scale Remedial Action Plan. In that context, a working group has pointed out that "a good indicator need not be quantifiable, particularly in the social-political-cultural domains. For example, 'feeling well' may be an indicator of human health in the ecosystem, but it is hard to put a number on it. The quantifiability criterion may be too restrictive."[70] These examples signal a growing awareness of the place of qualitative approaches in the development of sustainable development indicators.

What role can we expect phenomenology to play within the process of developing sustainability indicators? I see at least two directions for phenomenological inquiry. The first relates to the articulation of implicit judgments and worldviews that underly the identification and prioritization of indicators in general. The second area of phenomenological concern addresses the actual generation of qualitative indicators. Let me address each point in turn.

The Phenomenological Exposition of SDI Assumptions

While experts aim to generate objective, empirically verifiable and realistic indicators of sustainability, the process is hardly value neutral. As we have seen in previous chapters, the world is always interpreted within a horizon of transcendental understanding, and, in this respect, the selection and classification of indicators cannot proceed as if it were merely a technical matter of identifying a single set of "correct" variables. Inasmuch as we choose to bound phenomena in a particular manner, we cannot help but project prethematic assumptions that arise on the basis of our spatial and temporal situatedness. Which issues we consider to be of particular concern, how we define those issues in terms of specific indicators, and their temporal and geographical scales are all affected by implicit worldviews that arise on the basis of one's background, culture, and overall environment.

For example, a major issue to be confronted is the implicit role of positivist methodologies in the development of many indicators. To be sure, quantifying visible elements of change is important in the process of articulating and assessing environmental impacts of human development. Nevertheless, focusing exclusively on individual, empirically definable entities may risk reducing complex processes into oversimplified inventories of isolated, single components. A failure to address the relation *between* such components similarly presents a danger that indicators may be described and assessed out of context. To define indicators exclusively in positivist terms and statistical measures is already to have made a judgement call that implicitly stipulates that originative thinking has no place beside calculation in our reflections on sustainable development. We have already seen that this conclusion is hardly self-evident.

Value judgments affect the process of indicator development in a variety of ways. For instance, at the very source of the process, our own backgrounds and interests influence our initial observations of environmental phenomena. In perceiving a polluted body of water, a chemist may see a source of contaminants while political scientists may structure their perceptions around the problem of jurisdictional responsibilities. To decide between competing claims or to assign importance of one view over another is also to engage in judgment calls and, ultimately, in ethical decisions about which perspective more justifiably reflects significant indicators. To say that we may wish to avoid an either/or decision by accepting both the chemist's and the political scientist's assessments does not help in the long run. Ultimately, we must keep our compilation of indicators to some workable length and so, once again, we are obliged to make judgment calls and decisions regarding which indicators deserve greater priority among the myriad of benchmarks that one could, in theory, continue to develop *ad nauseum*.

Even within the confines of their own disciplines, experts often will assign different weighting coefficients to specific indicators, and, once again, value judgments will color these assessments. Sometimes indicators evolve on the basis of a ratio between current and desired conditions. Stipulating what is "desired" inevitably assumes some ethical decisions about what "ought" to be our ultimate targets.[71]

In all of these cases, there is a need to seek to articulate implicit judgments, both in order to avoid a situation where taken-for-granted attitudes may insidiously prejudice the supposedly "objective" process of generating sustainable development indicators, and to allow for an opportunity to communicate and clarify underlying ethical positions that may require resolution well in advance of assigning measures or "benchmarks." Phenomenological deconstruction of prethematic worldviews offers the possibility of moving beyond ontic, theoretical frameworks to illumine ontological foundations of thinking that underlie methodological and conceptual presuppositions of indicator development.

This process constitutes a special challenge of addressing more than our explicit value judgments, which can be inconsistent and inadequately scrutinized, even when they are spelled out. In the following chapter, I offer some concrete examples of how the phenomenological methodology allows for such a deconstruction. In such cases, the task for phenomenology becomes one of investigating not only what is said, but more important, what remains unsaid in our deliberations on appropriate indicators.

Evolving SDIs: A Second Task for Phenomenology

In addition to the deconstruction of taken-for-granted assumptions in the generation of specific indicators, there is a second, perhaps even larger challenge that presents itself to phenomenologists, to contribute to the generation of more meaningful evaluations of progress toward sustainable development. The whole discussion on indicators seems to me to be driven by a generalized need to assess our level of success in moving toward sustainability. Indicators themselves are part of a broad, comprehensive process of "setting priorities and goals, of designing programs and allocating responsibilities, and monitoring the results."[72]

In the name of assessing the success of sustainable development policies and programs, we may choose to constrain ourselves to measuring ontic entities—whether these entities are road infrastructure expenditures or "rate of change of social norms."[73] On the other hand, we may also choose to supplement such assessments by illumining ontological foundations of place-based, human activities that, in the final analysis, determine whether specific policies and programs of sustainable development will realistically acknowledge and respond to powerful influences of taken-for-granted paradigms, expectations, and lived values.

Of course, we must recognize that, already, there are studies undertaken to measure human values and perceptions of ecosystems and human settlements. Some of these studies assume that such values can be measured in terms of participants' "willingness-to-pay" for the preservation of different environments.[74] Critics point out, however, that the issue of how much people are willing to pay for their subjective preferences or wishes is a different question from whether value judgments are justifiable in the long run.[75]

Similarly, standard questionnaires can collect information on what people say they value. On the other hand, it begins to be evident that what people explicitly state to be their values and what they value in practice can be two different matters. A recent study, for example, shows that strong majorities of the American public express their convictions that nature is a limited resource, that market processes devalue the environment, and that nonintervention is the preferred prescription for environmental care.[76] At the same time, only 18 percent of Americans express a willingness to work, earn, and consume less as part of an environmental strategy so that some authors wonder whether expressions of ethical obligations to preserve the natural environment are simply "empty truisms."[77]

In the light of these findings, there seems to me to be a strong need to do more than to merely catalog peoples' preferences or even to survey their explicitly expressed beliefs. More important is to delve deeper to investigate hidden paradigms so that policy decisions may proceed on the foundation of a genuine awareness of cultural trends and place-based ethical convictions. Methodologically, such investigation can proceed in a number of ways.

We have reviewed in previous chapters the role of place-based, bioregional narratives as tools for eliciting a broad spectrum of environmental perceptions and values. Phenomenological interpretation of narratives opens up the possibility of illumining sustainable development indicators that take into account more than explicitly ordered belief systems. Just as quantitative, statistical indicators necessarily bound data within categorical limits, traditional questionnaires structure peoples' beliefs within preconceived frameworks.[78] The deconstruction of bioregional narratives offers the possibility of illumining a broader arena of paradigms and perceptions that would not qualify for inclusion in positivist approaches to developing indicators but that would, nevertheless, constitute essential information and contextual background for a fuller understanding of our rate and potential for success in working toward sustainability.[79]

Another avenue for generating qualitative indicators of sustainable development that is almost completely absent from current discussions is the inquiry into foundations of art and poetry. In environmental deliberations in our age of technique, passing reference may be made to "aesthetic preferences" of particular landscapes but I would propose that phenomenological reflections on art and poetry would attain to much more than superficial catalogs of likes and dislikes of particular vistas.[80] Heidegger himself has described the origins of the work of art in terms of the most fundamental disclosure of Being and the "happening of truth."[81] As he has shown in his phenomenological description of Van Gogh's painting of peasant shoes, works of art illumine a society's worldviews in relation to questions of work, the meaning of creativity, and of dwelling itself. A phenomenology of art, consequently, will reveal more than incidental caricatures and arbitrary renderings of individual points of view because authentic artwork is an expression of a culture's interpretation of the meaning of Being itself.[82]

As ontologically expressive, "the nature of art is poetry. The nature of poetry, in turn," Heidegger tells us, "is the founding of truth."[83] To develop indicators of sustainability in the absence of some understanding of a society's interpretation of Being and truth is to risk engaging in idle chatter at the expense of an ontological rethinking of sustainable development in its very essence. "Do *we* dwell poetically? Presumably," Heidegger warns, "we dwell altogether unpoetically" and, yet, "poetry and dwelling belong together, each calling for the other."[84]

We can choose to mock these claims—does Heidegger mean that "we must sit down and read some poems before setting out to encounter nature?"—or we can recognize that "when nature speaks to us, it does so poetically—gathering itself together in its richly significant and manifold primordiality. . . . Only when nature is disclosed poetically can we reside near it, can we dwell with and within it."[85] To inquire into the poetic and artistic roots of our society is also to inquire into that society's fundamental claims with respect to what is real and what is true—and also, what is worth preserving in our journeys along the path to sustainability.

Similarly, I would suggest that phenomenological readings of our built spaces and the places wherein we choose to dwell can illumine much about our success in attaining sustainable development. Architectural and literary theorist Ellen Eve Frank suggests that "the layman, especially in the United States, has lost the art of reading monuments and that even in Europe, to some the art of reading old buildings has given way to commercial interests in the new."[86] Nevertheless, how we structure our human settlements in terms of spatial and operational arrangements speaks to how we envision relationships among human beings as well as between human beings and their environments.

Frank reminds us that "architects explicitly intended buildings to be symbolic, to stimulate trains of association, to be read; it was assumed that buildings would influence the people living in them; and choice of style—whether Gothic, Palladian, Venetian, Norman, Doric or whatever—was meant to indicate a political or national preference as well as to suggest something about the nature or state of industry, civilization, moral or religious values."[87] To deconstruct hidden paradigms that sustain architectural designs and planning offers the possibility of enlarging our understanding of current attitudes to natural and built spaces—and, ultimately, to specific evaluations of the meaning of the relationship between human beings and the places that they deem worthy of preservation.[88]

In 1967, architect Sigfried Giedion maintained that the main task facing contemporary architecture is, in fact, "the interpretation of a way of life valid for our period."[89] Philosopher Karsten Harries believes that this same task defines architecture to this day: "Should architecture not continue to help us find our place and way in an ever more disorienting world?"[90] Harries argues that architecture has an ethical function, by which he means that its task is to help to articulate a common *ēthos*. " 'Ēthos' here names the way human beings exist in the world: their way of dwelling."[91] If we agree that "indicators provide a summary indication of a condition or problem, and permit the observation of progress or change," then certainly investigating built forms as they articulate cultural norms and paradigms of dwelling becomes another essential moment of evaluating current visions of patterns of sustainable development.[92]

My general worry about the direction that much of the current work on indicators is taking is that it may be narrowing the scope by which we assess our success in evolving a sustainable society. Broader, qualitative evaluations may be critical in enlarging our understanding of the context within which specific, quantitative indicators arise. Moreover, phenomenological reflection on taken-for-granted assumptions of the meaning of the relation between human beings and the environment may provide a basis for generating additional qualitative indicators of sustainability from the holistic perspective of human perceptions and values.

To continue to develop sustainable development indicators in the absence of a phenomenological reflection on qualitative aspects of environmental issues is, in any case, to risk remaining within a positivist paradigm that, in the end, may oversimplify and hypostatize complex processes. As a result, the very essence of the enterprise of generating indicators as an evaluation of our success in moving toward sustainability may be threatened. Overall, we cannot afford to forget that, in addition to calculative measurements of rates of success, originative thinking about qualitative aspects of dwelling is needed if sustainable development is to lead to a genuine caring for the earth.

10

Phenomenology, Sustainability, and the Lived World

The philosopher no longer has a right to independence vis-à-vis social practice.
Philosophy inserts itself into it.
—Henri Lefebvre, *Writings on Cities*

A philosophical position that does no more than merely speculate on matters of life in abstraction from the demands of the lived world engages in a forgetting of the genuine task of thinking. Certainly, the urgency of environmental problems makes special demands on philosophers to recall the need of seeking concrete ways in which their positions can be seen to *matter*. Environmental philosophers Lisa Newton and Catherine Dillingham are, in my view, quite right to suggest that "the first assignment for any work on the environment is to clarify questions . . . and focus emotion through the lens of logic into practical policy. Since the time of Socrates, that happens to be the traditional assignment of the discipline of philosophy."[1]

It is true that that philosophical applications are more than a simple matter of analyzing theoretical issues and then unilaterally applying them to specific cases. Instead, those cases inform one's philosophical position, which, in turn, guides subsequent problem solving. In this chapter, I offer examples of some environmental work that has been informed by phenomenology. The cases are not intended to be prototypes for future phenomenological inquiry in environmental decision-making. Instead, it is my more modest hope that these instances may further illumine for the reader some *possibilities* for meaningful, phenomenological inquiry when it comes to dealing in the lived world with questions of environmental policy development and decision-making.

Three cases are presented. The first two give some indication of how a phenomenological deconstruction of taken-for-granted paradigms may inform interdisciplinary research and environmental planning.[2] The third case describes an instance where phenomenology provided prescriptive guidance in the development of a code of ethics for park visitors.[3] The chapter concludes with some final reflections on the place of phenomenology in promoting environmental awareness in our educational system.

The Ecowise Study of Sustainability of the Hamilton Harbour

In 1991, the Federal Ministry of Environment Canada joined with three major federal granting councils to fund advanced, interdisciplinary research and training in environmental studies. As part of Canada's Green Plan, $30 million was committed over six years to support "Tri-Council" grants, university faculty chairs, and doctoral fellowships.

Ten interdisciplinary research projects across the country were funded. One of the first to receive support was the $2.1 million "Ecowise" study, where over thirty university researchers from five Southern Ontario universities committed themselves to an examination of the sustainability of the Hamilton Harbour Ecosystem (HHE) in western Lake Ontario, part of the North American Great Lakes.[4]

The watershed supports a population of over 500,000 people within about 494 square kilometers. Approximately 52 percent of its 45-km-long shoreline consists of an industrial base, supported primarily by Stelco and Dofasco steel companies. The harbour serves as a port and as a recreational center, but inasmuch as it continues to offer a site for the disposal of industrial and municipal waste, it is known for its environmental problems. In this regard, it has been designated as an "area of concern" by the International Joint Commission (IJC) who has deemed that harbour contaminants exceed IJC objectives.

In 1986, an agreement was struck between the federal and provincial governments to begin the cleanup of major, polluted sites in Ontario. The Hamilton Harbour Remedial Action Plan (RAP)—one of the most advanced of Canadian RAPs—was developed in response to this agreement. Community leaders worked to evolve fifty recommendations for cleanup action, ranging from carp control and marsh vegetation restoration to public education.[5] One of the principal objectives of the Ecowise project was to "study, assist and assess the implementation of the Hamilton Harbour Remedial Action Plan."[6]

The project specifically aimed to advance knowledge about the interrelations between human and nonhuman components of the ecosystem; to develop new techniques and methodologies for studying and restoring ecosystems; and to increase understanding about the development and management of interdisciplinary research activities.[7] The team of thirty researchers was divided into four major research groups: Human Values and Perceptions; Contaminants; Biotic Recovery; and Policy Analysis and Economics. A fifth group that intersected the other four, was responsible for communication, education, and dissemination of research findings, as well as for "integration." The task of providing an integrative framework became my responsibility on the project.

It was clear to most researchers that the project was to consist of more than a multidisciplinary collection of discrete viewpoints. The integrative framework for the project, therefore, was to seek to do more than catalog individual researchers' work. Instead, our aim was to elicit a holistic overview of the research study, as well as of the ecosystem itself, as it was perceived by researchers. The assumption was that the framework would ensure that disciplinary perspectives were only more meaningful as genuine, rather than accidental, parts of the interdisciplinary project as a whole.[8]

My research assistants and I aimed to ensure that the holistic overview with which we were engaged was neither a universalizing abstraction, nor a super-part imposed top-down upon a variety of perspectives. Instead, we hoped to encourage a synergistic belonging of the individual projects to the research as a whole.[9] While remaining sensitive to the plural demands of different languages, assumptions, and research methods of each researcher, the aim was to evolve a synthesis that remained respectful of such pluralist foundations and avoided the straitjacket of an artificially imposed model. To elicit such a collective vision of the Hamilton Harbour as perceived by the researchers, we engaged in a phenomenological interview process with the investigators individually (see fig. 10.1) in order to illumine (1) their vision of the sense of place of the Hamilton Harbour ecosystem; and (2) their understanding of how their research was intended to impact upon that ecosystem.[10]

Each participant told a unique story, as he or she was encouraged to speak to several central themes. For instance, they were asked to imagine that they were describing Hamilton to a friend, visiting for the first time: what would that general description consist of? What would one point out to the friend to be the key landmarks and central issues affecting development? What one-word descriptors would one use to communicate essential aspects of the sense of place? On the issue of scales, what might one identify as the smallest area of significance—and the larger areas of significance? On this point, we wanted to know at what point the researchers felt that they no longer were really within the area of the Hamilton Harbour Ecosystem. These and similar questions prompted a narrative that was interrupted as little as possible, in the hope that spontaneous reflections might illumine hidden assumptions and fundamental perceptions of essential elements of the ecosystem under study.

The description of place that emerged from a phenomenological "deconstruction" of taped interviews was not an objective, "complete" picture; indeed, it was never meant to be so.[11] However, what did evolve was a collective vision ("from the inside out," to use geographer Edward Relph's phrase) of essential descriptors of place in the absence of which Hamilton Harbour Ecosystem could not be what it is for them.[12] This process of deconstruction evolved over many days of individual

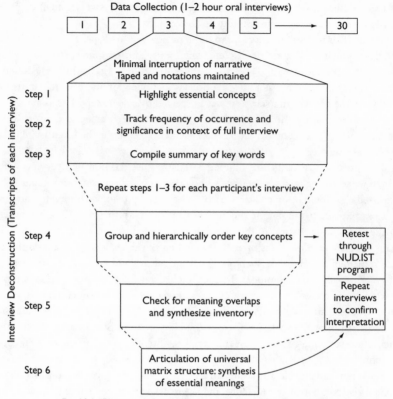

Fig. 10.1. Phenomenological Method: Interviews Ecowise Project

analysis and collective comparison of the interview transcripts. Keyword responses were identified and, eventually, grouped under broader categories of meaning. Care was taken to preserve a balance between the need of synthesis and the desire to preserve the integrity of the original interviews.

A final "check" of the process was twofold: on the one hand, original interview transcripts were passed through the recently developed "NUD.IST" software program for managing and organizing qualitative research data.[13] In addition, a second set of interviews confirmed components and classifications with each researcher. Eventually, the interactions between these descriptors were mapped on a four-dimensional, computerized matrix, constituting an interdisciplinary, integrative overview of key elements of the Hamilton Harbour ecosystem. Over 5,000 interactions between more than eighty descriptors of the Hamilton Harbour ecosystem were mapped within the matrix.

A number of key patterns emerged from this process. Despite the fact that the project members included researchers from the social sciences and humanities, by far the largest emphasis, as well as the longest list of elements that evolved from the interviews were related to the physical natural environment, and indeed, were very much *harbor*-related. While, on one level, everyone "knew" that an interdisciplinary project such as Ecowise "ought" to study the human/environment relation, our overview essentially indicated that the importance of the human settlement side of the equation was underrated in favor of the harbor itself.

During the original interviews, this conclusion was evident on a number of levels: several researchers simply disliked the city and avoided taking visitors into the urban areas. Other responses indicated that if the visitors were to be taken to the downtown at all, it was by car, and one would drive through, rather than linger in any area of significance. Similarly, while key landmarks were noted in terms of some significant architectural features, on the whole, issues such as urban planning, religion, community, and social services received little emphasis in comparison with issues of wildlife, water quality, and habitat preservation. Subjects such as the built environment, networks, and technology each represented less than 1 percent of the project's research focus, compared to the physical natural environment, which represented more than 70 percent of ecosystem descriptors and interactions plotted on the matrix.

This study suggests that even though there is an *explicit* recognition of the interrelation between the urban and natural environments, priority may be given *implicitly* to traditional natural science perspectives on rehabilitation of an ecosystem. On a project essentially directed toward remediation of the ecosystem (rather than preventive measures), much attention was given to contaminant characteristics, with far less attention directed to contaminant *sources*. Flagging such issues on a project of this size allows, in the best scenario, for the possibility of redirecting some research in order to ensure a broader range of study. At the very least, it brings to researchers' attention issues and opportunities that might otherwise have been ignored. It also suggests possibilities for future avenues of research of those areas that were, in the end, inadequately addressed as part of this particular project.

Phenomenological Readings of Suburbs

Another example where phenomenology has been shown to inform concrete, environmental planning and policy development is evident in the examination of perceptions of suburbs. As we publicly reflect on issues of sustainable development, suburban sprawl often is a legitimate target of criticism with respect to such impacts as depletion of agricultural lands or the destruction of ecosystem habitats. Lewis Mumford has charged that "the suburb served as an asylum for the preservation of illusion. Here, domesticity could flourish, forgetful of the exploitation on which so much of it was based."[14] In the end, the suburb for Mumford "was not merely a child-centered environment; it was based on a childish view of the world."[15]

As much as one might feel compelled to side with Mumford and critique suburbia, such a move does not really shed light on why suburban living continues to be so attractive to so many residents. Brian Berry has cataloged the cultural preferences of suburbanites, identifying a number of factors that explain the appeal of this residential choice.[16] From a love of newness and a preservation of individualistic value systems, to an appeal of rural ideals and freedom to move in larger spaces, suburbs embody the American dream of upward social mobility and material security.

Other empirical studies of suburbs have been undertaken to describe conditions and aspirations of suburban living.[17] As phenomenologist Robert Mugerauer points out, "however accurate in assessing peoples' responses to residential environments, these works do not exhibit the patterns of residents' direct, value-laden experiences and perceptions which occur as part of their life-world. The latter requires a complementary, qualitative approach, such as taken in phenomenology."[18]

Mugerauer's own work involved comprehensive interviews with residents of two communities, Riverside and Park Forest, Illinois. He explains that the project team "made every effort to become full partners in a dialogue, not to ask leading questions and not to formulate, much less try out, hypotheses about what we were hearing. Our goal was to listen and to hear what respondents wanted to say about their place and lives."[19]

The study showed how preferred areas were judged on the strength of the beauty of the place. Contrary to stereotypical descriptions, residents here were surprisingly self-reflective, revealing a passionate commitment to their community's landscapes. Mugerauer reports that "despite the stereotype of the suburb as a no-where, as a place with homogeneous and sterile landscape . . . Riverside and Park Forest showed themselves to be very agreeable places. . . . These suburban communities appear to know who they are and actively work, largely by retelling their narratives of identity and by nurturing and renewing the landscape—a landscape that is integral not just to where they are, but to who they are."[20]

Interviews of residents, however, are not the only sources for phenomenological investigations of suburbs. David Seamon points out that "concrete techniques by which the phenomenologist attempts to arrive at genuine contact can include reflection . . .[and] careful observation of places or environments."[21] Others similarly have suggested that we can learn much about the phenomenon of dwelling through a phenomenological reading of specific settings.[22]

The notion of "reading" human settlements may sound unorthodox to some people and even untrustworthy as an approach to understanding sense of place. Nevertheless, John Ruskin reminds us "how much less the beauty and majesty of a building depend upon its pleasing certain prejudices of the eye, than upon its rousing certain trains of meditation in the mind."[23] Recall Ellen Eve Frank's compelling testimony to the need to recover the "lost art of reading monuments."[24] While "the alphabet has gone out of use," the idea of reading places suggests that environments are meaningful texts on a variety of levels.

A phenomenological reading of places certainly will seek to avoid totalizing discourse. First-hand descriptions, however, should also consist of more than merely subjective, arbitrary constructs. The possibility should present itself of replicating the interpreter's reading of a place and so, in this sense, a phenomenological reading is a preliminary—although often revealing—step in the process of interpreting the meaning and organization of our lived spaces.

In this light, I undertook to explore a suburban community near Toronto, to see if I might better understand suburbanites' preferences through a careful reading of its physical design. The area that I investigated was the central area of Mississauga, firmly anchored in its city hall and one of the largest shopping malls in eastern Canada. Perhaps the fact that the City Center is defined by such a mall reflects the consumerist society that sustains it. On the other hand, the architectural design of the city hall is meant to be reminiscent of a barn and silo. It looms majestically on the landscape, as if to definitively secure the picture of a rural alternative to the urban, concrete jungle (see fig. 10.2).

The primary mode by which one moves through this community is, as with most suburbs, the automobile. The houses bear witness to this fact in the front-and-center garage design of their homes (see fig. 10.3).[25] One senses that the human activity is concentrated, however, not on the street but within the home. Dolores Hayden has written how "a civilization has created a utopian ideal based on the house, rather than the city or the nation."[26] As I make my way through Mississauga, I note how each house seems to turn its back to the street: the main entrance is in a state of recession, far behind the garage, so that the facade of the home and a significant part of the front yard accommodate the car. The larger backyard appears to be the protected, social nexus for the family gatherings.

In some sense, one might say that the community as a whole turns its back to the city as well. Overall, the image avoids the urbane cosmopolitanism of Toronto and supports a private, rural image. While wide main streets are clearly automobile centered, at the same time, each house is designed as if to say: dispense with the automobile and the outside world to which it connects, immediately at the start of the private lot, and then move inside or to the private, usually fenced back yard.

In the yard, we can contemplate nature in solitude, away from the necessary chaos of the city to which we must return ultimately but which, for now, can be excluded from our family's world. In the suburb is where we plant our flowers, cultivate our plants and trees, and barbecue summer meals. This is our refuge from the harried world, a world suitably suppressed for the time being.

Figure 10.2. Mississauga City Hall

Figure 10.3. Front- and-center garage design.

Inside the standardized, but spacious home, cathedral ceilings in the main entrance halls seem to elicit a vision of grandeur. The sense is that the human being matters here, has a dignified presence within the confines of the home. More than mere utilitarian functions are well served within this technologically sophisticated dwelling place. Private bedrooms for the children, play areas segregated from wood-paneled dens—all offer the resident a legible, spatial organization to support freedom of choice for a range of activities. The house is spacious but designed with postmodern touches of wood, archways, and bay windows to provide a sense of enclosure and quasi-historical reminders of receding traditions.

In all of this, I am reminded of the words of Gaston Bachelard, who reflected how "our house is our corner of the world. As has often been said, it is our first universe, a real cosmos in every sense of the word. . . . And always, in our daydreams, the house is a large cradle."[27] Similarly, Pater muses upon how "the quiet spaciousness of the place is itself like a meditation, an 'act of recollection,' and clears away the confusion of the heart."[28] In Mississauga, there is a clear sense of home as haven, as a refuge from the outside world. Each single detached house appears fully self-contained, guarding carefully the privacy of interior and backyard spaces. The streets—essentially empty of people—have clearly not been designed in any major way for pedestrian use. On the contrary, they signify that the foundation of living is not to be found within the public realm but within the home itself. The house is meant to secure—to cradle—the sense of Insideness as shelter and serves as a primordial center for dwelling.

In some sense, the image of the settlement as a whole is of the nonthreatening: the homogeneity from one identical garage to the next seems to signify that nothing is unexpected. No risks are implied by virtue of enigmatic spatial patterns to disrupt the notion of a perfectly ordered and safe community. The message is of a secure environment, of shelter, of refuge, of insideness and a cradling against any threats from the outside world.

Not only do spatial images of security and control present themselves to the mind, coinciding temporal images are communicated as well. Things appear to move more slowly here than in the city. In a sense, one feels that time stands still. From house to saplings to recently poured asphalt, the overriding image is of newness. Any hint of intuition of the past is frozen in discreet, architectural gestures of traditions gone by. For instance, the unused, artificial shutter, the wooden details, the bay windows aim to recover some sense of warmth elicited by historical houses, but as discrete moments, they are solitary remembrances of eras and time frames no longer genuinely accessible in today's harried world.

There is little sense of futural projection within this ordered community, aiming to minimize unnecessary diversity or unknown possibility. If the future is constituted as a horizon of openness, this means that with authentic futurity comes uncertainty and vulnerability.[29] Images of exposure and defenselessness are subdued within Mississauga. Quite the contrary, there is a pervading sense of safety in homecoming. To some extent, the present appears to be secured in the tidiness of a manicured environment, preserving an image impervious to substantive change and to danger.

There is a sense of belonging here that arises precisely in spite of Toronto the urbane. Mississauga seems to want to stand as the alternative to high density, high-stress living. In the community symbolized by the free enterprise of the Square One shopping mall, one is free to move where one pleases with the high mobility offered by the car. One is free to purchase or at least to survey a variety of commodities at will in the central core. One is free to withdraw into the cocoon of one's private home and yard and exclude unwelcome aspects of today's hectic world. One is free to dream in peace.

In summary, a phenomenological reading of this suburban community reveals the following:

1. Anchorage in a commercial center: Square One shopping mall provides a commercial and entertainment center for the community at large. Its city hall stands out from the landscape to visually concentrate the image of the center from afar.

2. Point-oriented relation of inside to outside community: The automobile—central to the house and community design—constitutes the locus for geographical point-to-point interaction with the cosmopolitanism of Toronto. Otherwise, there appears to be a sense that Mississauga's community identity is distinctive precisely by virtue of providing an escape from the urbanity of the large city.

3. The rural ideal preserved: The city hall, adjacent to Square One and visible from many vantage points as one approaches the community by car, looms large as a symbol of a silo in an agricultural field. Despite the high level of technical unsustainability of suburbs, the community message at its core is that the quiet sense of the earth is to be preserved here.

4. Privacy and enclosure: Backyards ensure a sense of shelter from the outside world. Interiors of homes encapsulate the sense of refuge, shelter, and protection, while at the same time, the interior spatial organization reflects a respect for individual, human dignity.

5. Reflective of time as the present: The past is secured in architectural features reminiscent of a past era, frozen in discrete images. The future as sheer possibility and openness implies risk that is absent, overall, from this community, which projects an image of security in full presence.

6. Freedom as autonomy: From images of free enterprise to free mobility, the tyranny of urbanization and high-density living is denied in favor of the sovereignty of the individual and the family.

Edward Relph suggests that "phenomenology is a way of thinking that enables us to see clearly something that is, in effect, right before our eyes yet somehow obscured from us—something so taken for granted that it is ignored or allowed to be disguised by a cloak of abstractions."[30] The very preliminary, phenomenological reading of a suburb presented above is not meant to be a universal, abstract description of all suburban environments. Nevertheless, it may prompt readers to consider whether similar images might converge in their own, first-hand experiences of suburban dwelling places.

Such images are hardly incidental parts of the planning process. There is a genuine need for architects and planners to better understand how human beings actually experience their environment. Planner Jack Nasar points out that "we need to know how the public evaluates the cityscape and what meanings they see in it: the *evaluative image* of the city. . . . Research on the evaluative image of the city might have little practical value if design professionals shared the values of the public and delivered those values in designs and plans. This has not been the case."[31] The phenomenological deconstruction of environmental perception offers the hope that we may come to better understand the foundations of residents' lived experiences of the places wherein they seek to dwell so that, in the long run, planners may better respond to such experiences in the design and building of our human settlements.

Environmental Codes of Ethics

The previous examples have focused on the possibility of a phenomenological deconstruction of attitudes that may be taken-for-granted on a number of levels. On the other hand, in discussing the generation of sustainable development indicators in the previous chapter, I have suggested that phenomenology also offers the positive possibility of moving beyond description to a prescriptive role as well.

A recent project offers one example of how the phenomenological approach can be essential to the process of generating guidelines that are responsive to human and environmental needs. In this case, the guidelines emerged in the form of a code of ethics for a provincial park in southern Ontario (see fig. 10.4). At first glance, it seems that any codified system of rules is the ultimate example of essentialist thinking that is the very target of phenomenological criticism. Imposing abstract, ethical principles on the community's lived experience of place seems about as far from the spirit of phenomenological thought as one might imagine.

Nevertheless, we are thrown sometimes into situations that are unexpected and that, furthermore, yield surprising results. This project offered an unusual opportunity for phenomenological reflection that was initiated in response to a very concrete, community need. The study arose in response to the publication, in 1991, by the Ontario Ministry of Nature Resources, of a Management Plan for Short Hills Provincial Park. Covering 688 hectares on the southwest edge of St. Catharines in the Regional Municipality of Niagara, the park is widely recognized as a significant, natural area of the region as a whole.

The management plan acknowledged that there was clear, public endorsement for preserving the park as a "wild, natural area, with only very basic facilities to support trail use."[32] At the same time, there was a clear need to continue to support a variety of "high quality, day-use recreational and interpretive experiences," ranging from hiking, horseback riding, sport fishing, cross country skiing, mountain biking, nature and heritage appreciation as well as outdoor education.[33] The plan concluded that there was a need to explore ways of reconciling the ecocentric needs of protecting the park's natural features, while also accommodating legitimate, recreational and educational activities of visitors. Since conflict over trail use had already been evident, the Ministry's goal also was to seek ways to "minimize conflict between trail users" themselves.[34]

Traditional ways of minimizing or resolving such social and environmental conflicts typically include policing procedures and negative reinforcement techniques. For example, a warden in Short Hills Park administers fines for littering or for unlawful trespassing of snowmobilers, motorcyclists, and overnight campers. Top-down law enforcement is not, however, the only way of encouraging appropriate conduct among park visitors. Studies have shown that the majority of people modify their actions in response to prompts, cues, information dissemination, and better education about behavior expectations.[35] Planner Oscar Newman reminds us that, after all, the root of the word "policing" is *polis*, meaning community.[36] In this light, we decided to seek the community's help in jointly evolving, "bottom-up," a code of ethics to help increase environmental awareness and reduce potential conflicts in Short Hills Park.

In general terms, a code of ethics is a written articulation of moral guidelines, designed to lead to minimally acceptable standards of human conduct. It serves to provide a common vocabulary about right and wrong, to clarify ethical issues, to suggest a framework for conflict resolution, and to promote environmental awareness.[37] On the other hand, if codes are to be more than mere window-dressing or abstract, ineffective constructs, they must be meaningful as part of a larger process of promoting awareness and preserving a community's collective wisdom.

Park-centered codes of ethics are particularly rare. Environmentalist David Johnson notes that "unlike most other aspects of human existence [enjoyment of outdoor activities] does not have a long-established, tight code of laws regulating it. Rules are still few and loose."[38] Johnson argues that, precisely on this account,

A Code of Ethics for Short Hills Provincial Park

As a friend of Short Hills Park, I understand that:

- The park is a unique, natural environment to be preserved for its own sake, as well for future generations.
- My responsibility is of a care-taker, to actively seek to promote the ecological health and diversity of the park.

I pledge to:

- show respect; tread lightly.
- pack out at least what is packed in.
- keep wildlife wild, by observing from a safe and non-interfering distance.
- observe, not disturb natural features in the park. Memories outlast specimens.
- preserve the peace in the park. Be considerate of others.
- protect the park from disruptive activities, such as forest fires or vandalism.
- become better informed about the needs of Short Hills Park, and share my knowledge with others.

Some Guidelines for Conduct

1. Show Respect; Tread Lightly.
    1.1 Remain on established trails.
    1.2 Respect the rules of multi-use trails. Meet and pass with respect. Use caution and speak quietly in approaching, to pacify the horses. Cyclists will remain in single file to the right of trails, announcing themselves in advance of bends, and yielding to others.
    1.3 Avoid using trails when wet, especially when cycling or horseback riding.
    1.4 Avoid trespassing on private property.

2. Pack out at least what is packed in.

    2.1 Avoid all littering.

    2.2 If possible, leave the park cleaner than you found it.

3. Keep wildlife wild, by observing from a safe and non-interfering distance.

    3.1 Avoid feeding wildlife, as it upsets the natural food chain.

    3.2 Control all pets brought into the park.

4. Observe, but do not disturb natural features in the park.

    4.1 Preserve plants and flowers.

    4.2 Natural systems, as well as cultural artifacts will remain duly undisturbed in the park.

    4.3 Refrain from polluting the environment in any way.

5. Preserve the peace in the park. Be considerate of others.

    5.1 Be courteous in sharing trails.

    5.2 Use common sense in announcing yourself, particularly on narrow trails with limited visibility.

    5.3 Curtail rowdiness.

6. Protect the park from disruptive activities.

    6.1 Fires are prohibited in the park.

    6.2 Report to the Park Superintendent, at the telephone number below, any vandalism encountered within the park.

7. Become better informed and share your knowledge about Short Hills.

    7.1 Be aware of and sensitive to the needs of the park. Be open to new knowledge about the park.

    7.2 Support environmental education about Short Hills Park.

For further information, or to voice your views, please contact the Ontario Ministry of Natural Resources, PO Box 1070, Fonthill, Ont. LOS 1EO. Telephone: (905) 892-2656.

there may be a considerably higher need of ethics here than in more naturally re-strictive settings that are more heavily monitored. On the other hand, our view was that, if a park-based code of ethics was to be meaningful at all, it would need to be perceived not as a top-down tool for law enforcement, but instead as a re-flection of the community's *ēthos* that citizens could relate to and genuinely appro-priate as their own.

The process of evolving a code of ethics for Short Hills Park consisted of lengthy dialogues with community members and it was fundamentally place-based. Rather than constructing and imposing a system of abstract, codified rules, the intent was to rely upon an iterative approach to illumine implicit community values and expectations that could be seen to converge in a so-called code. Ques-tionnaires were designed to be more than tools for quantitative compilation of ex-plicit judgments. They invited respondents instead to share their stories in a narra-tive format that, in some cases, resulted in numerous pages of additional, descriptive entries. Questions were deliberately designed to illumine converging images of what constituted the sense of place for the park and to capture that understanding within guidelines for appropriate conduct.

In-depth, one- to two-hour-long interviews were organized with a cross sec-tion of visitor groups, so that participants were, once again, encouraged to spon-taneously share their stories about why Short Hills Park was meaningful to them. A workshop was organized in 1993, in an effort to bring groups together to dis-cuss how a code of ethics could help resolve social and environmental conflicts within the park. A final workshop one year later brought together community members who deliberated in small, four- to five-member working groups, over de-tails of the draft code.

Searches of existing codes of ethics of individual, organized groups of local visitors were carried out. In addition, we contacted superintendents from every major national park in the United States to learn from the American experience. As part of the process of evolving a code of ethics, a Friends of Short Hills group of volunteers was struck, who began the process of investigating ways and means of communicating the code to park visitors.

The process was a very lengthy one, and not without its difficulties. There was extensive discussion and, sometimes, dissension regarding proposed items in the code. For instance, the issue of "multi-use trails" attracted much thought and re-flection. While originally, we had suggested exclusive right-of-way to equestrians, those very equestrians noted that there would be occasions when they did not feel morally entitled to such right-of-way (with the approach of walkers along some trails, for instance).

On the issue of environmental preservation, there was some disagreement re-garding the degree to which the park should be developed to support recreational and educational activities. One respondent wrote that the "Board of Education is most anxious to add Short Hills to their list of resources. However, in order to facilitate school use, we need access to the park, parking for a bus and washrooms." While the Board representative appreciated the need to preserve the natural environment, he was equally concerned that pupils from elementary grades would be unable to access educational trails because of large distances required for walking from parking lots.

Others, like the Niagara Falls Nature Club, welcomed the wildness of the park. "The people of the Niagara Falls Nature Club," they wrote, "value and appreciate the opportunities in Short Hills Park to observe and study the birds, trees and wildflowers in a significantly sized natural habitat." In workshop discussions, a recurring theme was to what extent Short Hills—originally deemed to be a natural environment class park—could be developed to accommodate human (especially children's) needs.

There was constructive discussion about many specifics of wording of the code. The suggestion that encouraged visitors to "actively seek and protect" the park was felt by some community representatives to be an inappropriate call to political action since such political commitment should be freely chosen, rather than required by way of a pledge in an ethical code. Instead, it was agreed that the code could legitimately urge visitors to "become better informed and share your knowledge about Short Hills Park."

The process of evolving this environmental code of ethics emerged as part of a discursive process and practical negotiation among community representatives. These representatives showed a great deal of sensitivity, both to the needs of others and to the needs of the park itself. Local media reported on social conflicts in dramatic headlines: "Equestrians vs. Pedestrians" meant that the "Short Hills Battle" was a "sign to planners of disaster ahead."[39] Our experience, however, of the general sentiment and commitment among community members to resolve problems was markedly different than that expressed in such media reports. While recognizing one another's sometimes-competing claims, in every case, the opportunities provided in workshops for dialogue resulted in amiable and unanimous resolution of differences.

No doubt, some philosophers would be uncomfortable with this process of evolving ethical guidelines. The method of the phenomenogist, in this undertaking, was unusual in that it avoided any unilateral application of a systematic, philosophical theory to resolving practical, community problems. On the contrary, the aim was to elicit narratives that would help to clarify the meaning of the sense of place of Short Hills Park.

To be sure, the task of phenomenology in such a process includes critical analysis of conflicting claims, as well as identification of converging images. In guiding the process of negotation of a code of ethics, the phenomenologist needs to be self-reflexive and sensitive to the fact that all interpretation—including one's own—is value laden. Nevertheless, the iterative process of evolving a code of ethics for Short Hills Park does suggest the possibility that ethics is neither a linear product of philosophical theorizing, nor merely a sociological accumulation of viewpoints. Rather, what emerged on this project was a role for philosophy of mediating between concrete, place-based needs and critical thinking about broader implications of how best to collectively reconcile those needs.

I must add that the code of ethics that emerged from this work was not perceived as a self-standing tool, in isolation from other community processes. That our project spurred the development of the Friends of Short Hills volunteer group was an important consequence of the study that aimed for a larger regeneration of spirit of place in the park. In a similar project that is currently underway, investigating evaluative images of the 325-kilometer-long Lake Ontario Waterfront Trail, the plan is also to promote environmental awareness by publishing narratives that emerge from our interviews, that would be of interest to young children. Whether articulated in the form of guidelines for conduct, codes of ethics, or storybooks, the phenomenological exposition of an *ēthos* of place can illumine significant aspects of our lived world and promote environmental education—a theme to which we now turn.

Phenomenology and Environmental Education

With the introduction of originative thinking into discussions of sustainability, one would hope that policy formulation and program development would proceed with greater wisdom and foresight, and that the very meaning of intelligence might be reassessed in more than calculative terms. Some authors argue, however, that our educational system continues to foster interpretations of both intelligence and creativity that are counterproductive in promoting ecological awareness. If we are genuinely concerned to measure "indicators" of sustainability and to continue to promote policies that will encourage wise interventions, then it is important that we give some thought to how we are managing to promote ecological values among those generations who will themselves be responsible for environmental decision-making in the near future.

Of course, promoting environmental awareness is a matter for more than school teachers, since education extends beyond formal instruction to nonformal settings, such as workplaces, parks, and even shopping malls.[40] As I have noted above, the way in which we organize our natural and built environments not only reflects a culture's attitudes but shapes those attitudes as well. The news media constitutes a powerful influence in the shaping of values, and other trends in film, music, and theater equally impact upon peoples' implicit and explicit systems of beliefs.

Nevertheless, the school curriculum still can provide an obvious, major focus for discussion of education for sustainability and there are a number of recommendations that might be drawn on the basis of our phenomenological reflections.

Professor of Education C.A. Bowers highlights in a recent volume a number of concerns that could also arise for the phenomenologist, particularly in view of the critique of the limits of positivist thinking. Bowers agrees that people's thought processes and worldviews are embedded in taken-for-granted patterns of everyday life.[41] Since formal education "appears both very powerful in terms of conserving the deepest and largely unconsciously held patterns of modern culture and, at the same time, as one of the few public forums we have for developing a critical understanding of the crisis we are now in," there is good reason to pay heed to implicit and explicit messages that we are communicating to our children within their educational institutions.[42]

Bowers is concerned that our assessments of intelligence and creativity in our schools are based on a worldview that remains product-oriented, mechanistic, and subjectively centered on the autonomous individual.[43] For instance, the definition of creativity offered by a faculty member of the prestigious Merrill-Palmer Institute of Human Development and Family Life is symptomic of a commonly accepted paradigm that assumes that "to be creative means to experience life in one's own way, to perceive from one's own person, to draw upon one's own resources, capacities, roots. . . . Only from *the search into oneself* can the creative emerge."[44]

Critical of implicit paradigms that define creativity as culture-free and based on the original self-expression of autonomous individuals, Bowers points out that the modern way of representing the self-reliant, creative individual is only part of a complex, cultural myth that severs human beings from the environments within which they are implaced. We have seen in previous chapters of this volume some of the consequences of understanding other people, the city, environment, and sustainable development through a positivist worldview that disengages the human subjectivity as an ontic entity from the world.

Phenomenologists would likely argue for a view of creative thinking that is based, not on an isolated subjectivity but on a recognition of the fundamental relatedness between human beings and their ecological settings. They would agree with Bowers' suggestion that more attention should be given in schools to developing a critical understanding of the web of ideologies and traditions that affect our interpretations of creativity in the first place.[45] Furthermore, "teachers need to help students recognize that the achievements of the past are embedded in current practices, and that knowledge of these traditions may expand their own sense of meaning and depth of creative expression."[46]

Students should be encouraged to recognize that their existence depends upon a balanced interaction with historical traditions and environmental needs, and that creative activities unaccompanied by fundamental notions of respect and care, both for other people and for the natural world, may be inventive in some sense, but are misplaced in terms of genuinely originative acts of thinking. In Bower's words, "the destruction of the environment confronts us with the need to make a radical shift away from the current emphasis on individually-centred creativity, and toward a greater emphasis on using the arts as a form of cultural storage that enhances communication between generations, and across species, about how to live in ecologically sustainable relationships."[47]

If the lessons of sustainable development show that each generation is obliged to meet its own needs without jeopardizing the ability of future generations to meet their needs, then such an obligation most clearly requires a shift of emphasis from traditional liberal attitudes and self-determined concerns of autonomous individuals as the basis for moral action to a much broader starting point for ethics: a starting point that will recognize that individual human beings are fundamentally already implaced in a complex array of sociocultural, economic, technological, regulatory, and environmental relationships. Simply to show young people that the starting point for determining right from wrong, truth from opinion, and the real from the illusory means directing their attention beyond their inner selves as autonomous creatures is already to begin to sensitize them to the fact that they themselves are existentially defined by *relationships* that open up the possibility of care, rather than egotistic gratification, as the starting point for environmental awareness.

A similar rethinking is needed with respect to the meaning of intelligence. In a calculative era where cognitive science insidiously propogates a "mechanistic though equally culture-free view of intelligence," the prevailing assumption is that the student, as cognitive agent and autonomous individual, takes an active role in the *construction* of knowledge.[48] The current view implicitly represents the mind as a unique processor of raw data of experience and this processor is capable of objectively assembling individual bits of information, ideally, in a format that is unaffected by apparently subjective, cultural influences.

Nevertheless, it is important to recall our earlier discussions that showed how human beings are not simply subjectivities isolated from their historical traditions but are ontologically defined as implaced. In this respect, we are born into root metaphors of our culture that are encoded in the languages and analogs within which we learn to think and speak.[49] Our predominant, western, constructivist view of intelligence as tied to the processing of information of an autonomous individual is itself rooted in a fundamental metaphysical assumption that human subjectivities are ontic entities confronting an objective world.

Originative thinking beckons us to expand our visions and acknowledge the role of embodiment and implacement in defining genuine wisdom. Intelligence itself might then come to be viewed, less as *empowerment* of autonomous individuals than as *attunement* to the moral implications that are announced by virtue of our ontological relation to and embeddedness in a world of nature and historical traditions. I am reminded of the laments of a Bushman, whose people have become disassociated with the land that they once knew. "There's been so much lost in all the children's knowledge," he writes.[50] "If we can't use the land like we used to, we're going to lose the knowledge and it's going to be lost forever—what we can eat, what is good, what is dangerous. The women have to teach the little girls the foods of the veldt, where to get wood, how to find plants. The men must teach the boys where to get water, how to follow spoor and find game."[51]

This Bushman feels that his people have been punished for forgetting their essential ties to the land. Fostering intelligence in this man's world means recalling traditions and ties to a world that is being forgotten. "The old people," he reports, "would like to take the children into the veldt and bring the children's hearts back to the dances and the music and the stories. . . . The day that the children feel the spirit in the dances, that is the day that the Father will forgive them. That is what the punishment is for. For forgetting the dance."[52]

In a similar manner, perhaps it is our own duty to remind our children of the dance, of the interplay between human beings and the environments in which they are implaced. A goal for environmental education, then, becomes one of sensitizing students to taken-for-granted ontological assumptions that ground their being-in-the-world. Genuine "critical thinking" is fostered, not simply by memorizing rules of logic, but by recognizing relationships, interdependencies, and patterns of interaction that define our complex world.

Educator David Orr recommends that we "help students to unlearn indifference to place and learn to 'live well in a place'—to inhabit as caring stewards, rather than merely to reside as user-consumers."[53] Orr and others point out that all education inevitably teaches our children something about the relationship between human beings and their environments, as well as about ethical expectations that emerge from within that relationship.[54] Rethinking cultural myths, sensitizing our students to the historical traditions that they inevitably appropriate, and teaching them to be aware that the human being is more than an autonomous subjectivity but is fundamentally implaced in a spatial and temporal landscape—all of these factors deserve to be included implicitly and explicitly as part of our children's environmental curricula.

What are some examples of educational strategies that might encourage students to rethink their relationship to their world? Pamela Courtenay-Hall suggests activities that will engage the student from grade 3 to postsecondary levels, in appropriating the history of their local places. "Have students interview a wide variety of local people, especially elderly people" she suggests, "to find out what a particular local field, park, forest, river or their backyard means to them."[55] Beyond the interviews, she suggests that the students compare the perspectives that they have gathered together to identify recurrent themes and to evaluate them with respect to the welfare of the broader community and the landscape.[56] Encouraging students to better understand the places that they call home through small, group discussion of life experiences will hopefully ensure a more concrete understanding of environmental concerns than might be available through more abstract lessons.

Naturalist Paul Krapfel similarly offers some examples that reflect phenomenological sensibilities in environmental education.[57] He argues that there is a need for us to "shift assumptions within our culture," and he provides "tools for seeing" the world in a different manner.[58] "One evening," he writes, "I saw the Earth turning. Before that night, I had always seen the Sun *setting* toward a stationary horizon. But when I saw the Sun, instead, as stationary, then I saw my horizon *rising* toward the Sun."[59] In the first instance, he perceives the sun to be moving, whereas in the second, his world moves. "My eyes see the same thing—the gap between Sun and horizon closing. But what is moving? My brain must make an assumption. Shifting that assumption changes the world I see."[60]

Sometimes, our minds become entrenched in perceiving phenomena in traditional ways so that we become closed to alternative scenarios. The task of environmental education is certainly one of informing the student about scientific facts. A concomitant task, however, is to stretch students' minds to see the world differently than they ordinarily may do. For instance, the narratives of science teach us that the blowing wind moves the leaves on the trees but some native myths describe the same event in terms of the leaves conversing with one another. Originative thinking demands that we expand our environmental awareness through a variety of narratives. In the case of the leaves, a shift in thinking occurs when we see the movement of the trees as more than merely technical responses to external stimuli. The moving leaves, perceived as speaking to one another, help us to envision the tree as alive, with a language and a meaning essential to its being in nature.

In this respect, Krapfel encourages us to see the world "through the eyes of animals," and Courtenay-Hall suggests that students might create stories, poems, or plays that focus on the life of an animal interacting with a human being who does not understand or value it.[61] In both instances we are guided to see the world, not as a product for human use, but in terms of our relationship with beings that are other than ourselves.

Krapfel describes his experiences of discovering the wisdom of appropriate "fits" of trails to landscapes by tracing animals' patterns of movement.[62] He teaches his students to search for intermediate stages of a process of plant development as a "game" whereby attention is focused on the detailed "spirals of change" that mark the movement of nature.[63] Learning to investigate integrative patterns and to trace flows among phenomena, rather than hypostatizing relationships in technical, causal terms, becomes a phenomenological priority in environmental education. Krapfel calls for a new practice of "seeing a world of merging gradients rather than of separating edges."[64] In so doing, one hopes that students might approach sustainability, less as a fixed state of affairs than as a challenging journey with renewed responsibilities of understanding the world in truly originative ways.

Final Reflections

In a recent article, educational sciences professor Lucie Sauvé shows how diverse conceptions of environment, education, and sustainable development coexist in our school systems, influencing the manner in which educators understand and practice environmental education.[65] "Should this diversity be perceived as a problem?" she asks.[66] Professor Sauvé argues against a search for standarized definitions, suggesting instead that this diversity "needs to be acknowledged and considered as 'fuel' for critical reflection, discussion, contestation and evolution."[67]

Certainly, we must guard against indoctrination of any sort, since the starting point for all environmental education is, as Courtenay-Hall points out, "to approach open-mindedly."[68] Environmental phenomenology fosters a way of thinking that allows for a genuine listening to others. By illumining the temporal grounds of our being-in-the-world, phenomenological reflection reveals the historicity of understanding and the naïveté of universalizing "solutions" to problems of sustainability.

On the other hand, in a postmodern era, diverse interpretations of the environment are not always equally appealing nor easily reconciled in meaningful ways. In such a fast-changing world, working toward sustainable development can appear as a daunting task. Plural interpretations of right and wrong often conflict and decision-making in the face of uncertainty can overwhelm us and threaten our best intentions at times. In the face of a growing appeal of postmodernism, C. A. Bowers is particularly critical of this movement. He argues that, despite their accomplishments in illumining the significance of language and culture, postmodern thinkers "have not engaged the fundamental question of how to live in a sustainable relationship with other life forms we now understand as interdependent."[69] Remaining implicitly grounded in an anthropocentric paradigm, postmodernism offers little direction for environmental theory.[70] "We shall have to turn elsewhere," Bowers concludes, "for guidance in how to understand the nature of a more ecologically responsible form of creativity."[71]

This book argues that environmental phenomenology may provide a significant avenue for rethinking sustainability and environmentalism. The special task for phenomenology becomes one of promoting awareness of ontological relations and grounds of shared meaning so that sustainable development is not pursued haphazardly, with a focus merely on arbitrary, ontic realities. It is not an easy journey, maneuvering between a respect for plural interpretations, as well as a need to discover some patterns of moral order that are the condition of the possibility of dialogue among diverse interests. J. B. White has an important reminder when he writes: "when we discover that we have in this world no rock or earth to stand and walk upon, but only shifting sea and sky and wind, the mature response is not to lament the loss of fixity, but to learn to sail."[72] Environmental phenomenology, it seems to me, is well suited to help us, on the one hand, to respect the reality of flux and diversity while, on the other hand, it helps to keep us on course as we search for meaningful direction on the way to sustainability. My hope is that the reader will accept the challenge to look beyond narrow, ontic concerns to consider broader, ontological questions as we collectively engage in environmental decision-making. A genuine rethinking of sustainability, as we seek to build a wiser, common future, deserves no less.

Appendix: Heidegger's Politics

Martin Heidegger was by far the most influential philosopher of the 20th century. . . .
Heidegger was also a Nazi.
—Stephen Howe, "A Nazi Genius"

While few would argue that Heidegger supported anti-Semitism, it is true that he was a member of the National Socialist Party in Germany for a time. In choosing to write about his philosophy, one is compelled to answer to critics who, once again in recent years, have focused attention in this involvement.[1] One could argue that Heidegger's personal history is irrelevant to his phenomenological writings. Some have made the case, however, that his political interests were inextricably linked to his ontological reflections and so I feel that it is important to address these issues. I should say, at the outset, that I do not believe that his links to the party were a necessary consequence of his philosophy. They do show, however, that Heidegger was politically naive and his refusal to engage in any overt support of political activity after 1934 indicates to me that he recognized this fact.

Let me address the two major issues that arise with respect to Heidegger's Nazism. First, I feel that we should consider his personal aspirations in choosing to associate himself with National Socialism. One cannot help but wonder what it was that attracted this German intellectual to identify in any way with a political movement that has come to symbolize the roots of human evil. Second, and perhaps more significantly, it is important to consider some of the arguments that suggest that these political motivations were integrally related to his philosophy. If the ties between his politics and philosophy are real, then Heidegger's environmental phenomenology must be seriously questioned.

Heidegger's Personal Involvement with National Socialism

Heidegger joined the party in 1933 in conjunction with taking up a post as rector of the University of Freiburg. In his posthumously published interview with *Der Spiegel*, he points out that he was ambivalent about accepting this post.[2] On the one hand, he and others were concerned that if he did not take up this position, "the danger would be that a party functionary would be named rector."[3] On the other hand, he was concerned that he lacked sufficient experience in administration. Consequently, he hesitated and, in fact, expressed his wish to withdraw his candidacy for this position. Eventually, however, he was prevented from doing so by administrative regulations.[4]

What motivation compelled Heidegger to accept National Socialism in the first place? Certainly, the inspiration was *not* anti-Semitism. One must recall that Heidegger's phenomenological mentor, Edmund Husserl, was a Jew. Rumors that Heidegger had been motivated by some faint stirrings of anti-Semitism to forbid Husserl to enter or use the university library were described by Heidegger as "a slander."[5] In fact, there are numerous incidences recounted by Heidegger where, in every case, he refused to abide by the party's racist demands.[6]

Nevertheless, as rector of the university, Martin Heidegger did join the party in 1933 because, he states, "at that time, I saw no alternative. In the general confusion of opinions and of the political trends of 22 parties, it was necessary to find a national and, above all, a social point of view."[7] We must keep in mind that National Socialism emerged in response to different problems and failings from those that it eventually caused—specifically, wide-ranging unemployment; inept Weimar regimes; various weakening repercussions following the loss of World War I; and sociopolitically debilitating hyperinflation. For many Germans, as for Heidegger, the specter of National Socialism offered the promise of economic stability and promise, as well as renewed national pride.

Heidegger's naïveté with respect to the possibilities offered by the Nazi Party to renew a spirit of resolve and direction in Germany extended to his hopes for the university to take a leading role in such renewal. His rectoral address was entitled, somewhat controversially, "The Self-Assertion of the German University." He agrees with the *Der Spiegel* interviewer's assessment that Heidegger drew the university into something that he felt at the time to be "a new dawn . . . you wished to see the university assert itself against currents which were overpowering and which would have no longer allowed the university to keep its own identity."[8]

Philosopher Graeme Nicholson points out that, as rector of the university, Heidegger genuinely believed himself to be capable of exerting influence on the broader, social happenings in the country, by way of the university.[9] His rectoral address clearly indicates that his means for achieving such an impact was going to be linguistic: "He seeks to appropriate portions of the Nazi vocabulary and interweave them with the vocabulary of his own philosophy, speaking as a law-giver to the university community. If practice and life within the university can be shaped by this double language, the result will be an impact upon the Nazi language itself. . . . Thus, he takes the street words *Führer, Volk* and *Kampf*—all imbued with National Socialist feeling—and makes a rhetorical transformation of them which hopes to foreshadow a transformation in life of what the words denote."[10]

Ultimately, Nicholson points out that, in his naive assumption of authoritative rule of the university, Heidegger "risked his philosophy by putting it to the test, and it lost" because it did not and never could have accomplished his anticipated role of political guide against the ruthlessness of Hitler.[11] After a year in office, Heidegger reports, "I recognized my political error and resigned my rectorship in protest against the state and the party."[12] In 1936, he began his Nietzsche lectures. "Anyone with ears to hear," he points out, "heard in these lectures a confrontation with National Socialism."[13]

Heidegger maintained that he was "constantly under surveillance," and that he was later categorized by the Nazi Party under the category of "completely dispensable people."[14] He did cause a stir in the academic community in 1953 when, in a lecture, he referred to the "inner truth and greatness" of the National Socialist movement.[15] Nevertheless, his statement was part of a critique of how the movement had evolved, rather than a simple expression of support, and he was addressing, not a political question, but the essence of the encounter beween global technology and modernity.

In a letter to his former student and famous Marxist author Herbert Marcuse, Heidegger accepts that he was negligent in not taking a more forceful stand against National Socialism: "You are entirely correct that I failed to provide a public, readily comprehensible counter-declaration; it would have been the end of both me and my family. On this point, Jaspers said: that we remain alive in our guilt."[16] As for any statement after 1945, any recanting "was for me impossible: the Nazi supporters announced their change of allegiance in the most loathsome way; I, however, had nothing in common with them."[17]

Heidegger's story is not a simple one. He maintained that he "expected from National Socialism a spiritual renewal of life in its entirety, a reconciliation of social antagonisms and a deliverance of Western Dasein from the dangers of communism."[18] Karl Jaspers remarks upon this naive expectation: "To a certain extent, I acknowledge the personal excuse that Heidegger was according to his nature unpolitical; the National Socialism which he embraced had little in common with existing National Socialism."[19]

Other publications, however, continue to struggle to comprehend Heidegger's naïveté and many critics simply believe that he should have been wiser to events in which he chose to be involved.[20] Nevertheless, for now, my suspicion is that he allowed his ego and his ambitions for university direction of a political movement to stand in the way of careful consideration of Nazi propaganda. The broader question, however, is to what extent his personal error reflects upon his philosophy. I turn now to this issue.

Heidegger's Philosophy and the National Socialist Movement

In his letter to Heidegger, Marcuse points out that "we cannot make the separation between Heidegger the philosopher and Heidegger the man, for it contradicts your own philosophy."[21] Certainly Heidegger's phenomenology was not meant to be a free-floating, abstract exercise, theoretically divorced from the lived social and political world in which it was to find its meaning. Are we to conclude, however, that Heidegger's links to National Socialism reflect a deep and insidious evil within his own philosophical project?

Some critics have accused Heidegger of implicitly succumbing, in his philosophy, to modernist tendencies. If one accepts such a reading of Heidegger as a closet modernist, then the links are easier to make between his phenomenological and political statements. For example, the title of his *Der Spiegel* interview and statements contained therein stipulated that "Only a God Can Save Us." The notion of "overcoming" a western philosophical tradition through a saving grace—and the concomitant, popular description of Nazis as saviors—were all ideas firmly embedded in metaphysical residues of thinking and a modernist conception of a single, liberating, transcendent source of inspiration.

Marcuse himself broke with Heidegger's teachings when, in his words, he "realized that Heidegger's concreteness was to a great extent a phony, a false concreteness, and that in fact his philosophy was just as abstract and just as removed from reality, even avoiding reality, as the philosophies which at that time had dominated German universities."[22] Marcuse maintained the principal concepts such as *Dasein, Das Man, Sein, Existenz* were " 'bad' abstracts in the sense that they are not conceptual vehicles to comprehend the real concreteness in the apparent one. They lead away."[23]

Even Jaspers remarked that Heidegger's later thinking proceeded "with the mystagogy of a magician," and in this respect, perhaps one could argue once again that Being is a modernist relic to the extent that it remained divorced from the concreteness of lived reality.[24] The conclusion would be, then, that the ontological was severed from the ontic by Heidegger, and that the search for Being was, in essence, not very different from the Nazi quest for glory, purification, and generalized renewal of that which was most meaningful—though now lost to German society.

Another set of criticisms emerge on the basis of an accusation that Heidegger's *Daseinanalytic* remained, in essence, traditional metaphysical humanism and self-defeating subjectivism.[25] Nazism istself is seen, in this scenario, as a parallel sort of humanism "that rests on a determination of *humanitas* which is, in its eyes, more powerful, i.e. more effective, that any other."[26] National Socialists believed that the new heros would be the western saviors from Spenglerian decline and Heidegger's implicit reliance on Dasein as the location of the source of Being was simply another expression of self-defeating, metaphysical humanism that we have already criticized in previous chapters of this book. Finally, one might wish to conclude that, with his discussions of Being as Nothing, Heidegger was succumbing to a nihilism no different from that found in Nazism.

While I wish to argue that these criticisms distort Heidegger's philosophy, I must admit that there are cases where I do see links between the times when

Heidegger published and taught, and his own academic publications. I think Marcuse is right to point out, when he surveys the contents of *Sein und Zeit*, that terms such as Idle talk, falling, Being-toward-death, anxiety, dread and boredom—all reflected the fears and frustrations of the German people at the time.[27] I do not believe (and neither did Heidegger) that, as philosophers, we write in some state that is detached from our own historical and geographical grounding.

Nevertheless, some of the most scathing attacks seem to be developed on the basis of a critique of an underlying metaphysicizing and modernism that supposedly underlies Heidegger's thought. Previous chapters of this book show how Heidegger's ontology cannot indicate a severance from the ontic, and a mystical "realm" unto itself. The book also shows how Dasein is seriously misinterpreted when defined in a merely humanistic fashion as a center of subjectivity. Furthermore, nothingness is hardly a nihilistic endeavor but, rather, points to a process of seeking and a movement toward the retrieval of ontological meaning. I am not particularly apologetic that Heidegger has avoided going as far as the postmodernists in escaping modernism. My own view is that there is a deep need to go back to Heidegger, after postmodernism, to appropriate certain messages that are too vital to forget—the obvious example being the question of the meaning of Being itself.

In short, to endeavor to link Heidegger's philosophy to Nazism on the basis of his supposed modernist leanings is to distort his ontological writings and to risk bypassing phenomenological reflections that remain significant to environmental philosophy to this day. To be sure, the recent publications and renewal of interest in Heidegger's ties to National Socialism mean that there is now a permanent mark on the man. I believe that, sadly, Heidegger may deserve this sentence because, after all, he took the risk of immersing himself in political activities and in supporting Hitler for a time.

Nevertheless, to remodel his philosophy on simplistic, modernist terms or to reject the body of his work on the basis of his human failings would be, in my view, too high a sacrifice for phenomenology and an unfounded one as well. Heidegger himself remarked to Marcuse that the latter's letter "shows me precisely how difficult it is to converse with persons who have not been living in Germany since 1933 and who judge the beginning of the National Socialist movement from its end."[28] Graeme Nicholson similarly notes that "it is always hard to remember that events now in the past were once in the future."[29] With hindsight, one wishes that Heidegger would have acted differently than he did. Before we accuse Heidegger too readily, however, of the perils of human error that he himself addressed in his writings, we might wonder whether our own children will be able to forgive us, when they perceive with hindsight again, our own environmental sins and blindness to long-term impacts of self-gratification at the expense of environmental care.

Notes

Introduction

1. World Commission on Environment and Development, *Our Common Future* (New York: Oxford University Press, 1987), p. 43.
2. *Macleans*, 15 May 1946. Reported more recently in *Macleans*, 7 August 1995, p. 24.

Chapter 1. The Challenge of Sustainability

The epigraph is from Maurice Sendak, *I Dream of Peace* (New York: UNICEF/HarperCollins, 1994). This book publishes paintings by children of the former Yugoslavia, who have been assisted by programs of art therapy and counseling to overcome some of their traumatic experiences of the recent war. I have rarely encountered a more moving testimony to the horrors of conflict as well as the enormous faith in the promise of peace.

1. Plato, *Theatet.* 155d. "For this is especially the *pathos* of a philosopher, to be in wonder. For there is no other beginning of *philosophia* than this."
2. Friedrich Nietzsche, "Of the Three Metamorphoses," *Thus Spoke Zarathustra*, book 1, trans. W. Kaufmann (New York: Viking Press, 1970), p. 139. Nietzsche's child is not innocent as unknowing or unaware but rather stands within the metamorphosis of spirit itself.
3. Cf. Martin Heidegger, *An Introduction to Metaphysics* (New York: Doubleday/Anchor Books, 1961), p. 10. Heidegger writes: "It is absolutely correct and proper to say that "You can't do anything with philosophy." It is only wrong to suppose that this is the last word on philosophy. For the rejoinder imposes itself: granted that *we* cannot do anything with philosophy, might not philosophy, if we concern ourselves with it, do something *with us?*"
4. The World Commission on Environment and Development, *Our Common Future* (New York: Oxford University Press, 1987).
5. Cf. Martin Heidegger, "What is Metaphysics?" in *Existence and Being* (Chicago, Illinois: Henry Regnery Company, 1949), p. 325. Heidegger reminds us that "philosophy, according to Hegel, is the 'world stood on its head.'" Hegel's own remarks that the philosopher "walks on his head" occur in his *Phänomenologie des Geistes*, ed. Johannes Hoffmeister (Hamburg: Meiner, 1952), p. 25. Cf. also *Werke: Volständige Ausgabe durch einen Verein von Freunden des Verewigten*, 2d ed. (Berlin: Duncker & Humblot, 1940–47), p. 535. It is worth noting that, at one point, Hegel modifies this famous metaphor, suggesting on the contrary that Christian faith and philosophic thought would be described as being on their feet, in his description of evil as "the perversion of good, which possesses an actuality in its own right, but stood on its head." Cf. *Berliner Schriften*, ed. Johannes Hoffmeister (Stuttgart: Frommann, 1936), p. 314.

6. The World Commission on Environment and Development, *Our Common Future*.
7. Ibid., p. 43. Cf. also William E. Rees, "Defining 'Sustainable Development'" (British Columbia: University of British Columbia Centre for Human Settlements, May 1989).
8. World Commission on Environment and Development, *Our Common Future*, p. 44.
9. George E. Connell, "Letter from the Chair" in *National Round Table on the Environment and the Economy Annual Review 1994–95* (Ottawa, Canada: NRTEE, 1995), p. 4.
10. Ranjit Kumar, Edward W. Manning, Barbara Murck, *The Challenge of Sustainability* (Don Mills, Ontario: Foundation for International Training, 1993), p. 35.
11. Herman E. Daly and John B. Cobb, *For the Common Good: Redirecting the Economy toward Community, the Environment, and a Sustainable Future* (Boston: Beacon Press, 1989), p. 138.
12. Ibid.
13. Rees, "Defining 'Sustainable Development,'" p. 3.
14. Rajni Kothari, "Environment, Technology, and Ethics," in *Reflection on Nature: Readings in Environmental Philosophy*, Lori Gruen and Dale Jamieson, eds. (New York Oxford University Press, 1994), p. 228.
15. Ibid., p. 229.
16. William E. Rees, "Understanding Sustainable Development: Natural Capital and the New World Order," (unpublished discussion paper from the University of British Columbia, School of Community and Regional Planning).
17. Cf. Husserl, Edmund, *Ideas Pertaining to a Pure Phenomenology and to a Phenomenological Philosophy*, trans. F. Kersten (The Hague, Netherlands: Martinus Nijhoff, 1983).
18. Cf. Ricoeur, Paul, *Fallible Man: Philosophy of the Will*, trans. C. Kelbley (Chicago: Henry Regnery Co., 1967); Gadamer, Hans-Georg, *Truth and Method* (New York: The Seabury Press, 1975) and *Interpretation Theory* (Fort Worth, Texas: Christian University Press, 1977); Merleau-Ponty, Maurice, *Phenomenology of Perception*, trans. Colin Smith (London: Routledge & Kegan Paul, 1962); Sartre, Jean-Paul, *Being and Nothingness*, trans. Hazel E. Barnes (New York: Washington Square Press, 1956); Heidegger, Martin, *Being and Time*, trans. John Macquarrie and Edward Robinson (New York: Harper & Row, 1962).
19. Heidegger, Martin, *Basic Problems of Phenomenology* (Bloomington and Indianapolis: Indiana University Press, 1982), p. 328.
20. Cf. Martin Heidegger's comments in *Being and Time*, where he writes: "One can never carry on researches into the source and the possibility of Being in general simply by means of 'abstractions' of formal logic—that is, without any secure horizons for question and answer. One must seek a *way* of casting light on the fundamental question of ontology, and this is the way one must go. Whether this is the *only* way or even the right one at all, can be decided only *after one has gone along it*" (p. 487). Similarly, he writes elsewhere that "it may happen that when our thinking, set into motion by some particular matter, pursues it, it undergoes a change on the way. In what follows, it is for this reason advisable to pay close attention to the way and not so much to the content" (*Identity and Difference*, trans. J. Stambaugh [New York: Harper & Row, 1969], p. 23). For a discussion of Heideger's philosophy as a "way," see Otto Pöggeler's *Der Denkweg Martin Heideggers* (Pfullingen, 1963), pp. 7–15.
21. Spiegelberg, Herbert, *The Phenomenological Movement*, 2 vols. (The Hague, Netherlands: Martinus Nijhoff, 1960).

22. Heidegger, Martin, "Modern Science, Metaphysics and Mathematics," in *Basic Writings*, ed. David Farrell Krell (New York: Harper & Row, 1977), pp. 247–48.

23. Ibid.

24. Scientist Stephen Jay Gould writes that "The history of science has been transformed . . . by a recognition that, although nature surely embodies factual truth accessible to human investigation . . . science does not and cannot 'progress' by rising above social embeddedness on wings of timeless and international 'scientific method.' Science, like all human intellectual activity, must proceed in a complex social, political and psychological context; greatness must therefore be grasped as fruitful use, not as transcendence." See "The Paradox of Nature," in *Nature* 355 (16 January 1992).

25. The example comes from energy scientist Amory Lovins, "Technology Is the Answer (But What Was the Question?)" in *Environmental Science*, G. Tyler Miller, ed. (Belmont, Calif.: Wadsworth, 1991), pp. 56–57.

26. Robyn Eckersley, *Environmentalism and Policy Theory* (New York: State University of New York Press, 1992), p. 52.

27. Cf. Martin Heidegger, *An Introduction to Metaphysics* (Garden City, New York: Doubleday, 1961), pp. 89–90.

28. Martin Heidegger, "Truth in Platonism and Positivism," in *Nietzsche*, vol. 1 (New York: HarperCollins Publishers, 1991), p. 159.

29. Cf. section 125 of Nietzsche's *The Gay Science*: "God is dead! God remains dead! And we have killed him! . . . Don't we have to become gods ourselves just to seem worthy of it?" cited in Walter Kaufmann, *Existentialism from Dostoevsky to Sartre* (Cleveland and New York: The World Publishing Company, 1956).

30. Husserl, *Phenomenology*, p. 164.

31. Heidegger, *Being and Time*, p. 58.

32. Ibid.

33. Husserl, *Phenomenology*, pp. 142, 148. Other philosophers such as Locke, Hume, and Descartes were locked in a metaphysical dogmatism that ultimately prevented them from carrying out the phenomenological journey. Kant came closest in his *Critique of Pure Reason* to phenomenology but then "misinterpreted that realm as psychological and therefore he himself abandoned it."

34. Heidegger, *Being and Time*, introduction.

35. Jean-Francois Lyotard, *The Postmodern Explained* (Minneapolis: University of Minnesota Press, 1992), p. 15.

36. The expressions are Lyotard's. "The answer is this: war on totality. Let us attest to the unpresentable; let us activate the differends and save the honor of the name." Cf. Ibid., pp. 15–16.

37. Cf. Werner Marx, *Towards a Phenomenological Ethics: Ethos and the Life-World* (New York: State University of New York Press, 1992).

38. Robert Solomon, "Introduction" to *Phenomenology and Existentialism* (Lanham, Md.: University Press of America, 1980), p. 3.

39. Hok-Lin Leung, *City Images* (Kingston, Ontario, Canada: Ronald P. Frye & Company, 1992), p. 211.

40. Ibid.

41. Cf. Heidegger, *Being and Time*, where being human is described in terms of an originary

implacement in the world. Inasmuch as one is human, says Heidegger, one is a Being-in-the-world. Self and world, then, are not two distinct entities but belong together in a unity. See also *The Basic Problems of Phenomenology*, pp. 300–301.

42. Cf. in this connection Robet Mugerauer, who discusses "how to have plural meaning and yet a basis for saying that not just anything goes." *Interpretations on Behalf of Place: Environmental Displacements and Alternative Responses* (Albany, New York: State University of New York Press, 1994), p. 7.

43. Cf. Thomas Nenon's enlightening foreword to Werner Marx, *Phenomenological Ethics*, p. 6.

44. Ibid. Nenon points out that this description of phenomenology in terms of "possibilities as such" differs from the Husserlean conception that emerged as a "form of transcendental philosophy that establishes the *necessary* conditions for the possibility of certain kinds of entities through an analysis of the conditions for the possibility of the genesis of such things within consciousness."

45. The image is used also by Martin Heidegger, in "The Way Back into the Ground of Metaphysics," in *Existentialism from Dostoevsky to Sartre*, ed. Walter Kaufmann (New York: World Publishing Company, 1956).

46. Reported in G. Conrad Brunk, Lawrence Haworth, and Brenda Lee, *Value Assumptions in Risk Assessment: A Case Study of the Alachlor Controversy* (Waterloo, Ontario: Wilfrid Laurier University Press, 1991).

47. Ibid., p. 10.

48. Alan Durning, *How Much Is Enough?* (New York: W. W. Norton, 1992) cited in Peter Freund and George Martin, *The Ecology of the Automobile* (Montreal: Black Rose Books, 1993), p. 103. I refer the reader particularly to chapters 5 and 6 of this book, entitled "The Ideology of Automobility" and "The Phenomenology of Automobility" respectively.

49. Cf. Peter Calthorpe, "The Post-Suburban Metropolis," in *Whole Earth Review* (Winter 1991): 44–51; Dolores Hayden, *Redesigning the American Dream: The Future of Housing, Work, and Family Life* (New York: W. W. Norton and Company Ltd., 1984); Kenneth Jackson, *Crabgrass Frontier: The Suburbanization of the United States* (New York: Oxford University Press, 1985).

50. Cf. *The Intensification Report* (ISSN 1192–6961) published bimonthly by the Canadian Urban Institute, 2nd Floor, West Tower, City Hall, Toronto, Canada. M5H 2N1.

51. Cf. R. Simpson, "Residential Intensification: The Wrong Planning Debate," in *The Intensification Report* (ISSN 1192–6961), vol. 1, no. 1, March 1993 (Toronto, Canada: Canadian Urban Institute).

52. Surveying eight major Canadian cities, the poll shows not a single case of higher average preference rating of the downtown over suburban living. Cf. Angus Reid Group, *Urban Canada Study*, 1991, reported in Jeffrey Patterson, "Introducing Sustainable Cities," in *Sustainable Cities: IUS Newsletter Supplement*, no. 1, December 1991 (University of Winnipeg: Institute of Urban Studies).

53. Canadian Institute pf Planners, *Reflections on Sustainable Planning* (Ottawa: Canadian Institute of Planners, 1990).

54. See *Sustainable America: A New Consensus for Prosperity, Opportunity, and a Healthy Environment for the Future* (Washington, D.C.: Government Printing Office, February 1996).

55. World Commission on Environment and Development, *Our Common Future*, pp. xiii, 111.

56. Ibid., pp. 6, 9, 21.

57. Ibid., p. 46.
58. Thomas S. Kuhn, *The Structure of Scientific Revolutions* (Chicago: University of Chicago Press, 1970).
59. Ibid., p. 11.
60. Hans-Georg Gadamer, *Truth and Method* (New York: The Seabury Press, 1975), p. 340.

Chapter 2. The Brundtland Report

1. World Commission on Environment and Development, *Our Common Future* (Oxford, New York: Oxford University Press, 1987).
2. Margaret Catley-Carlson, president of the Canadian International Development Agency (CIDA), calls the book :"the most important document of the decade on the future of the world," and a "'must-read' for just about anyone who's concerned with where our planet is heading." "Building a Sustainable Environment," presented to a meeting of the Fourth World Congress on the Conservation of the Built and Natural Environments, 23 May 1989, Toronto, Canada.
3. Cf., for example, Lester Brown's *Building a Sustainable Society* (New York: W. W. Norton, 1980); and the International Union for the Conservation of Nature and Natural Resources, *World Conservation Strategy* (Geneva, Switzerland: IUCN, 1980).
4. The World Commission on Environment and Development, *Our Common Future*.
5. Donella H. Meadows; Dennis L. Meadows, Jorgen Randers; William W. Behrens III, *The Limits to Growth* (New York: Universe Books, 1972).
6. Cf. Ibid., p. 21. Significantly, in the sequel to *Limits to Growth*, the authors similarly speak about a choice faced by the world, that is, "the choice is between *models*" (italics mine). See *Beyond the Limits: Confronting Global Collapse, Envisioning a Sustainable Future* (Post Mills, Vt.: Chelsea Green, 1991) by Donella H. Meadows, Dennis L. Meadows, and Jorgen Randers.
7. Meadows, Meadows, and Randers, *The Limits to Growth*, p. 142.
8. Willy Brandt and the Independent Commission on International Development Issues, *North-South: A Program for Survival* (Cambridge, Mass.: The MIT Press, 1980).
9. Ibid., p. 29.
10. Ibid., p. 25.
11. World Commission on Environment and Development, *Our Common Future*, p. 2.
12. Joseph C. Dunstan, Katherine L. Jope, Geoffrey M. Swan, "Why Sustainability?" in *The George Wright Forum* 10, no. 4 (1993): 9–18.
13. Ibid., p. 14.
14. World Commission on Environment and Development, *Our Common Future*, p. xi.
15. Ibid., p. 38.
16. Cf. Ibid., p. 342. "Problems of today do not come with a tag marked energy or economy or CO_2 or demography, nor with a label indicating a country or a region. The problems are multi-disciplinary and transnational or global."
17. Ibid., p. 38.
18. Ibid., p. 4.
19. Cf. ibid., p. 9.
20. Ibid., p. 309.
21. Ibid., p. 247.

22. Ibid., p. 235.

23. Ibid., p. 246.

24. Ibid., p. 37.

25. On issues relating to women, see ibid., p. 257; on indigenous peoples, see p. 114; on economics, see p. 67ff; and on justice and equity, see pp. 261, 67, 46.

26. Meadows, Meadows, and Randers, *Beyond the Limits*, p. 23.

27. World Commission on Environment and Development, *Our Common Future*, p. 45.

28. Ibid.

29. As John Kenneth Galbraith writes, "Pessimism in our time is infinitely more respectable than optimism: the man who foresees peace, prosperity and a decline in juvenile delinquency is a negligent and vacuous fellow. The man who foresees catastrophe has a gift of insight which insures that he will become a radio commentator, an editor of *Time*, or go to Congress." Cited in Thomas C. Emmel, *Global Perspectives on Ecology* (Palo Alto: Calif.: Mayfield Publishing company, 1977).

30. Cf. World Commission on Environment and Development, *Our Common Future*, p. 237. Also D. Brooks, "Beyond Catch Phrases: What Does Sustainable Development Really Mean?" in *IDRC Reports* (October 1990).

31. T. Trainer, "A Rejection of the Brundtland Report," *IFDA Dossier* (International Foundation for Development Alternatives) (May/June 1990): 71–84.

32. Ibid., p. 72; Maureen Reed, "Sustainability and Community: Still Searching for Meaning," in *Environments*, 21, no. 2 (1991)).

33. Stephen Viederman, "A Sustainable Society: What Is It? How Do We Get There?" in *George Wright Forum* 10, no. 4 (1993): 34–47.

34. Joy A. Palmer, "Destruction of the Rainforests," in *The Environment in Question: Ethics and Global Issues*, ed. David E. Cooper and Joy A. Palmer (London and New York: Routledge, 1992), p. 92.

35. World Commission on Environment and Development, *Our Common Future*, p. 58.

36. Ibid.

37. Dunstan, Jope, and Swan, "Why Sustainability?" pp. 9–18.

38. World Commission on Environment and Development, *Our Common Future*, p. 45.

39. Dunstan, Jope, and Swan, "Why Sustainability?" p. 10.

40. World Commission on Environment and Development, *Our Common Future*, p. 23.

41. Ibid., p. 22.

42. Cf. *Being and Time*, Division 2, trans. John Macquarrie and Edward Robinson (New York and Evanston: Harper & Row, 1962) as well as *The Concept of Time*, trans. William McNeill (Oxford: Basil Blackwell, 1992).

43. Heidegger, *The Concept of Time*, p. 20E. Cf. also *Being and Time*, p. 434.

44. Ibid. I shall have more to say about temporality and historicity in part II.

45. Heidegger, *Being and Time*, p. 22ff.

46. Ibid.

47. Heidegger, "Memorial Address" in *Discourse in Thinking* (New York: Harper & Row, 1966).

48. Ibid.

49. See Martin Heidegger, "Rapture as Aesthetics," in *Nietzsche*, vol. 1, trans. David Farrell Krell (San Francisco: Harper & Row, 1979), p. 92.

50. Heidegger, "Memorial Address," p. 54.

51. I shall return to a more comprehensive discussion of the significance of the question of the meaning of Being for Heidegger in part II.

52. World Commission on Environment and Development, *Our Common Future*, pp. 54–55.

53. Ibid., pp. xi, 11, 95–117.

54. *Webster's Ninth New Collegiate Dictionary* (Springfield, Mass.: Merriam-Webster, 1985).

55. Martin Buber, *I and Thou*, trans. Walter Kaufmann (New York: Charles Scribner's Sons, 1970), p. 59.

56. Martin Heidegger tells us that "[t]he whole of modern metaphysics taken together . . . maintains itself within the interpretation of what it is to be and of truth that was prepared by Descartes." See "The Age of the World Picture," in *The Question Concerning Technology and Other Essays*, trans. William Lovitt (New York: Harper & Row, 1977), p. 127.

57. Descartes writes, for example: "It is some time ago now since I perceived that, from my earliest years, I had accepted many false opinions as being true, and that what I had since based on such insecure principles could only be most doubtful and uncertain; so that I had to undertake seriously once in my life to rid myself of all the opinions I had adopted up to then, and to begin afresh from the foundations." From the "First Meditation," *Discourse on Method and Meditations*, trans. F. E. Sutcliffe (Middlesex, England: Penguin Books, 1968), p. 95.

58. Ibid., "Second Meditation," p. 102.

59. Ibid., "First Meditation," pp. 96–98.

60. Descartes speculated that it was quite possible to "suppose, therefore, that there is, not a true God, who is the sovereign source of truth, but some evil demon, no less cunning and deceiving than powerful, who has used all his artifice to deceive me." Ibid., p. 100.

61. Ibid., pp. 106–7.

62. Descartes, *Discourse on Method, Selected Philosophical Writings*, trans. J. Cottingham et al. (Cambridge: Cambridge University Press, 1988), p. 28.

63. Heidegger writes: "The real system of science consists in a solidarity of procedure and attitude with respect to the objectification of whatever is." See Heidegger, *The Question Concerning Technology*, p. 126.

64. Ibid., p. 128.

65. Ibid., p. 129.

66. Ibid., pp. 129–130.

67. Ibid., p. 128. Heidegger refers to "man" here: "Man becomes the relational center of that which is as such." Ecofeminists argue convincingly of the centrality of the male image in modern thought. They also argue for the overturning of this image. For an overview of these issues and a bibliography of the field, see the American Philosophical Association's *Newsletter on Feminism and Philosophy* 90, no. 2 (fall 1991).

68. This point is clearly made in Thomas S. Kuhn's popular *The Structure of Scientific Revolutions* (Chicago: The University of Chicago Press, 1970).

69. Martin Heidegger, "Oh the Essence of Truth," in *Basic Writings*, ed. David Farrell Krell (New York: Harper & Row, 1977)., p. 122ff.

70. Heidegger, "The Age of the World Picture," p. 134.

71. Heidegger, M., "The Question Concerning Technology," *The Question Concerning Technology and Other Essays*, pp. 14, 16.

72. Ibid., pp. 14–15.

73. Ibid., p. 15.

74. Ibid., p. 16.

75. Ibid., p. 18ff.

76. Ibid., p. 28.

77. Heidegger, "Memorial Address," p. 46.

78. Cited in David Wann, *Deep Design: Pathways to a Livable Future* (Washington, D.C.: Island Press, 1996), p. 38.

79. Gaston Bachelard, *The Poetics of Space*, trans Maria Jolas (Boston: Beacon Press, 1964), pp. 67–68.

80. Heidegger, *Basic Writings*, p. 119.

81. Aristotle's *Metaphysics* Delta Book 7. The remarks here relating to Aristotelean and Thomistic philosophy are discussed in further detail in William Barrett's insightful work, entitled *Irrational Man* (New York: Doubleday, 1958). This, as well as a number of other passages in this chapter, are based on a paper by I. L. Stefanovic, which appeared originally as "Evolving Sustainability: A Re-thinking of Ontological Foundations," in the *Trumpeter* 8, no. 4, (fall 1991): 194–200.

82. Louis Million, *It Was Home: A Phenomenology of Place and Involuntary Displacement as Illustrated by the Forced Dislocation of Five Southern Alberta Families in the Oldman River Dam Flood Area* (Ph.D. diss., Saybrook Institute, California, 1992).

83. Jean-Paul Sartre, *Being and Nothingness*, trans. Hazel E. Barnes (New York: Simon and Schuster, 1956), p. 53ff.

84. William Barrett, *Irrational Man*, pp. 288–89.

85. Ibid., p. 289.

86. World Commission on Environment and Development, *Our Common Future*, p. 118.

87. Cf. Dreyer Kruger, *An Introduction to Phenomenological Psychology* (Pittsburgh: Duquesne University Press, 1979), p. 9ff.

88. Cited in Walter Kaufmann, *Existentialism from Dostoevsky to Sartre* (Cleveland and New York: The World Publishing Company, 1956), pp. 53–54.

89. The hero refuses even to be categorized as spiteful: "It was not only that I could not become spiteful, I did not know how to become anything: neither spiteful nor kind, neither a rascal nor an honest man, neither a hero nor an insect." Cf. ibid., p. 55.

90. Ibid., p. 65.

91. John Watson notes that "psychology as the behaviourist views it, would be a purely objective branch of natural science using experimental methods. Its theoretical goal is the prediction and control of behaviour." Cited in Kruger, *Introduction to Phenomenological Psychology*, p. 5.

92. Heidegger, "Memorial Address," p. 51.

93. Ibid., p. 50.

94. Heidegger, *Being and Time*, and *The End of Philosophy*, trans. Joan Stambaugh (New York: Harper & Row, 1973).

95. Cf. Heidegger, "The Age of the World Picture."

96. Heidegger, *Being and Time*, p. 257.

97. Martin Heidegger, *The Basic Problems of Phenomenology*, trans. Albert Hofstadter (Bloomington and Indianapolis: Indiana University Press, 1982), pp. 216, 221.

98. Heidegger, "Memorial Address," p. 46.

99. Martin Heidegger, "Modern Science, Metaphysics, and Mathematics" in *Basic Writings*, p. 254.

100. Ibid.

101. *Webster's Ninth New Collegiate Dictionary*. Italics are mine.

102. Heidegger, "Science, Metaphysics, and Mathematics," p. 253.

103. Ibid., p. 251.

104. Ibid., p. 252.

105. Ibid., p. 252. Mathematician Morris Kline has an interesting suggestion in this regard. He suggests that "the present state of mathematics has been aptly described by Weyl: 'The question of the ultimate foundations and the ultimate meaning of mathematics remains open; we do not know in what direction it will find its final solution, or even whether a final objective answer can be expected at all. 'Mathematizing' may well be a creative activity of man, like language or music, of primary originality, whose historical decisions defy complete objective rationalization.'" See Morris Kline, *Mathematical Thought*, vol. 3 (New York: Oxford University Press, 1972), p. 1210. My thanks to Dr. Boris Weisman for this reference.

106. Heidegger, "Science, Metaphysics, and Mathematics."

107. Tony Hodge, Susan Holtz, Cameron Smith, and Kelley H. Baxter, eds., *Pathways to Sustainability: Assessing Our Progress* (Ottawa: National Round Table on the Environment and the Economy, 1995), p. 7.

Chapter 3. Calculation and Sustainability

1. Jacques Maritain, "The Human Person and Society," in *Challenges and Renewals* (Cleveland and New York: The World Publishing Company, 1966), pp. 283–308.

2. Ibid., p. 287.

3. Ibid.

4. Margaret Catley-Carlson, "Building and Sustainable Environments" (paper presented at the meeting of the 4th World Congress on the Conservation of the Built and Natural Environments, Toronto, 23 May 1989,) p. 6.

5. World Commission on Environment and Development, *Our Common Future* (Oxford and New York: Oxford University Press, 1987), p. 281.

6. Louis P. Pojman, *Environmental Ethics: Readings in Theory and Application* (Boston and London: Jones and Bartlett Publishers, 1994), p. 281.

7. Arthur Simon, *Bread for the World* (New York: Paulist Press, 1975), cited in ibid., p. 281.

8. Ibid., p. 282.

9. Martin Heidegger, *Being and Time*, trans. J. Macquarrie and E. Robinson (New York: Harper & Row, 1962), p. 164.

10. Ibid., p. 165.

11. World Commission on Environment and Development, *Our Common Future*, p. 41.

12. This is sometimes referred to as the "argument from ignorance." Cf. J. R. Des Jardins, *Environmental Ethics* (Belmont, Calif.: Wadsworth, 1993), p. 77. Also Gregory Kavka, "The Futurity Problem," in *Obligations to Future Generations*, ed. R. I. Sikora and Brian Barry (Philadelphia: Temple University Press, 1978).

13. Des Jardins, *Environmental Ethics*, p. 78.

14. Ibid. Cf. also "Future Generations: The Non-Identity Problem" by D. Parfit, who argues that it makes no sense to say that future generations will be harmed by our actions, because those same actions will influence who in fact exists, composing such future generations. Even though an action we choose to pursue may be a bad one, "our choice will be worse for no one." *Ethical Issues: Perspectives for Canadians*, ed. Eldon Soifer (Peterborough, Ontario: Broadview Press, 1992), pp. 281–89.

15. The best discussion I have run across regarding the dangers of isolating "the duties which people owe each other *merely as thinkers* from those deeper and more general ones which they owe each other as beings who feel" is found in Mary Midgley, "Duties Concerning Islands," in *Environmental Ethics*, ed. Robert Elliot (New York and Oxford: Oxford University Press, 1995). Midgley describes how the social contract model is ultimately itself reductionist, and therefore cannot account for responsibilities not only to future generations, but to the dead, to children, to the insane, to animals, to plants, to ecosystems, and ultimately even to oneself and to God.

16. Ibid., p. 124.

17. Caroline O. N. Moser calls for distinguishing housing needs not only in terms of income, but also on the basis of gender. She writes how "for instance, policy-makers tend to identify target groups in terms of the income of the male breadwinner; project authorities design eligibility criteria for participating in sites and services projects in terms of the income of men and evidence of regular employment; and architects design houses to meet the needs of nuclear families, in which all productive work is undertaken by men outside the home." *Women, Human Settlements and Housing* (London and New York: Tavistock Publications, 1987), p. 13.

18. Cf. for example Karen Warren, "Feminism and Ecology: Making Connections," *Environmental Ethics* 9 (spring 1987): 3–20. Also "The Power and Promise of Ecological Feminism" in *Environmental Ethics* 12 (summer 1990): 125–46.

19. Cf. Jim Cheney, "Nature/Theory/Difference: Ecofeminism and the Reconstruction of Environmental Ethics" in Karen Warren, *Ecological Feminism* (London and New York: Routledge, 1994), p. 159.

20. Cf. for example "Is Ecofeminism Feminist?" by Victoria Davion, in Karren Warren, *Ecological Feminism*, pp. 8–28; Val Plumwood, "Feminism and Ecofeminism," *The Ecologist* 22, no. 1 (January–February 1992): 8–13. I recommend to the reader Val Plumwood's *Feminism and the Mastery of Nature* (London: Routledge, 1993) as a thoughtful defense of critical ecofeminist theory.

21. See for example, Douglas J. Buege's excellent piece entitled "Rethinking Again: A Defense of Ecofeminist Philosophy," in Karen Warren, *Ecological Feminism*, p. 42ff, where he argues that ecofeminists' strength lies precisely in their variety of "innovative ways that allow for the diverse voices of society to speak and be heard" (56). See also Jim Cheney's paper "Nature/Theory/Difference: Ecofeminism and the Reconstruction of Environmental Ethics" in the same volume, where he criticizes the totalizing discourse of contemporary philosophy, and shows how ecofeminism may lead us to a greater awareness of the social and historical embeddedness of human beings.

22. Cited in Dreyer Kruger, *An Introduction to Phenomenological Psychology* (Pittsburgh: Duquesne University Press, 1979), p. 15.

23. See *Building Momentum: Sustainable Development in Canada* (Ottawa: Minister of Public Works and Government Services Canada, 1997), pp. 11–13.

24. Cited in the World Commission on Environment and Development, *Our Common Future*, p. 38.

25. David E. Cooper, "The Idea of Environment" in *The Environment in Question: Ethics and Global Issues*, ed. D. E. Cooper and Joy A. Palmer (London and New York: Routledge, 1992), p. 167.

26. Cf. Heidegger, *Being and Time*.

27. This is definitively argued in Edward Casey, *Getting Back into Place: Toward a Renewed Understanding of the Place-World* (Bloomington and Indianapolis: Indiana University Press, 1993).

28. Michael Hough, *City Form and Natural Process* (London and New York: Routledge, 1984, 1989), pp. 18–19.

29. Ibid.

30. Ibid., p. 18.

31. R. Repetto, *World Enough and Time: Successful Strategies for Resource Management*, cited in *Canadian Centre for Human Settlements Research Bulletin*, May 1989 (The University of British Columbia: UBC Centre for Human Settlements), p. 5.

32. Kelly Hawke Baxter, "Jobs, Prosperity, and a Sustainable Economy: It's All Common Sense" in *National Round Table Review* (Ottawa: National Round Table on the Environment and the Economy, fall 1993), p. 1.

33. This point is argued by some deep ecologists and finds its extreme expression in the ideology of EarthFirst!ers. See C. Manes, *Green Rage* (Boston: Little, Brown and Company, 1990).

34. Bill Devall and George Sessions, *Deep Ecology: Living as if Nature Mattered* (Salt Lake City: Peregrine Smith Books, 1985). See chapter 5 on the "basic principles" of deep ecology.

35. See Cooper, "Idea of Environment."

36. Dave Foreman, spokesman for EarthFirst!ers and a supporter of deep ecology, argues in his membership brochure that "humankind is no greater than any other form of life and has no legitimate claim to dominate Earth. . . . All human decisions should consider Earth first, humankind second." For a further discussion, cf. the Universityof Windsor's Martha F. Lee, "Environmental Apocalypse: A Case Study of Earth First!" presented at the Canadian Political Science Association meetings in Ottawa, 1993.

37. Cf. in this respect Douglas Torgerson, who explains that the paradox of ecocentric ethics is that it "de-centers the human, and at the same time, places humanity at the center of things. As soon as humanity is expelled from its privileged position, it is readmitted, so to speak, by the back door. Human reason is divested of its pretensions, but placed in judgment of all being. It could not be otherwise, for environmental ethics depends, after all, on ethical discourse. Discourse presupposes rational participants, and the only natural beings we know to be potentially qualified participants happen to be human beings." In "The Paradox of Environmental Ethics," *Alternatives* 12, no. 2 (winter 1985): 26–36.

38. Cf. Cooper, "Idea of Environment," pp. 165–80.

39. Ibid., p. 166.

40. Ibid.

41. Ibid., p. 167. Cooper reminds us further on of the significance of the French *environs*, as that which surrounds. Environment becomes linked to identity with place, which is the condition for environmental care.

42. Jim Cheney, "Postmodern Environmental Ethics: Ethics as Bioregional Narrative" in *Environmental Ethics: Convergence and Divergence*, ed. Susan J. Armstrong and Richard G. Botzler (New York: McGraw-Hill, 1993), p. 32.

43. Heidegger, *Being and Time*, division 1, chapter 2.

44. Henry David Thoreau, "Solitude" in *Walden*, cited in Casey, *Getting Back into Place*, p. 245.

45. Cf. G. P. Marsh, who claims how "in countries untrodden by man . . . geological influences [are] so slow in their operation that the geographical conditions may be regarded as constant and immutable." *Man and Nature*, ed. D. Lowenthal (Cambridge: Harvard University Press [1864] 1967), pp. 29–30.

46. Cited in Gerald Hodge, *Planning Canadian Communities* (Scarborough, Ontario: Nelson Canada, 1991), p. 72.

47. David Loenthal, "Daniel Boone is Dead," in *Natural History*, American Geographical Society (August–September 1968). Cited in Hough, *City Form*, p. 19.

48. Ibid.

49. Hough, *City Form*, pp. 15–16.

50. Sim Van Der Ryn and Stuart Cowan, *Ecological Design* (Washington, D.C.: Island Press, 1996), p. 62.

51. Ibid., p. 16.

52. Tony Hiss, *The Experience of Place* (New York: Alfred A. Knopf, 1990), pp. 61–62.

53. Gaston Bachelard, *The Poetics of Space*, trans. Maria Jolas (Boston: Beacon Press, 1964), p. xxxii.

54. Ibid., p. 47.

55. Wendy Dobson, "The Environment from an Economic Perspective," *Inside Guide* (Toronto), 3, no. 5 (winter 1989): 62.

56. A. G. Tansley, "The Use and Abuse of Vegetational Concepts and Terms," *Ecology* 16 (1935): 298.

57. Neil Evernden, *The Natural Alien: Humankind and Environment* (Toronto: University of Toronto Press, 1985), p. 142.

58. International Union for Conservation of Nature and Natural Resources (IUCN) with the United Nations Environment Program (UNEP); the World Wildlife Fund (WWF) in collaboration with the Food and Agriculture Organization of the United Nations (FAO) and the United Nations Educational, Scientific, and Cultural Organization (UNESCO), *World Conservation Strategy: Living Resource Conservation for Sustainable Development* (IUCN-UNEP-WWF, 1980). I am indebted to Dr. John Middleton of Brock University's Institute for Environmental Policy, for pointing this example out to me.

59. IUCN, UNEP, and WWF, *Caring for the Earth: A Strategy for Sustainable Living: Summary* (Gland, Switzerland: October 1991), p. 4.

60. This example is reported in J. C. Dunstan, K. L. Jope, and G. M. Swan, "Why Sustainability?" *The George Wright Forum* 10, no. 4 (1993): 11–12, and in J. W. Thomas, *Forest Ecosystem Management: An Ecological, Economic and Social Assessment*, Report of the Forest Ecosystem Management Assessment Team, 1993.

61. Ibid., p. 1.
62. Ibid.
63. Ibid.
64. Ibid., p. 12.
65. Cited in World Commission on Environment and Development, *Our Common Future*, p. 115.
66. See, for example, an outstanding doctoral thesis recently defended in the Department of Philosophy, University of Toronto, on the theme of "Ecoholism and its Critics" by Pamela Mae Courtenay-Hall, August 1995. Courtenay-Hall develops a typography of ecoholist perspectives, and argues that such perspectives are "deeply problematic." She does not propose that ecoholism be abandoned, but, instead, that it be more carefully formulated, recognizing some of the philosophical pitfalls of previous versions.

Chapter 4.The Possibilities of Originative Thinking

1. Quoted from *Macleans*, 27 March 1995, p. 21.
2. Webster's defines the word "meditate" as "to engage in contemplation or reflection . . . to ponder over." (*Webster's Ninth New Collegiate Dictionary* [Springfield, Mass.: Merriam-Webster, 1985]). The implication could be, then, that Heidegger's concept of meditative thinking is simply an abstract "pondering over" or "contemplation" of highly speculative, metaphysical concepts. One thereby misses much of the essence of what Heidegger was hoping to communicate in his own, much broader understanding of meditative thinking.
3. When Heidegger describes meditative thinking in terms of a "releasement toward things" (*die Gelassenheit zu den Dingen*) and "openness to the mystery," the suggestion is that everyday modes of comportment toward the world are rethought from the ground up. These characteristics of meditation "grant us the possibility of dwelling in the world in a totally different way. They promise us a new ground and foundation upon which we can stand." Martin Heidegger, *Discourse on Thinking*, ed. John M. Anderson and E. Hans Freund (New York: Harper & Row, 1966), pp. 55, 56.
4. Heidegger writes of a great danger that "the approaching tide of technological revolution in the atomic age could so captivate, bewitch, dazzle and beguile man that calculative thinking may someday come to be accepted and practiced *as the only* way of thinking." Ibid., p. 56.
5. World Commission on Environment and Development, *Our Common Future* (New York: Oxford University Press, 1987), p. 37.
6. Ibid., p. 62.
7. Tony Hodge, Susan Holtz, Cameron Smith, and Kelley Hawke Baxter, eds., *Pathways to Sustainability: Assessing Our Progress, National Round Table Series on Sustainable Development* (Ottawa, Canada: NRTEE, 1995), pp. 6, 12. The National Round Table on the Environment and the Economy was created in 1988 as an independent agency, mandated by the Parliament of Canada to report directly to the prime minister on principles and practices of sustainable development in Canada. For further information, write to NRTEE, 1 Nicholas St., Suite 1500, Ottawa, Ontario, Canada. K1N 7B7.
8. See, for example, the recent $30 million program of support for advanced Canadian

eco-research that was mandated as explicitly "cross-disciplinary." As part of Canada's Green Plan, "Tri-Council" funding was provided through three major funding agencies to support ten interdisciplinary research projects across the country, as well as a number of university faculty chairs and doctoral fellowships.

9. Cf. David Wann, *Deep Design: Pathways to a Livable Future* (Washington, D.C.: Island Press, 1996), p. 5. "A recurring effort of deep designers is to find the best individual components for a design, then integrate those components into a system. No design is an island. Every design is a system that is part of a larger system."

10. See Peter Passell, "The Wealth of Nations: A 'Greener' Approach Turns List Upside Down," *New York Times*, 19 September 1995, B5.

11. See *Sustainable America: A New Consensus for Prosperity, Opportunity, and a Healthy Environment for the Future,* the President's Council on Sustainable Development (Washington, D.C.: Government Printing Office, February 1996).

12. Cf., for example, H. Daly and J. Cobb, *For the Common Good: Redirecting the Economy Toward Community, the Environment, and a Sustainable Future* (Toronto: Oxford University Press, 1989) where an Index of Sustainable Economic Welfare (ISEW) is proposed. See also L. R. Brown, "Illusion of Progress" in *State of the World*, ed. Lester R. Brown et al. (New York: W. W. Norton & Company, 1990). The Physical Quality of Life Index is found in M. D. Morris, *Measuring the Condition of the World's Poor: The Physical Quality of Life Index* (New York: Pergamon Press, 1979). More recently, the Human Development Index is another example where a somewhat more comprehensive measure of a population's well-being has been developed. See United Nations Development Program (UNDP), *Human Development Report* (New York: Oxford University Press, 1990, 1991, and 1992).

13. Parmenides, fragment 8, lines 1–6, cited in Martin Heidegger, *An Introduction to Metaphysica* (New York: Doubleday, 1961), pp. 81–82). For key texts, see G. S. Kirk and J. E. Raven, *The Presocratic Philosophers* (Cambridge: Cambridge University Press, 1957).

14. Cf. Plato's *Republic*, bk. VII, 514a ff.

15. Plato, *Republic*, bk. VII, 421c, trans. W. H. D. Rouse, *Great Dialogues of Plato* (New York: Mentor books, 1956).

16. Cf. Aristotle, *Metaphysics*, bk. I, chap. 2.

17. Aristotle, *Metaphysics*, bk. I, chap. 1, 981b, trans. Richard McKeon, *Introduction to Aristotle* (New York: The Modern Library, 1947).

18. Aristotle, *Metaphysics*, bk. I, chap. 1, 982a, cited in ibid.

19. *Metaphysics*, bk. I, chap. 1, 982b, cited in ibid.

20. St. Thomas Aquinas, *Exposition of Aristotle's Metaphysics*, in *The Pocket Aquinas*, ed. Vernon J. Burke (New York: Washington Square Press, 1960), p. 146.

21. G. W. F. Hegel, *Werke: Vollständige Ausgabe durch einen Verein von Freunden des Verewigten*, 2nd. ed. (Berlin: Duncker & Humblot, 1940) 6, p. 353ff. The full quotation reads: "Everything rational shows itself to be a threefold union or syllogism, in that each of the members takes the place both of one of the extremes and the mediating middle."

22. K. Koffka, *Principles of Gestalt Psychology* (London: Kegan Paul, 1935).

23. "Ecological thought, historically, has tended to be holistic in outlook. Ecology is the study of the *relationships* of organisms to one another and to the elemental environment." See J. Baird Callicott, "The Conceptual Foundations of the Land Ethic," in

Environmental Philosophy: From Animal Rights to Radical Ecology, ed. Michael E. Zimmerman, J. Baird Callicott, George Session, Karen Warren, and John Clark (Englewood Cliffs, N.J.: Prentice Hall, 1993), p. 121. See also S. H. Anderson, R. E. Beiswenger, and P. W. Purdom, *Environmental Science*, 3rd ed. (Columbus: Merill Publishing Company, 1987), p. 5 and Bernard J. Nebel and Richard T. Wright, *Environmental Science* (Englewood Cliffs, N.J.: Prentice Hall, 1993), p. 12.

24. Frederick Clements, *Research Methods in Ecology* (Lincoln: University of Nebraska Press, 1905). Quoted in J. R. Des Jardins, *Environmental Ethics* (Belmont, Calif.: Wadsworth, 1993), p. 182.

25. Barry Commoner, *The Closing Circle: Nature, Man, and Technology* (New York: Bantam Books, 1972), pp. 29–35, 188. Cited in Carolyn Merchant, *Radical Ecology: The Search for a Livable World* (New York: Routledge, 1992), p. 76.

26. Merchant, *Radical Ecology*.

27. Bernard J. Nebel and Richard T. Wright, *Environmental Science: The Way the World Works*, 4th ed. (Englewood Cliffs, N.J.: Prentice Hall, 1993), p. 17.

28. Ibid.

29. Robert Gifford, *Environmental Psychology: Principles and Practice* (Boston: Allyn and Bacon, 1987), p. 6. An updated version of this wonderful overview of the field is forthcoming.

30. Kenneth E. Goodpaster, "From Egoism to Environmentalism," in *Ethics and Problems of the Twenty-first Century*, ed. K. E. Goodpaster and K. M. Sayre (Notre Dame, Ind.: University of Notre Dame Press, 1979), p. 30.

31. Ibid., p. 33.

32. Mary Midgley, "Duties Concerning Islands," in *Environmental Ethics*, ed. Robert Elliot (Oxford: Oxford University Press, 1995), p. 91.

33. Ibid.

34. See Aldo Leopold, *A Sand County Almanac: And Essays on Conservation from Round River* (New York: Oxford University Press, 1949).

35. Ibid., p. 216.

36. Arne Naess, "Ecosophy T: Deep Versus Shallow Ecology," in *Environmental Ethics: Readings in Theory and Application*, ed. Louis P. Pojman (Boston: Jones and Bartlett Publishers, 1994), p. 107.

37. Ibid., p. 105.

38. Arne Naess, "The Shallow and the Deep, Long-Range Ecological Movement," in *Environmental Ethics*, p. 103.

39. The best survey of the field that I have run across is in the form of an as-yet unpublished Ph.D. thesis, completed in 1995 by Pamela Courtenay-Hall through the Department of Philosophy, University of Toronto, entitled "Ecoholism and its Critics." This amazing work manages to consolidate the critiques of ecoholism in a hefty, 378-page thesis that is nonetheless succinct, clear, and persuasive.

40. Carolyn Merchant is hardly the only author who makes such a claim. One other example comes from John Briggs, who uses virtually the same language. He writes about a "holism in which everything influences, or potentially influences, everything else—because everything is in some sense constantly interacting with everything else." See John Briggs, *Fractals: The Patterns of Chaos: Discovering a New Aesthetic of Art, Science, and Nature* (New York: Simon & Schuster, 1992), p. 21.

41. Cooper, "The Idea of Environment" in *The Environment in Question: Ethics and Global Issues*, ed. D. E. Cooper and Joy A. Palmer (London and New York: Routledge, 1992), p. 166.
42. Ibid.
43. Ibid.
44. Ibid., pp. 168–69.
45. Ibid., p. 170.
46. Kristin Shrader-Frechette, "Individualism, Holism, and Environmental Ethics" in *Ethics and the Environment* 1, no. 1 (1996): 61.
47. Ibid.
48. Ibid.
49. Ibid., pp. 61–62.
50. Tom Regan, *The Case for Animal Rights* (Berkeley: University of California Press, 1983), esp. pp. 361–62. See also Regan's "Ethical Vegetarianism and Commercial Animal Farming" in *Contemporary Moral Problems*, ed. J. E. White (St. Paul, Minn.: West Publishing, 1985), pp. 279–88.
51. J. Baird Callicott, "The Conceptual Foundations of the Land Ethic," in *In Defense of the Land Ethic* (Albany, N.Y.: State University of New York Press, 1989), p. 87.
52. See, for example, Michael P. Nelson, "Holists and Fascists and Paper Tigers . . . Oh My!" in *Ethics and the Environment* 1, no. 2 (1996): 113.
53. William Aiken, "Ethical Issues in Agriculture" in *Earthbound*, ed. Tom Reagan (New York: Random House, 1984), p. 269.
54. Editors' introduction to Jim Cheney's "Postmodern Environmental Ethics: Ethics as Bioregional Narrative" in Susan J. Armstrong and Richard G. Botzler, *Environmental Ethics: Divergence and Convergence* (New York: McGraw-Hill, 1993), p. 86.
55. John P. van Gigch, *Applied General Systems Theory* (New York: Harper & Row, 1974), p. 11.
56. Henk Tennekes, "The Limits of Science" in *Ecology, Technology, and Culture: Essays in Environmental Philosophy*, ed. Wim Zweers and Jan J. Boersema (Cambridge, England: The White Horse Press, 1994).
57. Ibid., p. 87.
58. Ibid., p. 74.
59. Ibid.
60. Ibid., p. 78.
61. Ibid., p. 75.
62. Ibid., p. 84.
63. Ibid., p. 81.
64. Martin Heidegger, *Basic Problems of Phenomenology* (Bloomington and Indianapolis: Indiana University Press, 1982), p. 165.
65. Henri Bortoft, "Dwelling in Nature" in David Seamon and Robert Mugerauer, *Dwelling, Place and Environment: Towards a Phenomenology of Person and World* (Netherlands: Martinus Nijhoff, 1985), p. 282ff.
66. Ibid., p. 286.
67. Ibid., p. 290.
68. Ibid.
69. Ibid., p. 293.

Chapter 5. Ontological Foundations of Environmental Thinking

1. Martin Heidegger, *The Basic Problems of Phenomenology*, trans. Albert Hofstadter (Bloomington and Indianapolis: Indiana University Press, 1982), p. 164.

2. William H. Ittelson, "Perception of the Large-scale Environment," in *Transactions of the New York Academy of Sciences* 32 (1970): 807–15; "Environmental Perception and Urban Experience," in *Environment and Behaviour* 10 (1978): 193–213.

3. Heidegger, *Basic Problems of Phenomenology*.

4. Ibid., p. 162.

5. Ibid.

6. Ibid., p. 164.

7. Martin Heidegger, *Being and Time*, trans. John Macquarrie and Edward Robinson (New York and Evanston: Harper & Row, 1962), p. 98.

8. Ibid.

9. Ibid.

10. Ibid.

11. Heidegger, *Basic Problems of Phenomenology*, p. 163.

12. Ibid.

13. For further discussion on the rich possibilities of reading specific elements of architectural design, see T. Thiis-Evanson, *Archetypes of Architecture* (Oslo: Norwegian University Press; New York: Oxford University Press, 1989).

14. Robert Gifford, *Environmental Psychology: Principles and Practice* (Newton, Mass.: Allyn and Bacon, 1987), p. 20.

15. See Henri Bortoft's *The Wholeness of Nature: Goethe's Way toward a Science of Conscious Participation in Nature* (New York: Lindisfarne Press, 1996).

16. The image is designed by Jackie Bortoft and is found in ibid., p. 50.

17. Ibid.

18. See part 3 in ibid.

19. Bortoft has a wonderful description of scientific findings, such as Galileo's discovery of the satellites of Jupiter or Copernicus's discovery of the earth rotating on its own axis and revolving around the sun. These examples are shown by Bortoft to have emerged, not simply because new sense data were presented to these scientists but rather, the organizing ideas brought to observational discoveries suggested new meanings and ultimately, radical interpretations of phenomena previously viewed from a different angle. See part 3 of ibid. and p. 131.

20. Heidegger, *Being and Time*, p. 99.

21. Heidegger, *Basic Problems of Phenomenology*, p. 164.

22. Heidegger writes that "temporality is the primordial 'outside-of-itself' in and for itself. We therefore call the phenomena of the future, the character of having been and the Present the 'ecstases' of temporality." *Being and Time*, p. 377.

23. Ibid., p. 402.

24. Ibid., p. 377. See also p. 375: "The primordial unity of the structure of care lies in temorality."

25. Webster's Ninth New Collegiate Dictionary defines eternity as "infinite time."

26. Heidegger, *Being and Time*, p. 400. "Tenses, like the other temporal phenomena of language . . . do not spring from the fact that discourse expresses itself 'also' about

'temporal processes,' processes encountered 'in time. . . . Discourse *in itself* is temporal."

27. Ibid., p. 377.

28. See Heidegger's "What is Metaphysics?" where he addresses the question: "What about Nothing?" *Existence and Being* (Chicago: Henry Regnery Company, 1949).

29. Heidegger, *Basic Problems of Phenomenology*, p. 300.

30. Ibid., pp. 299, 300.

31. I often challenge my students to give me an example of consciousness pure and simple, in the absence of intentional projection. The instance that they most often cite is of the state of meditation in some Eastern religions, where one aims to achieve a condition where consciousness is undirected toward anything in particular. I think that Heidegger's notion of transcendence, as ontologically grounded, can account for even this state of meditation. While not directed toward anything in particular, one's awareness presumably does not cease. That awareness continues to be temporally constituted and therefore, in some sense, is anticipatory and futural. If it were not, one would be dead!

32. Ibid., p. 299. Heidegger writes: "*Transcendere* means to step over; the transcendens, the transcendent, is that which oversteps as such. . . . The world is transcendent because, belonging to the structure of being-in-the-world, it constitutes stepping-over-to . . . as such. The Dasein itself oversteps in its being and thus is exactly *not the immanent*."

33. Heidegger, *Being and Time*, p. 279.

34. For more on this nothing of beholdenness, see Thomas Langan's *Being and Truth* (Columbia: University of Missouri Press, 1996).

35. Heidegger, *On Time and Being* (New York: Harper & Row, 1972), pp. 14, 15.

36. Ibid., p. 16.

37. By the end of the summer, the number of people charged for obstructing the logging bridge at Clayoquot Sound totaled eight hundred. See Alan Drengson and Duncan Taylor, "Shifting Values: Seeing Forests and Not Just Trees," in *Canadian Issues in Environmental Ethics*, ed. Alex Wellington, Allan Greenbaum, and Wesley Cragg (Peterborough, Ontario: Broadview Press, 1997), p. 35ff.

38. Ibid., p. 100.

39. Martin Heidegger, *An Introduction to Metaphysics* (New York: Doubleday & Company, 1961), pp. 11–12.

40. Ibid., p. 12.

41. Bruce V. Foltz, *Inhabiting the Earth: Heidegger, Environmental Ethics, and the Metaphysics of Nature* (Atlantic Highlands, N.J.: Humanities Press, 1995), p. 130. I recommend this book to the reader—particularly chapters 7 and 8 on "Heidegger's Deconstruction of the Metaphysics of Nature: Toward a New Topology of the Natural" and "Dwelling Poetically upon the Earth: Toward a New Environmental Ethic."

42. See Martin Heidegger, "Parmenides," *Gesamtausgabe*, II, Abt., Bd. 54 (Frankfurt: V. Klostermann, 1982), p. 211. See also ibid. p. 136f.

43. Martin Heidegger, "Building Dwelling Thinking," in *Poetry, Language, Thought* (New York: Harper & Row, 1971), p. 149.

44. Cf. Foltz, *Inhabiting the Earth*, p. 132ff.

45. When I find myself in a new wilderness environment for the first time, I can sometimes feel overwhelmed by the unknown elements to the point of feeling horror in the

face of the unpredictable. I know of cases where urban dwellers have completely lost their composure and experienced genuine terror in the face of the mystery of the wilderness. Such instances constitute for me a primordial plunge into a relation with the givenness of nature from which we are typically sheltered in our built environments. In a similar vein, I am reminded of the different personal reactions between my husband and me to a winter storm by the lake a few years ago. We battled huge winds and horizontally blown snows to make the five-minute walk to the lake. My husband stood beside the crashing waves and gale-force winds exhilarated by the power of nature. I stood in horror, contemplating the finitude of my existence and my sense of being powerless in this overwhelming setting. Nature experienced as mysterious can be exhilarating but it can be horrifying as well.

46. Reported in *The Economist*, 2 August 1997, p. 63.

47. Ibid., p. 64.

48. Heidegger distinguishes between his notion of the Same and identity. "The same is not the merely identical. In the merely identical, the difference disappears. In the same, difference appears." Instead of metaphysically contemplating "the unifying unity of perdurance," Heideger urges us to move beyond the theologic conception of unity and holistic thinking. See *Identity and Difference*, trans. J. Stambaugh (New York: Harper & Row, 1969).

49. World Commission on Environment and Development, *Our Common Future* (Oxford: Oxford University Press, 1987), p. 109.

50. Principle 7 of the Rio Declaration, approved by the United Nations Conference on Environment and Development in Rio de Janeiro, Brazil, June 3–14, 1992, and later endorsed by the 47th session of the United Nations General Assembly on December 22, 1992. Cited from Louis J. Pojman, *Environmental Ethics* (Boston: Jones and Barlett Publishers, 1994), p. 503.

51. Cited in the promotional literature for the ISEH, University of Guelph, Ontario, Canada.

52. See World Commission on Environment and Development, *Our Common Future*, pp. 11, 16–17, 54, 56, 96–7, 103, 105–6, 109, 183–84, 211, 231, 263.

53. David J. Rapport, "What Is Ecosystem Health?" in *Ecodecision* (winter 1997): 45.

54. Hans-Georg Gadamer, *The Enigma of Health: The Art of Healing in a Scientific Age*, trans. J. Gaiger and N. Walker (Stanford, Calif.: Stanford University Press, 1996). I review this book in further detail in *Humane Health Care International* 13, no. 2 (summer, 1997).

55. Gadamer, *The Enigma of Health*, p. 96.

56. Ibid., p. 43.

57. Ibid., p. 34.

58. Ibid., p. 73.

59. Ibid., p. 73.

60. Rapport, "What Is Ecosystem Health?," p. 46.

61. Ibid., p. 45.

62. I must say on this last point that the phenomenon of absence that is being described here is other than mere privation. A graduate student, apparently critical of Gadamer, raised an interesting example where, he felt, health is felt to be not absent but fully

present. The student felt that when he emerged from his fitness session, his whole sense of self was pervaded by a sense of the presence of well-being. Good health was not, thereby, taken for granted but celebrated in the fullness of this moment of vitality, vigor, and general elation. The presence of health that this student described was not, however, analogous to the appearance of a present-at-hand state. Indeed, I would say that the very presence of well-being exceeded his capacity to reduce it to such a state. Ontologically, just as the presence of good health signifies more than the present-at-hand representation of a delimited object, absence refers to more than merely the privative state of a present-at-hand object. The phenomenon of "absence" to which Gadamer is referring points to the withdrawal of Being itself that exceeds all attempts of reductionist, ontic categories.

Chapter 6. Ontology and Ethics

1. Thomas Langan, "Transcendence in the Philosophy of Heidegger," in *New Scholasticism* 32 (1958): 53–54.
2. Emmanuel Levinas, "Ethics as First Philosophy," cited in *The Continental Philosophy Reader*, ed. Richard Kearney and Mara Rainwater (London and New York: Routledge, 1996), p. 134.
3. Hodge's claim "is that Heidegger falls short of the possibilities of his own thought by proposing to retrieve the tradition and to step back into the ground of metaphysics, while failing to pose the correlative question: what is ethics? He fails to affirm the coterminous necessity of taking a step forward into the potentiality of ethics. I suggest that his Nazi adventure is a result of this failure." Joanna Hodge, *Heidegger and Ethics* (London and New York: Routledge, 1995), p. 3. The reader is referred to the appendix of this volume for some of my own thoughts on Heidegger's Nazi association.
4. Heidegger declares: "There is no problem more elementary and concrete than that of Being." See "A Cassirer-Heidegger Seminar," trans. C. H. Hamburg, *Philosophy and Phenomenological Research* 25 (1964): 217.
5. See L. Van de Water, who argues that Heidegger is misled in his critique of metaphysics—a critique that "causes him to fall into an empty and abstract 'Being'! As a disciple of Husserl, he intends to philosophize by starting merely from the things themselves, but in fact he does it in such a way that they ultimately escape him. . . . The final result of all this is that anything precise can no longer be said about Being. Even the word 'Being' is still too concrete, it is too much of a being; therefore, it is better to drop it. . . . Because this Being has neither name nor content, and is only itself, the Being of each being is likewise empty." "Being and Being Human: An Impasse in Heidegger's Thought?" in *International Philosophical Quarterly* 13 (spring 1973): 395–97.
6. Martin Heidegger, *Being and Time*, trans. J. Macquarrie and E. Robinson (New York: Harper & Row, 1962), pp. 29, and 193–94.
7. Ibid., p. 58.
8. Joanna Hodge, *Heidegger and Ethics*, p. 26. A helpful explanation of the difference between ontology and the ontic realm is also articulated by J. L. Mehta. Truth in the ontic sense is understood as the "pre-predicative manifestness of essents, in which propositional truth is rooted." Ontology concerns "the overtness of Being which

renders ontic truth itself possible." See *The Philosophy of Martin Heidegger* (New York: Harper & Row, 1971), p. 89.

9. Martin Heidegger, *The Basic Problems of Phenomenology*, trans. Albert Hofstadter (Bloomington and Indianapolis: Indiana University Press, 1982), p. 19.

10. Ibid., p. 327.

11. Martin Heidegger, *Identity and Difference*, trans. Joan Stambaugh (New York: Harper & Row, 1969), pp. 68–69.

12. Martin Heidegger, "The Origin of a Work of Art," in *Poetry, Language, Thought*, trans. Albert Hofstadter (New York: Harper & Row, 1971), p. 39.

13. Martin Heideger, "The Thing," in *Poetry, Language, Thought*, p. 174.

14. Ibid., p. 181.

15. Ibid., p. 170.

16. Ibid., p. 181.

17. Rubert Mugerauer, *Interpretations on Behalf of Place: Environmental Displacements and Alternative Responses* (New York: State University of New York Press, 1994), p. 108.

18. Ibid.

19. Ibid., p. 114.

20. Ibid.

21. Heidegger, *Identity and Difference*, p. 69.

22. Ibid.

23. Gaston Bachelard's exploration of the phenomenology of roundness in his *Poetics of Space* is not unrelated, in my view, to Heidegger's notion of circling. Citing figures from Jaspers to Van Gogh, Bachelard explores how, in order to see that "Being is round," one cannot argue for this claim in the mode of mathetmatician, but instead, one must do so as a "dreamer of words." For a more extensive discussion of converging images of Bachelard and Heidegger, see my *The Event of Death: A Phenomenological Enquiry* (The Hague: Martinus Nijhoff, 1987), p. 317ff.

24. Heidegger's full quotation is a reference to the hermeneutic circle of understanding: "In the question of the meaning of Being, there is no 'circular reasoning' but rather, a remarkable 'relatedness backward or forward' which what we are asking about (Being) bears to the inquiry itself as a mode of Being of an entity." See *Being and Time*, p. 28.

25. Heidegger, "The Origin of the World of Art," p. 77.

26. Ibid., p. 62.

27. Ibid., p. 63.

28. Ibid.

29. Ibid.

30. Ibid., pp. 69–70.

31. Martin Heidegger, "Language," in *Poetry, Language, Thought*, p. 208.

32. Ibid., p. 209.

33. Ibid., p. 207.

34. Heidegger, "The Thing," p. 174.

35. Heidegger, *Being and Time*, p. 37.

36. Ibid.

37. Ibid.

38. Martin Heidegger, "Letter on Humanism," in *Basic Writings*, ed. David Farrell Krell (New York: Harper & Row, 1977), p. 228.

39. Heidegger, *Being and Time*, p. 364.

40. Ibid., p. 59. Heidegger tells us that the expression of "descriptive phenomenology: is "at bottom, tautological."

41. Plato *The Republic*, bk. I, 352c. Translated by W. H. D. Rouse, *Great Dialogues of Plato* (New York: The New American Library of World Literature, 1956).

42. Martin Heidegger, "The Way Back into the Ground of Metaphysics," in *Existentialism: From Dostoevsky to Sartre*, ed. Walter Kaufmann (New York: The World Publishing Company, 1956), p. 215.

43. See *Die Grundbegriffe der Metaphysik. Welt—Endlichkeit—Einsamkeit* (1929–30. *Gesamtausgabe*, II. Abteilung, Band 29/30, ed. Friedrich-Wilhelm von Hermann (Frankfurt: Klostermann, 1983), p. 54.

44. Bruce V. Foltz, *Inhabiting the Earth: Heidegger, Environmental Ethics, and the Metaphysics of Nature* (Atlantic Highlands, N.J.: Humanities Press, 1995), p. 168. Foltz quotes Heidegger from *Heraklit*: "Ēthos is the bearing within all the comportment that belongs to this abode in the midst of entities."

45. Heidegger, "Letter on Humanism," p. 233.

46. Ibid., p. 232.

47. Ibid., pp. 234–35. Final italic emphasis mine.

48. Joanna Hodge, *Heidegger and Ethics*, p. 18.

49. Jean-Paul Sartre, "Existentialism is a Humanism," in Kaufmann, *Existentialism: From Dostoevsky to Sartre*, pp. 295–98.

50. Ibid., p. 296.

51. Ibid.

52. Ibid.

53. Heidegger, "Letter on Humanism," p. 231.

54. On the other hand, neither should values be seen as free-floating and independent of facts. For a fascinating debate on these and related issues, see Kristin Shrader-Frechette, "Ecological Risk Assessment and Ecosystem Health: Fallacies and Solutions," in *Ecosystem Health* 3, no. 2 (June 1997): 73–81; Bryan Norton, "Relativism, Realism, and Ecological Risk: A Response to Shrader-Frechette," in *Ecosystem Health* 3, no. 3 (September 1997): 129–32; J. Baird Callicott, "Fallacious Fallacies and Nonsolutions: Comment on Kristen Shrader-Frechette's 'Ecological Risk Assessment and Ecosystem Health: Fallacies and Solutions'" in ibid., pp. 133–35.

55. Cited in *Eco-health: News and Views* 3, no. 2 (fall 1997), the Newsletter of the International Society for Ecosystem Health, in their report on the third biennial symposium of the International Society for Ecosystem Health, hosted by the University of California, Davis, in Sacramento, 14–16 September 1998.

56. Federation of Canadian Municipalities, *The Ecological City: Canada's Overview* (Ottawa: Canada Mortgage and Housing Corporation), May 1995.

57. Heidegger, "Letter on Humanism," p. 228.

58. Ibid.

59. Recall the comments of Tom Regan who suggests that "the development of what can properly be called an environmental ethic requires that we postulate inherent value in nature"; otherwise, we allow ourselves to slip into a "management ethic" for the "use

of the environment," rather than an ethic of the environment per se. See "The Nature and the Possibility of an Environmental Ethic," *Environmental Ethics* 3 (1981), p. 34.

60. John Stuart Mill, *Utilitarianism* (New York: Bobbs-Merrill, 1957).

61. For example, as an alternative to hedonistic utilitarianism that validates pleasure as the only good valued for its own sake, preference utilitarians emphasize human desires instead. The latter is, clearly, more closely allied to the economic theory of the free market, particularly in environmental matters, when one sets out to investigate human values in terms of willingness-to-pay. For example, in matters of environmental cleanups, the issue is not so much what brings the greatest pleasure but, rather, what do you *want* or *prefer* and how much are you willing to pay for it?

62. Werner Marx, *Towards a Phenomenological Ethics: Ethos and the Life-World*, trans. Ashaf Noor (New York: State University of New York Press, 1992), p. 43.

Chapter 7. The Emergence of Place

1. Joseph R. Des Jardins publishes a popular and informative introduction to the field and his description of environmental ethics is not uncommon. He writes that "in general, environmental ethics presents and defends a systematic and comprehensive account of the moral relations between human beings and their *natural* environment" (italics mine). See *Environmental Ethics: An Introduction to Environmental Philosophy* (Belmont, Calif.: Wadsworth Publishing company, 1993), p. 13.

2. Comments presented to the Great Lakes Megalopolis Symposion, Toronto City Hall, Canada, 24–27 March 1975.

3. John Muir, *Our National Parks* (Madison: University of Wisconsin Press, 1981), p. 1.

4. Shane Phelan, "Intimate Distance: The Dislocation of Nature in Modernity," in *In the Nature of Things: Language, Politics, and the Environment*, Jane Bennett and William Chaloupka, eds. (Minneapolis: University of Minnesota Press, 1993), p. 45. Phelan does not himself uphold the view quoted but discusses it in terms of "several meanings of nature" in political theory.

5. Edward Casey, *Getting Back into Place: Toward a Renewed Understanding of the Place-World* (Bloomington and Indianapolis: Indiana University Press, 1993), p. 180.

6. Harvey Cox recalls vividly a conversation that he had in 1964 with one of the women who had survived the Nazi destruction of the tiny village of Lidice in Czechoslovakia. "The Germans had arbitrarily picked this hamlet to be the example of what would happen to other villages if deeds like the assassination of Reinhard Heydrich recurred. They came into the town, shot all the men over twelve, then shipped the wives to one concentration camp and the children to another. They burned the village completely, destroyed all the trees and foliage and plowed up the ground. Significantly, they demanded that on all maps of Czechoslovakia the town of Lidice must be erased. . The woman survivor confessed to me that despite the loss of her husband and the extended separation from her children, the most shocking blow of all was to return to the crest of the hill overlooking Lidice at the end of the war—and to find nothing there, not even ruins." See Harvey Cox, "The Restoration of a Sense of Place: A Theological Reflection on the Visual Environment," *Religious Education*, 11 January 1966, reprinted in *Ekistics* (1968): 422–24.

7. Philosopher Don Ihde brilliantly shows how an instrumentally embodied science can

bring us close to an image of the world as a whole that is more than a mere reduction of world to "picture," as Heidegger contended. Global imaging technologies may distance us from the world if the planet is simply represented as an ontic entity. However, if those technologies are capable of mediating bodily perceptions through instrumentation, it becomes possible not simply to "look at a picture" but to "look through the image" and encounter the planet itself as home through a "seeing which understands." See Don Ihde, "Whole Earth Measurements," presented to the Society for Phenomenology and Existential Philosophy Annual Meeting, 1995; published in *Philosophy Today* 41, no. 1 (spring 1997): 128–34. Other works by Ihde include *Technology and the Lifeworld* (Indiana University Press, 1990) and *Philosophy of Technology* (Paragon House, 1993).

8. World Commission on Environment and Development, *Our Common Future* (Oxford: Oxford University Press, 1987), p. 235.

9. In his ground-breaking work on place, Philosopher Edward Casey raises some doubt as to whether the phrase "wild places" is an unwarranted oxymoron. "Is 'wilderness' a cultural category or an abiding independent reality?" I suspect that wilderness invokes both responses. For the moment, let me say that place will be understood as neither a subjectivistic, cultural projection on the world nor an objectivistic, independent reality. Phenomenology demands that place not be reduced to either subjective or objective categories. See *Getting Back into Place*, p. 191.

10. Cf. David Seamon, "Phenomenology and Environment-Behavior Research: in *Advances in Environment, Behavior, and Design*, vol. 1, ed. Ervin H. Zube and Gary T. Moore (New York: Plenum, 1987), p. 10.

11. Cf. Edward Relph, *Places and Placelessness* (London: Pion, 1976); Robert Mugerauer, *Interpretations on Behalf of Place* (New York: State University of New York Press, 1994); Edward Casey, *Getting Back into Place* and *The Fate of Place* (Berkeley: University of California Press, 1997). See also Michael Hough, *Out of Place: Restoring Identity to the Regional Landscape* (New Haven and London: Yale University Press, 1990); Doreen Massey, *Space, Place, and Gender* (Minneapolis: University of Minnesota Press, 1994); John Brinckerhoff Jackson, *A Sense of Place, a Sense of Time* (New Haven and London: Yale University Press, 1994).

12. See, for example, *Places, A Quarterly Journal of Environmental Design*, as well as *Ethics, Place, and Environment*, commenced in 1998 through Carfax Publishing Limited in Oxford, U.K. (Information is available on the World Wide Web at: http://www.carfax.co.uk/epe-ad.htm.) One example of a recent conference session convened on the theme of place includes a workshop on "Rethinking Place and Placelessness: Phenomenological Reflections" at the Environmental Design Research Association (EDRA) Annual Meeting in Montreal, Canada, 7–11 May, 1997).

13. G. Clay, "Sense and Nonsense of Place," in *Landscape Architecture* 32 (1983), 110–13.

14. Amos Rapoport, "A Critical Look at the Concept 'Place,'" *The National Geographic Journal of India* 40 (1994).

15. Casey, *Getting Back into Place*, p. 19.

16. Ibid., pp. 17–18.

17. Harvey Cox points out how, on a psychological level, this truism becomes evident in studies of individuals who are deprived, even for a short time, of sense perception

and environmental objects to which to relate. Studies indicate that the individual "quickly loses his touch with reality and degenerates into a quasi-catalyptic state. . . . This astonishingly rapid disintegration of personality has been observed, for example, in the so called 'sensory deprivation' laboratory of Dr. Abraham Maslow of Brandeis University. His experiments with many subjects seem to indicate that the normal functioning of personality depends on the subject's half-conscious awareness of a background of sensory items of orientation. Ordinarily, a person is not aware of this background, but when it is taken away or markedly altered, his perception of reality is dangerously undermined." See Cox, *Restoration of a Sense of Place*, p. 422.

18. Ibid;, pp. 13, 15.

19. Martin Heidegger, "The Way Back into the Ground of Metaphysics," in *Existentialism from Dostoevsky to Sartre*, ed. Walter Kaufmann (New York: The World Publishing company, 1956), p. 214.

20. Heidegger explains that "the proposition 'man exists' means: man is that being whose Being is distinguished by the open-standing standing-in in the unconcealedness of Being, from Being, in Being." Ibid.

21. Gaston Bachelard, *The Poetics of Space*, trans. Maria Jolas (Boston: Beacon Press, 1964), p. 137.

22. Martin Heidegger, "Building Dwelling Thinking," in *Poetry, Language, Thought*, trans. Albert Hofstadter (New York: Harper & Row, 1971), p. 148.

23. See, for example, Webster's Ninth New Collegiate Dictionary's definition of "build" as "to cause to be constructed." (Springfield, Mass.: Merriam-Webster, 1985).

24. As architect Philip Johnson acknowledges, "the job of the architect is to create beautiful buildings. That's all." Cited in Robert Gifford, *Environmental Psychology: Principles and Practice* (Boston: Allyn & Bacon, 1987), p. 345.

25. Cited in ibid., p. 340.

26. Environmental psychologist Robert Sommer acknowledges that "social design," rather than traditional, merely formal design, "is working with people rather than for them; involving people in the planning and management of the spaces around them; educating them to use the environment wisely and creatively to achieve a harmonious balance between the social, physical and natural environment." Cited in ibid., p. 342.

27. See the work of Constantinos Doxiadis who maintained that the basic "ekistic" functions, present in every human settlement, included social, cultural, economic, technological, and regulatory elements. *Ekistics: An Introduction to the Science of Human Settlements* (New York: Oxford University Press, 1968).

28. Cited in Christian Norbert-Schulz, *Meaning in Western Architecture* (New York: Rizzoli, 1974), p. 127.

29. Cited in Ellen Eve Frank, *Literary Architecture: Essays Toward a Tradition* (Berkeley: University of California Press, 1979), pp. 160–61.

30. Heidegger, "Language," in *Poetry, Language, Thought*, p. 206.

31. Cf. Heidegger, "What are Poets For?" in *Poetry, Language, Thought*.

32. Heidegger, "Building Dwelling Thinking," pp. 149–50.

33. Christian Norbert-Schulz, *The Concept of Dwelling: On the Way to Figurative Architecture* (New York: Rizzoli, 1985), p. 12.

34. Heidegger, "Building Dwelling Thinking," p. 149.

35. Bachelard, *Poetics of Space*, p. 186.

36. Heidegger writes: "The Greeks early called this emerging and rising in itself and in all things *physis*. It clears and illuminates, also, that on which and in which man bases his dwelling. We call this ground the *earth*." See "The Origin of the World of Art," in *Poetry, Language, Thought*, p. 42.

37. Ibid.

38. Ibid.

39. Jay Macpherson, "Cold Stone," in *An Anthology of Versa*, ed. Roberta A. Charlesworth and Dennis Lee (Toronto: Oxford University Press, 1964), p. 174.

40. Yi-Fu Tuan, *Space and Place: The Perspective of Experience* (Minneapolis: University of Minnesota Press, 1977), p. 107.

41. Ibid.

42. Rudyard Kipling, "Cities and Thrones and Powers," in Charlesworth and Lee, p. 208.

43. Heidegger, "The Origin of the Work of Art," pp. 39, 36.

44. Ibid., p. 42.

45. Ibid.

46. Heidegger, "Building Dwelling Thinking," p. 149.

47. See L. J. Karmel, "Effects of Windowless Classroom Environment on High School Students," in *Perceptual and Motor Skills* 20 (1965): 277–78.

48. Gifford, *Environmental Psychology*, p. 289.

49. See J. H. Heerwagen and G. H. Orians, "Adaptations to Windowlessness: A Study of the Use of Visual Decor in Windowed and Windowless Offices," in *Environment and Behavior* 18 (1986): 623–39. There have been numerous studies, leading to the general conclusion that people prefer settings with windows. See T. Ruys, "Windowless Offices," in *Man-Environment Systems* 1 (1970): 49. L. J. Karmel, "Effects of Windowless Classroom Environment on High School Students" in *Perceptual and Motor Skills*, pp. 277–78. For studies documenting the therapeutic effects of hospital windows, where patients with pleasing landscape views reported shorter stays, lower doses of painkillers, and generally fewer complaints to nurses, see R. S. Ulrich, "View through a Window May Influence Recovery from Surgery," *Science* 224 (1984): 420–21.

50. See Stevenson Swanson, "To Bring Back Starry Skies, Local Ordinances Restrict Excess Illumination," in *Washington Post* 25 December 1997, A19.

51. Heidegger, "Building Dwelling Thinking," p. 150.

52. For a discussion of how a community is able to preserve the interplay of mystery and disclosure to its advantage, see my article "Phenomenological Encounters with Place: Cavtat to Square One," *Journal of Environmental Psychology* 18 (1998): 31–44.

53. Heidegger, "Building Dwelling Thinking."

54. Casey, *Getting Back into Place*, pp. 6, 9.

55. Ibid., p. 7.

56. Ibid.

57. Ibid., pp. 13, 21.

58. Ibid., p. 13.

59. Ibid., p. 10.

60. Ibid., p. 12. Further discussion of Augustine recurs toward the end of the chapter as well.

61. For a discussion of how time is concretized in different spatial designs, see my preliminary remarks in "Temporality and Architecture: A Phenomenological Reading of Built Form," in *Journal of Architectural and Planning Research* 11, no. 3 (autumn, 1994): 211–25.

62. Frank, *Literary Architecture*, p. 225.

63. D. Parkes and N. Thrift, "Putting Time in Its Place," in *Making Sense of Time*, ed. T. Carlstein, D. Parkes, and N. Thrift (London: Edward Arnold Ltd., 1978), p. 119.

64. For a discussion of time as a collection of now-points, see Martin Heidegger, *Being and Time*, trans. J. Macquarrie and E. Robinson (New York and Evanson: Harper & Row, 1962), pp. 475ff.

65. Casey, *Getting Back into Place*, p. 11.

66. Ibid., p. 20. Of course, Casey carefully avoids the hypostatization of place that this phrase may suggest.

67. It occurs to me that, to Casey's credit, we must acknowledge that the very notion of horizon is, in some sense, placial. At the same time, as I intend to show, time and place must be seen to be interwoven, if they are understood ontologically. In other words, neither time nor place can stand alone but they belong together in their very essence. I will return to this discussion shortly.

68. René Dubos, *Celebrations of Life* (New York: McGraw-Hill, 1981), p. 37.

69. Heidegger, *Being and Time*, p. 377.

70. John Brinckerhoff Jackson, professor of landscape studies, agrees that time and movement are of increasing importance in western society, as less significance is attached to concepts of place and permanence. For a collection of essays on the vernacular landscape of parking lots, suburban garages, and roads, as well as a discussion of changing dwelling forms in New Mexico, see *A Sense of Place, A Sense of Time* (New Haven, Conn.: Yale University Press, 1994).

71. Casey, *Getting Back into Place*, p. 289.

72. Ibid., p. 288.

73. Ibid.

74. *Webster's Ninth New Collegiate Dictionary*, p. 1129.

75. Heidegger writes: "Dasein is essentially not a Being-present-at-hand; and its 'spatiality' cannot signify anything like occurrence at a position in 'world-space.'" See *Being and Time*, p. 138.

76. Ibid., p. 138ff.

77. Ibid., p. 146.

78. Ibid.

79. Ibid.

80. Ibid.

81. Ibid., p. 136. The translators of *Being and Time* explain that they are translating *Gegend* as "region," although no English word quite corresponds to the German original. "Whereabouts" comes closer in meaning but it is not incorporated in the English translation because "region" is less awkward and more familiar to most readers.

82. Heidegger, "Building Dwelling Thinking," pp. 156–57.

83. Ibid., p. 157.

84. Pierre-Jean Jouve, *Lyrique*, cited in Gaston Bachelard, *The Poetics of Space*, p. 211.

85. See, for example, *Being and Time*, where he writes that "Being-in . . . is a state of Dasein's Being; it is an *existentiale*. So one cannot think of it as the Being-present-at-hand of some corporeal Thing (such as the human body) 'in' an entity which is present-at-hand" (p. 79).

86. It is true that sometimes we feel that we can have "eyes at the back of our heads" but we also instinctively recognize the predominance of our forward-facing stance in such cases as in elevators, when we typically face the doors instead of turning our backs to them.

87. Casey deliberates at length on "The Body in Place" in part 2 of *Getting Back into Place* and I refer the reader to his third and fourth chapters for a detailed discussion on directions and dimensions. I similarly recommend a doctoral thesis, defended 30 May 1997 at the University of Toronto, by David Morris, entitled *Sense of Space: An Essay on Spatial Perception and Embodiment in the Spirit of Merleau-Ponty's Phenomenology of Perception*.

88. Joseph Grange, "Place, Body, and Situation" in *Dwelling, Place, and Environment: Towards a Phenomenology of Person and World*, ed. David Seamon and Robert Mugerauer (Dordrecht: Martinus Nijhoff Publishers, 1985), p. 74. This chapter as a whole is a brilliant exposition of body as *flesh*.

89. The phenomenologist who has written most eloquently and extensively on lived space and embodiment is Maurice Merleau-Ponty, especially in his *Phenomenology of Perception*, trans. Colin Smith (New York: Humanities Press, 1962). Also, it is Gabriel Marcel who writes: "My body is *my* body just in so far as I do *not* consider it in this detached fashion, do not put a gap between myself and it. To put this point in another way, my body is mine in so far as for me my body is not an object, but rather, I *am* my body." See *The Mystery of Being*, vol. 1, trans. G. S. Fraser (Chicago: Henry Regnery, 1960), p. 123; and for a lengthier discussion of the distinction between "being" and "having," see *Être et avoir* (Fernand Aubier: Editions Montaigne, 1935).

90. Quoted in *Neighbourhood, City, and Metropolis*, ed. R. Gutman and D. Popenoe (New York: Random House, 1970), p. 710.

91. Similar accounts of the force of potential or actual displacement are numerous within the literature. In Canada, a famous incident occurred several decades ago in Africville, Nova Scotia, when buildings were leveled to the ground in the forced relocation of an entire community of predominently black people whose place was similarly labeled by politicians as a "slum." The extent of loss of dignity and direction of members of the community are brilliantly portrayed in a 1991 National Film Board of Canada documentary entitled *Remember Africville* (order # C9191 086). The film grew out of an exhibit "Africville: A spirit That Lives On" and a conference "Africville: Lessons for the Future" held at Mount Saint Vincent University, 1989. A doctoral thesis, referenced earlier, is also particularly insightful in its depiction of the meaning of loss of place. See Louise Million's "It was Home: A Phenomenology of Place and Involuntary Displacement as Illustrated by the Forced Dislocation of Five Southern Alberta Families in the Oldman River Dam Flood Area" (Ph.D. diss., Saybrook Institute, California, 1992).

92. Cited in Julian Burger, *First Peoples: a Future for the Indigenous World* (New York: Doubleday, 1990), p. 122.

93. Ibid.

94. Ibid., p. 126.

95. Ibid., p. 32.

96. See Dolores Hayden, *The Power of Place: Urban Landscapes as Public History* (Cambridge: MIT Press, 1995).

97. Quotation from Kenneth T. Jackson, *Crabgrass Frontier: The Suburbanization of the United States* (New York: Oxford University Press, 1985). See also Sim Van der Ryn, *Communities: A New Design Synthesis for Cities, Suburbs, and Towns* (San Francisco: Sierra Club Books, 1986); and Peter Calthorpe's *The Next American Metropolis: Ecology, Community, and the American Dream* (New York: Princeton Architectural Press, 1993).

98. Recall the earlier reference in chapter 1 to the Canadian Institute of Planners' call to "find out why people prefer low density suburbs." *Reflections on Sustainable Planning* (Ottawa: Canadian Institute of Planners, 1990).

99. Recgnizing the diversity of actual built settlements that fall into the category of suburbs, I use the latter term cautiously. Although some theorists have tried to evolve universal definitions of suburbia, these definitions often suffer, precisely because they are insensitive to the diversity of forms that suburbs can take. A definition that appeals to me because of its breadth is one supplied by Kenneth Jackson, who writes: "suburbia is both a planning type and a state of mind based on imagery and symbolism" (4–5). Jackson explores this vision in his *Crabgrass Frontier.* .

100. See, for example, Brian Berry's catalog of cultural preferences of suburbanites, found in *The Human Consequences of Urbanization* (New York: St. Martin's Press, 1973).

101. Jackson, *Crabgrass Frontier.*

102. See Dolores Hayden, *Redesigning the American Dream: The Future of Housing, Work, and Family Life* (New York: W. W. Norton and Company, 1984).

103. Ibid.

104. Bachelard, *Poetics of Space*, pp. 4–5.

105. Ibid., p. 7.

106. See "The Phenomenology of Automobility," in Peter Freund and George Martin, *The Ecology of the Automobile* (Montreal: Black Rose Books, 1993), esp. p. 99.

107. Bachelard, *Poetics of Space.*

108. "Afterword," in *The Human Experience of Space and Place*, ed. Ann Buttimer and David Seamon (New York: St. Martin's Press, 1980, p. 194.

109. Mick Smith, "The Myth of Postmodernism," In *Postmodern Environmental Ethics*, ed. Max Oelschlaeger (New York: State University of New York Press, 1995), p. 265. The chapter is a thought-provoking reply to Jim Cheney's similarly engrossing "Postmodern Environmental Ethics: Ethics as Bioregional Narrative," found in the same volume.

110. Cited in Ellen Eve Frank, *Literary Architecture: Essays Toward a Tradition* (Berkeley: University of California Press, 1979), p. 81.

111. Bachelard, *Poetics of Space*, p. 13.

112. Ibid., p. 35.

113. Heidegger, "Building Dwelling Thinking," p. 147.

114. Casey, *Getting Back into Place*, p. 300.

115. Heidegger, *Being and Time*, p. 140.

116. Casey, *Getting Back into Place*, p. 63.

117. Heidegger, *Being and Time*, p. 139.
118. Grange, "Place, Body, and Situation,". 73.
119. Ibid.
120. Ibid.

Chapter 8. Place-Based Ethics

1. Mick Smith, "Against the Enclosure of the Ethical Commons: Radical Environmentalism as an 'Ethics of Place,'" in *Environmental Ethics* 19, no. 4 (winter 1997): 353.
2. A book that brought this issue of endocrine modulators to public attention is *Our Stolen Future* by Theo Colborn, Dianne Dumanoski, and John Peterson Myers (New York: Penguin Books, 1996). Some articles with general discussion of the issue include the following: Stephen H. Safe, "Environmental and Dietary Estrogens and Human Health: Is there a Problem?" in *Environmental Health Perspectives* 103, no. 4 (1995): 346–51; John Heinze, "Hormone Mimics: Health and Environment" in *Chemical Times and Trends* 19, no. 3 (1996): 42–46.
3. Sheila Jasanoff, "Acceptable Evidence in a Pluralistic Society," in *Acceptable Evidence: Science and Values in Risk Management*, ed. Deborah G. Mayo and Rachelle D. Hollander (New York: Oxford University Press, 1991), p. 29. I highly recommend this book to the reader who is interested in how ethics plays a central role in decision making when scientific evidence is inconclusive, particularly in the areas of environmental risk assessment and management.
4. See "Development and the Environment," *The Economist*, 21 March 1998, p. 64ff.
5. David M. Smith, "Geography and Moral Philosophy: Some Common Ground," in *Ethics, Place, and Environment* 1, no. 1 (March 1998): 29.
6. Jim Cheney, "Postmodern Environmental Ethics: Ethics as Bioregional Narrative" in *Postmodern Environmental Ethics*, ed. Max Oelschlaeger (New York: State University of New York Press, 1995), p. 29. Holmes Rolston III, "The Human Standing in Nature: Storied Fitness in the Moral Observer," in *Values and Moral Standing*, ed. Wayne Sumner, Donald Callen, and Thomas Attig (Bowling Green, Ohio: The Applied Philosophy Program, Bowling State University, 1986).
7. Arran Gare, "MacIntyre, Narratives, and Environmental Ethics," in *Environmental Ethics* 20, no. 1 (spring 1998): 3.
8. Ibid., p. 4. Gare credits Ulrich Beck for this image of bicycle and jet. See Ulrich Beck, "From Industrial Society to Risk Society," *Cultural Theory and Cultural Change*, ed. Mike Featherstone (London: Sage, 1992), p. 106.
9. Recent articles address environmentalism as it impacts on feminist issues, economics, theology, geography, and psychology. See volume 19, no. 3, fall 1997 and volume 20, no. 1., spring 1998.
10. The University of Toronto, for example, offers second and third year undergraduate courses in environmental ethics, whose enrollments consist sometimes of over 80% non-philosophy specialists. A graduate course in environmental philosophy is cross-listed in the Department of Philosophy and the Institute for Environmental Studies. Information on other courses in this field is available through the website of the course syllabi, provided by the International Society for Environmental Ethics.

11. Gare. "MacIntyre, Narratives, and Environmental Ethics."

12. The debate about moral monism versus pluralism was initiated principally through Christopher Stone's book *Earth and Other Ethics: The Case for Moral Pluralism* (New York: Harper & Row, 1987).

13. Christopher D. Stone, "Moral Pluralism and the Course of Environmental Ethics," in *Postmodern Environmental Ethics*, p. 253.

14. Ibid., p. 251.

15. Cf. Joseph R. DesJardins, *Environmental Ethics*, 2nd ed. (Belmont, Calif.: Wadsworth Publishing company, 1997), p. 250.ff.

16. Cf. Hans-Georg Gadamer, *The Enigma of Health: The Art of Healing in a Scientific Age*, trans. G. Gaiger and N. Walker (Stanford, Calif.: Stanford University Press, 1996).

17. Christopher D. Stone, "Moral Pluralism," p. 257.

18. Holmes Rolston III, *Environmental Ethics: Duties to and Values in the Natural World* (Philadelphia: Temple University Press, 1988), p. 2.

19. Holmes Rolston III, "The Human Standing in Nature: Stories Fitness in the Moral Observer," in *Values and Moral Standing*, Wayne Sumner, Donald Callen, and Thomas Attig, eds., p. 98.

20. The distinction was formalized by philosopher David Hume, *A Treatise on Human Nature* (London: Oxford University Press, 1749) 3, part 1, sect. 1. More recent, twentieth-century arguments advancing these ideas are found in G. E. Moore, *Principia Ethica* (London: Cambridge University Press, 1903).

21. One might make a case, for instance, that Aldo Leopold's land ethic commits this fallacy, inasmuch as we are told that "a thing is right when it tends to preserve the integrity, stability and beauty of the biotic community. It is wrong when it tends otherwise." Here, the ethical and natural intertwine. See A. Leopold, *Sand County Almanac with Essays on Conservation from Round River* (New York: Oxford University Press, 1949).

22. Calvin O. Schrag, *The Self after Postmodernity* (New Haven, Conn.: Yale University Press, 1997), pp. 8–9. This book is a thought-provoking and carefully constructed argument that I enthusiastically recommend to readers who are interested in exploring the notion of a self that is a "response both to the discourse of modernity and to the postmodern challenge."

23. Ibid., p. 31.

24. Cf. Aristotle's *Nicomachean Ethics* I, 4. "[A]ll knowledge and every pursuit aims at some good, what it is that we say political science aims at and what is the highest of all goods achievable by action."

25. Hans-Georg Gadamer, *Truth and Method* (New York: The Seabury Press, 1975), p. 280.

26. Joseph J. Kockelmans, "The Foundations of Morality and the Human Sciences," in *Foundations of Morality, Human Rights, and the Human Sciences*, ed. Anna-Teresa Tymieniecka and Calvin O. Schrag (Dordrecht: D. Reidel Publishing Company, 1983), p. 381.

27. Ibid.

28. Ibid., p. 382.

29. Ibid.

30. Cf. in particular Eugene T. Gendlin, "Process Ethics and the Political Question" in *The Moral Sense in the Communal Significance of Life* (Dordrecht: D. Reidel Publishing Company, 1986), p. 265ff.

31. Ibid., p. 265.

32. Ibid., pp. 265–66.

33. Ibid., p. 267.

34. Ibid.

35. Ibid.

36. Ibid., p. 274–75.

37. Hans-Georg Gadamer, *Truth and Method*, p. 284.

38. The craftsman who produces his craft in the manner of a work of art is, presumably, not the subject of Gadamer's argument here. Rather, I assume that he is referring to the technician who is able to assemble an object by following a manual of instructions and the objects themselves could be duplicated by anyone following such a manual.

39. Hans-Georg Gadamer, *Truth and Method*, p. 286.

40. Ibid., p. 284.

41. Ibid., p. 286.

42. Ibid.

43. Eugene T. Gendlin, "Process Ethics," p. 275.

44. Edward S. Casey, *Getting Back into Place: Toward a Renewed Undersanding of the Place-World* (Bloomington and Indianapolis: Indiana University Press, 1993), p. 260ff.

45. Ibid., p. 263.

46. Ibid., pp. 260, 263, 264.

47. Ibid., p. 265. In the context of his "preservation" movement, John Muir argued for the inherent value of all living things and he was opposed to viewing the natural environment as a mere commodity. For a good introduction to Muir's thinking, see Michael Cohen, *The Pathless Way* (Madison: University of Wisconsin Press, 1984). For more on Leopold, see *The Sand County Almanac*.

48. Casey, *Getting Back into Place*, p. 264.

49. Ibid., p. 265.

50. Ibid.

51. Ibid., p. 266. To what extent such husbandry really remains ecocentric is, in my view, questionable. As I have pointed out in earlier chapters, there are huge philosophical problems that arise in the field of environmental ethics when one assigns value to the natural environment "first." These problems may not be insurmountable but they need to be addressed by Casey before he proclaims himself to be ecocentric.

52. Ibid.

53. See particularly Jim Cheney's "Postmodern Environmental Ethics."

54. Ibid., p. 33.

55. Ibid., p. 35.

56. "The notion of socially constructed selves," Cheney remarks, "gives way to the idea of bioregionally constructed selves and communities." Ibid., p. 38.

57. Ibid., p. 37.

58. In this connection, phenomenology has some affinity with virtue ethics, which emphasizes the importance of building character rather than constructing an inventory of principles and rules.

59. Yvonne Dion-Buffalo and John Mohawk, "Thoughts from an Autochtonous Centre: Postmodernism and Cultural Studies," *Cultural Survival Quarterly* (winter 1994) 33–35,

cited in Frédérique Apfell-Marglin, "Counter-Development in the Andes," *The Ecologist* 27, no. 6 (November/December 1997): 221–24.

60. Apffel-Marglin, "Counter-Development in the Andes." Dr. Apffel-Marglin was invited to Peru in 1994 as part of a project to create "Centres for Mutual Learning."

61. Ibid., p. 221.

62. Ibid.

63. Ibid.

64. Ibid., p. 222.

65. Ibid., p. 221.

66. Ibid., p. 223.

67. Ibid. Apffel-Marglin takes special note of the "immense diversity" of conversations that emerge between the Andean farmer and the weather and the landscape—and the wealth of resources that emerge as a result of this interaction. "Indeed, the Andes have been identified by the great Soviet plant geneticist Vavilov as one of the eight centres of origin of cultivated plants. The enormous variety of cultivated plant species continues to astonish plant geneticists today."

68. Ibid., p. 222.

69. Ibid. At the same time, Apffel-Marglin rightly points out that "a dialogical stance is not an oppositional or an essentialist stance either, rejecting whatever comes from a foreign source."

70. Sylvia Bowerbank, "Telling Stories about Place," *Alternatives Journal* 23, no. 1 (winter 1997): 28, 30. While rare, stories about places are, nevertheless, emerging in the environmental literature. I refer the reader to an interesting, recent example of a book by Hok-Lin Leung entitled *City Images* (Kingston, Ontario, Canada: Ronald P. Frye & Company, 1992). Leung writes: "This book is about the views and images of ordinary citizens: the way they see the city and the meaning they give to what they see." It reports on images of Ottawa, the capital city of Canada, from a variety of perspectives, from a blind person, to artist, senior citizen, to taxi driver. It is an interesting approach to understanding perceptions of the city and what its citizens see to be meaningful about their ways of life. Other fascinating articles that expand on questions of narratives specifically in environmental ethics include: Arran E. Gare, "MacIntyre, Narratives and Environmental Ethics" in *Environmental Ethics* 20, no. 1 (spring 1998): 3–21; Mick Smith, "Against the Enclosure of the Ethical Commons: Radical Environmentalism as an 'Ethics of Place,'" *Environmental Ethics* 19, no. 4 (winter 1997): 339–53; Bryan G. Norton and Bruce Hannon, "Environmental Values: A Place-Based Approach," *Environmental Ethics* 19, no. 3 (fall 1997): 227–45. Finally, a new journal is highly recommended to the reader. It is entitled *Ethics, Place, and Environment*. Volume 1, no. 1 was published in March 1998, and contains superb articles of interest to geographers, philosophers, and others who wish to explore the relation between ethics and place.

71. Bowerbank, *Telling Stories about Place*, p. 32.

72. Ibid., p. 31.

73. Ibid.

74. William E. Rees, "Ecological Footprints and Appropriated Carrying Capacity: What Urban Economics Leaves Out," in *Environment and Urbanization* 4, no. 2 (October 1992): 121.

75. See, for example, Lawrence Durrell, *The Greek Islands* (New York: Viking Press, 1978) and Robert D. Kaplan, *The Ends of the Earth: A Journey at the Dawn of the Twenty-first Century* (New York: Random House, 1996). Quotes are from the preface.

76. Don Ihde, "Whole Earth Measurements" (paper presented at the annual meeting of the Society for Phenomenology and Existential Philosophy, 1995). Published as "Whole Earth Measurements: How Many Phenomenologists Does it Take to Detect a 'Greenhouse Effect?'" in *Philosophy Today* 41, no. 1 (spring 1997): 128–34.

77. Ihde, "Whole Earth Measurements," p. 132.

78. Bowerbank, *Telling Stories about Place*.

79. Ibid.

80. Martin Heidegger, *Basic Problems of Phenomenology* (Bloomington and Indianapolis: Indiana University Press, 1982), p. 23.

31. Ibid., p. 21.

82. Ibid., p. 23.

83. Mick Smith, "The Myth of Postmodernism," in *Postmodern Environmental Ethics*, ed. Max Oelschlaeger (New York: State University of New York Press, 1995), p. 267. In this fascinating article, Smith argues that the dichotomy that has evolved between modernism and postmodernism "is itself unconvincing." He also shows how Cheney naively romanticizes primitive societies and engages in his own form of essentializing when he describes modernism as inherently divorced from place.

84. Ibid., pp. 270–71.

85. Ibid., p. 270.

86. Ibid., p. 271.

87. Ibid.

88. Ibid.

89. Ibid.

90. Ibid., p. 272.

91. Werner Marx, *Towards a Phenomenological Ethics*, trans. Ashraf Noor (New York: State University of New York Press, 1992).

Chapter 9. Phenomenology and Sustainability

1. World Commission on Environment and Development, *Our Common Future* (New York: Oxford University Press, 1987), p. 321.

2. Ibid.

3. Ibid., p. 43.

4. Ibid., p. 46.

5. See, for example, Frédérique Apffel-Marglin, "Counter-Development in the Andes," *The Ecologist* 27, no. 6 (November/December 1997): 221–24. Also, the International Society for Ecology and Culture provides a nonprofit program of volunteer assistance in what they describe as "hands-on training in counter-development." See back cover of *The Ecologist* 28, no. 3 (May/June 1998).

6. Ibid.

7. Apffel-Marglin's description of the PRATEC initiatives in the Andes, reported in the last chapter, constitutes a case in point where the richness and diversity of local cultures is recognized and revived.

8. Thomas Langan, *Tradition and Authenticity in the Search for Ecumenic Widsom* (Columbia: University of Missouri Press, 1992), p. 68.

9. Ibid.

10. Ibid., p. 67.

11. Ibid. Langan's volume *Tradition and Authenticity* is the first in a series. On the first page, he describes it as a "decidedly not trendy" book "about development." The second book of the series addresses the origins of *Being and Truth*. I enthusiastically recommend the work of Langan to readers who have an interest in exploring the deeper, philosophical issues that underlie the search for ecumenic wisdom in a global context of appropriating also the wide diversity of contemporary cultures and religious traditions.

12. Langan, *Tradition and Authenticity*, p. 27.

13. See Martin Heidegger, "On the Essence of Truth," in *Existence and Being* (Chicago: Henry Regnery Company, 1949), especially p. 316ff. "Man errs. He does not merely fall into error, he lives in error always. . . . Error is part of the inner structure of Dasein. . . . The dissimulation of what-is concealed in totality comes into force through the revelation of what-is at any moment, and this revelation, because it is a forgetting of the dissimulation, leads to error." Error for Heidegger is not merely the occasional mistake but, rather, "the open ground, the basis of Wrong. Wrong is not just the isolated mistake, it is the empire, the whole history of all the complicated and intricate ways of erring."

14. Ibid., p. 319.

15. *Webster's Ninth New Collegiate Dictionary* (Springfield, Mass.: Merriam-Webster, 1985), p. 347.

16. Ibid.

17. Ibid. I should note here that Thomas Langan's book *Tradition and Authenticity* specifically links personal and social development, showing how the condition for authentic self-development is a coming to terms with implicit and explicit traditions within which we are immersed.

18. I am reminded of a revealing article, recently published in *Saturday Night* (March 1998), pp. 46–54 and p. 71) by philosopher Mark Kingwell who, as part of a larger project on investigating happiness and the search for self-development, enrolled himself in the "Option Institute and Fellowship" in Sheffield, Mass., where the search for happiness became a Faustian pursuit of an elusive state that, after all, cannot always be commanded at will. The full version of the article appears as "I Want it Now," chapter 2 of Kingwell's book entitled *Better Living: In Pursuit of Happiness from Plato to Prozac* (Toronto: Viking Press, 1998), pp. 39–93.

19. It is not difficult to imagine that citizens of the developing world might themselves find the term "counter-development" to be heavy-handed and misplaced to the extent that it could be seen to suggest that western society will continue to benefit from technological and economic "development" while developing countries will satisfy themselves with a state of affairs that runs "counter" to overall societal improvement. Both "development" and "counter-development" really do need to be articulated more carefully by proponents of sustainability in order that misinterpretations be avoided.

20. World Commission on Environment and Dvelopment, *Our Common Future*, p. 46.

21. Langan, *Tradition and Authenticity*, p. 124.

22. Ibid.

23. Ibid., pp. 26–27.

24. Ibid., p. 125.

25. Ibidl, p. 11.

26. Ibid., p. 12.

27. Heidegger suggests that it is precisely in the face of such dread that we deny our own Being-toward-death, escaping into the inauthentic delineation of death as a present-at-hand event. See *Being and Time*, trans. John Macquarrie and Eward Robinson (New York: Harper & Row, 1962), particularly division 2, sections 1 and 2.

28. Martin Heidegger, *The Concept of Time*, trans. William McNeill (Oxford: Blackwell, 1992), p. 12E.

29. Langan, *Tradition and Authenticity*, p. 1.

30. Ibid., pp. 1–2.

31. World Commission on Environment and Development, *Our Common Future*, p. 43.

32. Langan, *Tradition and Authenticity*, p. 231.

33. Ibid.

34. World Commission on Environment and Development, *Our Common Future*, p. 43.

35. Ibid.

36. In the developing world, the tragedy is that basic survival is often accomplished in a self-defeating manner. Geoffrey Bruce of the Canadian International Development Agencypoints out how "small farmers are held responsible for environmental destruction as if they had a choice of resources to depend on for their livelihood, when they really don't. In the context of basic survival, today's needs tend to overshadow consideration for the environmental future. It is poverty that is responsible for the destruction of natural resources, not the poor." Cited in ibid., p. 127.

37. Ibid., pp. 54–55.

38. Ibid., p. 54.

39. Martin Heidegger, "Hölderlin and the Essence of Poetry," in *Existence and Being* (Chicago: Henry Regnery Company, 1949), p. 289. Heidegger is here reflecting on Hölderlin's poetic description of "the time of the gods that have fled and of the god that is coming."

40. Martin Heidegger, "Remembrance of the Poet," in ibid., pp. 266–67. "The 'need' [*Not*] is the mysterious call 'to' the others . . . to become hearers. . . . The deliberating ones and the slow ones are for the first time the careful ones. Because they think of that which is written of in the poem, they are directed with the singer's care towards the mystery of the reserving proximity."

41. Heidegger, *Being and Time*, p. 274.

42. Heideger, *The Concept of Time*, p. 9E.

43. Heidegger, "On the Essence of Truth," p. 318; and Thomas Langan, *The Meaning of Heidegger* (New York: Columbia University Press, 1961), p. 100. Langan explains that "this need is that of a positive freedom seeking to fulfill its needs, born of finitude, from out of its strictly limited resources. When Heidegger insists that *das Nichts* is not a purely nugatory Nothing, he is thinking of the positive generation of light originated by the call of that need. The Being disclosed in the opening cleared by nothingness, by the need grounding freedom, is that Being by which and for the sake of which we exist: hence the justification for the religious language" (p. 101).

44. Heidegger, "Remembrance of the Poet," p. 266. The religious language continues in "Hölderlin and the Essence of Poetry," although Heidegger is referring to a specific poem that invokes religious images. Heidegger writes: "It is the time of the gods that have fled *and* of the god that is coming. It is the time *of need*, because it lies under a double lack and a double Not: the No-more of the gods that have fled and the Not-yet of the god that is coming" (see p. 289).

45. Martin Heidegger, *The Question Concerning Technology*, trans. W. Lovitt (New York: Harper & Row, 1977), p. 28. See also "Building Dwelling Thinking" in *Poetry, Language, Thought*, trans A. Hofstadter (New York: Harper & Row, 1971), p. 150, where Heidegger writes: "Saving does not only snatch something from a danger. To save really means to set something free into its own presencing. To save the earth is more than to exploit it or even wear it out. Saving the earth does not master the earth and does not subjugate it, which is merely one step from spoilation."

46. Heidegger, "The Origin of the Work of Art," in *Poetry, Language, Thought*, p. 46.

47. Martin Heidegger, *Vorträge und Aufsätze*, cited in *Inhabiting the Earth: Heidegger, Environmental Ethics, and the Metaphysics of Nature*, trans Bruce V. Foltz (Atlantic Highlands, N.J.: Humanities Press, 1995), p. 161.

48. World Commission on Environment and Development, *Our Common Future*, p. 343.

49. Bedrich Moldan and Suzanne Billharz, eds., *Sustainability Indicators: Report of the Project on Indicators of Sustainable Development* (New York: John Wiley & Sons, 1997), p. 1.

50. Ibid.

51. Monika Luxem and Birgitte Bryld, "The CSD Work Programme on Indicators of Sustainable Development," in *Sustainability Indicators*, p. 6.

52. Moldan and Billharz note that "these processes are parallel and complementary: working on indicators helps us to see the important processes and linkages among aspects of sustainable development at many levels and to appreciate fully the complex interactions among its different dimensions." Ibid., p. 5.

53. Readers may wish to visit the Indicators of Sustainability Website for further discussion of definitions at: http://www.subjectmatters.com/indicators/-index.html.

54. D. Tunstall sees an indicator as a "statistical measure"; Adriaanse implies that it is a meter or measuring instrument—a "fraction" comparing quantities; Ott describes an indicator as a single "quantity" derived from one variable and used to reflect some attribute. See D. Tunstall, *Developing and Using Indicators of Sustainable Development in Africa: An Overview*; A. Adriaanse, *Environmental Policy Performance Indicators*; W. R. Ott, *Environmental Indices: Theory and Practice*, all cited in *Sustainability Indicators*, p. 14.

55. OECD 1994 definition, cited in David Dilks, *Measuring Urban Sustainability: Canadian Indicators Workshop*, workshop proceedings 19–21 June 1995 (Ottawa, Canada: Canada Mortgage and Housing Corporation and Environment Canada, 1996), p. 2.

56. United Nations Centre for Human Settlements, *Indicators Programme: Monitoring Human Settlements Volume 1—Introduction, Background, and Rationale* (Nairobi, Kenya: UNCHS and the World Bank, 1995); and UNCHS *Indicators Programme: Monitoring Human Settlements: Key Indicators—Abridged Survey* (Nairobi, Kenya: UNCHS and the World Bank, 1995).

57. United Nations Development Programme (UNDP), *Human Development Report* (New York: Oxford University Press, 1990).

58. Ibid., p. 1.

59. Ibid., pp. 1, 9.

60. Myriam Linster, "OECD Indicators for the Integration of Environmental Concerns into Transport Policies," in Moldan and Billharz, *Sustainability Indicators*, p. 237. See also the Organization for Economic Cooperation and Development, *Environmental Indicators: OECD Core Set* (Paris, 1994).

61. Dilks, *Measuring Urban Sustainability*, p. 2.

62. Molan and Billharz, *Sustainability Indicators*.

63. Jacksonville Community Council, 1992, cited in Dilks, *Measuring Urban Sustainability*.

64. Adapted from D. Tunstall, "Developing Environmental Indicators: Definitions, Frameworks, and Issues" (draft paper) background materials for the World Resources Institute Workshop on Global Environmental Indicators, Washington, D.C., 7–8 December 1992, World Resources Institute, Washington, D.C.); and Moldan and Billharz, *Sustainability Indicators*, p. 15.

65. Moldan and Billharz, p. 17; Dilks, *Measuring Urban Sustainability*, p. 27.

66. Moldan and Billharz, *Sustainability Indicators*, p. 17.

67. Dilks, *Measuring Urban Sustainability*, p. 36.

68. Ibid., p. 35. Other types include: predictive or forward-looking; retrospective; objective; input versus output; index or composite indicators.

69. Ibid., p. 15.

70. The McMaster Tri-Council Eco-Research Program for Hamilton Harbour, *The Indicators Session of the Second Annual Ecowise Workshop*, April 25–26, 1995, p. 2.

71. Moldan and Billharz, *Sustainability Indicators*, p. 19ff.

72. Jan Bakkes, "Research Needs," in Dilks, *Measuring Urban Sustainability*, p. 379.

73. One rare example of normative and ethics indicators is found in the work of Hartmut Bossel, "Finding a Comprehensive Set of Indicators of Sustainable Development by Application of Orientation Theory," in ibid., p. 101ff. Examples of such indicators include: "frequency of violation of basic human rights," "future discount applied in policy decisions," "fairness level" (percent of population seeing systems as 'extremely unfair,') and "rate of change of social norms and behaviour" (consumer appliance inventory). Once again, most of these indicators seem to be ontic categories, capable of statistical measurement.

74. Such a study was conducted by economists as part of the Tri-Council McMaster Eco-research of the Hamilton Harbour ecosystem, *Indicators Session*.

75. See Mark Sagoff's excellent criticisms and positive critical analysis of the difference between preferences and wants on the one hand, and morality on the other, neatly summarized in his well-known article "At the Shrine of Our Lady of Fatima, or Why Political Questions Are Not All Economic," published originally in *Arizona Law Review* 23 (1981): 1283–1298, reprinted in *Environmental Ethics*, ed. Louis P. Pojman (Boston: Jones and Bartlett Publishers, 1994), pp. 443–50. See also his thoughtful book *The Economy of the Earth: Philosophy, Law, and the Environment* (New York: Cambridge University Press, 1988), 100–101, where he points out that, in terms of fundamental questions of ethics, "it is not just what the person *wants* but what he or she *thinks* that counts."

76. See Willet Kempton, James Boster, and Jennifer Hartley, *Environmental Values in American Culture* (Cambridge: The MIT Press, 1995). Reviewed by Bron Taylor in *The Ecologist* 27, no. 1 (January/February 1997): 38–39.

77. Ibid. I should point out that surveys that report a drop in citizens' interest in environmental concerns can be misleading. Often, people will suggest that the environment falls lower on their lists of priorities, because they feel that it is already attracting sufficient public money and is being "settled" appropriately. See, for example, the reports of Evert Carll Ladd and Karlyn Bowman, "Public Opinion on the Environment," *Resources for the Future* no. 124 (summer 1996): 5–7. (*Resources for the Future*, 1616 P Street NW, Washington, D.C. 20036–1400.) They write: "In the late 1960s and early 1970s, the idea that we should make a substantial commitment to the environment was not widely shared. Today it is. . . . The transformation of the environment from an issue of limited concern to one of universal concern is complete, and today, survey after survey shows that most Americans have turned their attention to other things."

78. Canadian urban planner Hok-Lin Leung points out that "the standard questionnaire survey assumes that the investigator knows what the question is and all that is needed is the answer. But we really can't predict what our internal viewers will tell us. There are no boxes to be checked off. Moreover, the question-and-answer survey approach can only entertain answers that are couched in terms of yes or no. It does not allow answers such as 'yes and no' or 'it depends.'" Leung quotes Studs Terkel who points out that "the question-and-answer technique may be of value in determining favored detergents, toothpaste and deodorants, but not in the discovery of men and women." See Hok-Lin Leung, *City Images* (Kingston, Ontario: Ronald P. Frye & Company, 1992), pp. 5, 7.

79. For further discussion on methodological aspects of phenomenological deconstruction of narratives through interview techniques, see Robert Bogdan and Steven J. Taylor, *Introduction to Qualitative Research Methods: A Guidebook and Resource* (New York: John Wiley & Sons, Inc., 1998). For a presentation of some of my own work in conducting interviews within a phenomenological framework, see "Interdisciplinarity and Wholeness: Lessons from Eco-research on the Hamilton Harbour Ecosystem" in *Environments: A Journal of Interdisciplinary Studies* 23, no. 3 (1996): 74–94.

80. Hartmut Bossel, for example, includes in his "comprehensive list of indicators" a listing of psychological indicators that includes "regional landscape aesthetics (on a scale of 'pleasing' to 'ugly')." See "Finding a Comprehensive Set of Indicators," p. 103.

81. Heidegger, "The Origin of the Work of Art," p. 56.

82. David Seamon points out that, while written texts that describe environments and actual landscapes dominate phenomenological research focusing on environmental themes, other visual media such as artworks and photography can be equally illumining. See "Awareness and Reunion: A Phenomenology of the Person-World Relationship as Portrayed in the New York Photographs of André Kertész," in *Place Images in Media: Portrayal, Experience and Meaning*, ed. Leo Zonn (Savage, Maryland: Rowman & Littlefield, 1990), pp. 31–61.

83. Heidegger, "The Origin of the Work of Art," p. 75.

84. Martin Heidegger, ". . . Poetically Man Dwells . . ." in *Poetry, Language, Thought*, p. 227.

85. Bruce V. Foltz, *Inhabiting the Earth* (Atlantic Highlands, N.J.: Humanities Press, 1995), p. 158.

86. Ellen Eve Frank, *Literary Architecture: Essays Toward a Tradition* (Berkeley: University of California Press, 1979), pp. 255–56.

87. Ibid., p. 257.

88. For some examples of human settlement "readings," see Francis Violich, "'Urban Reading' and the Design of Small Urban Places: The Village of Sutivan" in *Town Planning Review* 54 (1983): 41–60; Ingrid Leman Stefanovic, "The Experience of Place: Housing Quality from a Phenomenological Perspective," *Canadian Journal of Urban Research* 1, no. 2 (December 1992): 145–61; *Dwelling, Seeing, and Designing: Toward a Phenomenological Ecology*, ed. David Seamon (New York: State University of New York Press, 1993).

89. Sigfried Giedion, *Space, Time, and Architecture*, cited in Karsten Harries, *The Ethical Function of Architecture* (Cambridge: MIT, 1997), p. 2.

90. Ibid.

91. Ibid.

92. Dilks, *Measuring Urban Sustainability*, p. 2.

Chapter 10. Phenomenology, Sustainability, and the Lived World

1. Lisa H. Newton and Catherine K. Dillingham, *Watersheds: Classic Cases in Environmental Ethics* (Belmont, Calif.: Wadsworth Publishing Company, 1994), p. 2.

2. The first case relating to the Hamilton Harbour Ecosystem was originally reported in a number of articles, including "Interdisciplinarity and Wholeness: Lessons from Eco-Research," *Environments* 23, no. 3 (1996), 74–94; "An Integrative Framework for Sustainability: The Case of the Hamilton Harbour Ecosystem" (proceedings of the conference on "Synthesis of Tradition and Modernity for a Sustainable Society," organized by the Commonwealth Association of Architects in India and the World Society for Ekistics, 1995), pp. 19–26; and "New Project Management Frontiers in Interdisciplinary Research," with Michael Stefanovic (proceedings of the annual meeting of the Project Management Institute, 13–18 October 1995, New Orleans), pp. 625–32. The second case relating to a phenomenological reading of Mississauga was originally reported in "The Experience of Place: Housing Quality from a Phenomenological Perspective," in *Canadian Journal of Urban Research* 1, no. 2 (December 1992): 145–61 and "Phenomenological Encounters with Place: Cavtat to Square One," in the *Journal of Environmental Psychology* 18 (1998): 31–44.

3. The research was originally reported in "A Code of Ethics for Short Hills Park" (proceedings of the *Leading Edge '94* conference, organized by the Ontario Ministry of Environment and Energy, 1995), pp. 278–90; and in "Encouraging Environmental Care," in *Canadian Issues in Environmental Ethics*, ed. Alex Wellington, Allan Greenbaum, and Wesley Cragg (Peterborough, Canada: Broadview Press, 1997), pp. 246–48. An earlier version of the last article was also printed in *The George Wright Forum* 13, no. 2 (1996).

4. The full, formal project title was "Hamilton Harbour: Towards Restoring and Sustaining a Healthy Ecosystem."

5. *Remedial Action Plan for Hamilton Harbour*, RAP Stage 2, November 1992.

6. Cited in the original proposal and application for a research grant to the Tri-Council, Ottawa, Canada, for the study of "Hamilton Harbour: Towards Restoring and Sustaining a Healthy Ecosystem," 1992.

7. Ibid.

8. For a thoughtful discussion of the difference between multidisciplinarity, interdisciplinarity, transdisciplinarity, cross-disciplinarity, pluridisciplinarity, and other similar variations, see Julie Thompson Klein, *Interdisciplinarity: History, Theory, and Practice* (Detroit: Wayne State University Press, 1990).

9. I would like to credit my two research assistants—Carolyn Johns and Bertrand Leman—for their invaluable assistance on this project.

10. The phenomenological interview process schematically portrayed in figure 10.1 builds on a similar diagram that was presented to the Environmental Design Research Association Annual Meeting by Dr. Margaret Boschetti in a paper on "Possessions and Place-Making," in an "Intensive" on "Recovering Sense of Place: Research in Environmental and Architectural Phenomenology." Further information about Dr. Boschetti's own phenomenological interview process can be obtained from her through the School of Human Environmental Sciences, East Carolina University. See also Guba, Egona, and Yvonna Lincoln, *Fourth Generation Evaluation* (London: Sage Publications, 1989), p. 152 for a discussion of the "hermeneutic dialectic circle," which similarly seeks an alternative methodology for research based on phenomenological foundations, as well as such works as *Introduction to Qualitative Research Methods*, 3rd ed., Steven J. Taylor and Robert Bogdan (New York: John Wiley & Sons, 1998).

11. When Heidegger speaks of the "destruction" of the history of ontology, he is referring to the phenomenological task of uncovering the hidden origins that remain forgotten and yet continue to have influence upon the apparently self-evident truths of a particular tradition. (Cf. *Being and Time* (New York: Harper & Row, 1962), p. 43ff.) Arising out of this interpretation, I use the word "deconstruction" to indicate the parallel historical task of illumining essential, taken-for-granted meanings that constitute the condition of the possibility of explicitly articulated beliefs.

12. Edward T. Relph, "Modernity and the Reclamation of Place" in *Dwelling, Seeing, and Designing: Toward a Phenomenological Ecology*, ed. David Seamon (Albany: State University of New York Press, 1993), p. 34.

13. The NUD.IST program stands for "nonnumerical unstructured data indexing, searching, and theorising." The softward system was designed by Tom Richards, Department of Computer Science and Computer Engineering, and Lyn Richards, Department of Sociology, La Trobe University, Bundoora, Vic 3083, Australia.

14. Lewis Mumford, *The City in History: Its Origins, Its Transformations, and Its Prospects* (New York: Harcourt, Brace & World, 1961), p. 494.

15. Ibid.

16. Brian Berry, *The Human Consequences of Urbanization* (New York: St. Martin's Press, 1973).

17. See, for example, J. B. Lansing, R. W. Marans, and R. B. Zehner, *Planned Residential Environments* (Ann Arbor: University of Michigan, 1979): P. Calthorpe, *The Next American Metropolis: Ecology, Community, and the American Dream* (New York: Princeton Architectural Press, 1993); K. T. Jackson, *Crabgrass Frontier: The Suburbanization of the United States* (New York: Oxford University Press, 1985); D. Hayden, *Redesigning the American Dream: The Future of Housing, Work, and Family Life* (New York: W. W. Norton and Company Ltd., 1984).

18. Robert Mugerauer, "Midwestern Suburban Landscapes and Residents' Values," in

Coming of Age: Environmental Design, ed. Robert Selby (Chicago: University of Illinois, 1990).

19. Ibid.

20. Ibid.

21. David Seamon, "The Phenomenological Contribution to Environmental Psychology," *Journal of Environmentsl Psychology* 2 (1982): 121.

22. See, for example, M. Dozio, P. Federson, and K. Noschis, "Everyday Life on an Insignificant Public Square: Venice," *Ekistics* 198, pp. 66–76; J. Nogué i Font, *Una Lectura geogràphico-humanista del apistage de la Garrotxa* (Barcelona: Collegi Universitari de Girona, 1985); Fran Violick, *Dalmatia: A Search for the Meaning of Place* (Baltimore: Johns Hopkins Press, 1996); and Fran Violich "'Urban Reading' and the Design of Small Urban Places: the Village of Sutivan," *Town Planning Review* 54 (1983): pp. 41–60.

23. John Ruskin, "The Poetry of Architecture," *Works*, I, 17, cited in Ellen Eve Frank, *Literary Architecture*.

24. Ibid., p. 255ff.

25. For an interesting discussion on "The Phenomenology of Automobility," see part 2 of Peter Freund and George Martin, *The Ecology of the Automobile* (Montreal/London: Black Rose Books, 1993).

26. Dolores Hayden, *Redesigning the American Dream: The Future of Housing, Work, and Family Life* (New York: W. W. Norton and Company, 1984), p. 18.

27. Gaston Bachelard, *The Poetics of Space*, trans. Maria Jolas (Boston: Beacon Press, 1964), pp. 4, 7.

28. Walter Horatio Pater, "A Prince of Court Painters," *Imaginary Portraits* (London and New York: 1887) cited in Ellen Eve Frank, *Literary Architectures*, p. 32.

29. On this theme, see Martin Heidegger's *Being and Time*, especially division 2: Dasein and Temporality.

30. Edward T. Relph, "Geographical Experiences and Being-in-the-World: The Phenomenological Origins of Geography," in *Dwelling, Place, and Environment: Towards a Phenomenology of Person and World*, ed. David Seamon and Robert Mugerauer (The Hague, Martinus Nijhoff, 1985), pp. 15–16.

31. Jack L. Nasar, *The Evaluative Image of the City* (London: Sage Publications, 1998), pp. 2, 17.

32. Ontario Ministry of Natural Resources, *Short Hills Provincial Park Management Plan* (Fonthill, Ontario: OMNR, 1991), p. 2.

33. Ibid., pp. 4, 7.

34. Ibid., p. 4. Examples of conflicts between trail users included complaints by hikers of damage to trails by equestrians; mountain bikers startling horses; and similar instances relating to the sharing of multiuse trails in particular.

35. See S. C. Hayes and J. D. Cone, "Decelerating Environmentally Destructive Lawn-Walking Behaviour" in *Environment and Behaviour* 9 (1977): 91–101; J. W. Reich and J. L. Robertson, "Reactance and Normal Appeal in Antilittering Messages" in *Journal of Applied Social Psychology* 9 (1979): 91–101; A. W. Magill, "Methods to Control Negative Impacts of Recreation Use," in *River Recreation Management and Research Symosium* (January 24–7, 1977): 402–4.

36. Oscar Newman, *Defensible Space: Crime Prevention through Urban Design* (New York: Macmillan Publishing Company, 1972), p. 3.

37. For more on the advantages and disadvantages of codes of ethics, see Kenneth Kernaghan, "Managing Ethics: Complementary Approaches," *Canadian Public Administration* 34, no. 1 (spring): 132–45; Reg Lang and Susan Hendler, "Ethics and Professional Planners," in D. MacNiven, *Moral Expertise* (London: 1988); J. S. Beazley, "What Is This Thing Called Ethics and Sometimes, The Code of Ethics?" in *Photogrammetric Engineering and Remote Sensing* 57, no. 5 (May 1991): 497–99; Ralph Clark Chandler, "The Problem of Moral Reasoning in American Public Administration: The Case for a Code of Ethics," in *Public Administration Review* 43 (January/February 1983): 32–39.

38. David N. Johnson, "Outdoor Ethics and Public Education in Africa," in Proceedings of the International Conference on Outdoor Ethics, 8–11 November 1987, p. 22, Lake Ozark, Missouri. Sponsored by the Izaak Walton League of America.

39. Stories by Doug Draper, *St. Catherines Standard*, 26 June 1993.

40. Shopping malls often propagate consumer values and competition. Moreover, the shopping center in my own neighborhood is hardly atypical in actually housing a tutoring agency for after-school instruction, specifically in mathematics and scientific disciplines.

41. C. A. Bowers, *Educating for an Ecologically Sustainable Culture: Rethinking Moral Education, Creativity, Intelligence, and Other Modern Orthodoxies* (New York: State University of New York Press, 1995), p. 2.

42. Ibid., p. 3. Pamela Courtenay-Hall reminds us that the array of messages communicated through schools includes both the explicit as well as the implicit ("the hidden") curriculum, ranging from "the ways in which teachers interact with students; the ways students are expected to interact (or not interact) with each other; the ways in which the school day is organized; the emphasis placed on competition or cooperation, obedience to authority or independent thinking, artistic efforts, team sports or community volunteering, working with texts or working with people and projects. . . . In short, much of the learning that students do in schools comes not from the overt curriculum which teachers, textbooks, and class exercises aim to develop but, rather, from the various school and classroom policies and traditions that shape the school experiences of young people . . . policies and traditions involving how to eat, talk, sit, how to be (behave) in the classroom, how to be (behave) in the playground, how to locate oneself in the community. These policies and traditions are no less about gender, race, class and culture. And they *percolate* with issues of separation or integration, equity or disparity, marginalization or affirmation." See "Environmental Education in a Democratic Society," in *Canadian Issues in Environmental Ethics*, ed. Alex Wellington, Allan Greenbaum, and Wesley Cragg (Peterborough, Ontario: Broadview Press, 1997), p. 370.

43. Bowers, *Education for an Ecologically Sustainable Culture*, p. 46.

44. Ibid., p. 43.

45. Ibid., p. 72.

46. Ibid., p. 73.

47. Ibid., p. 11.

48. Ibid., p. 101. "It is now safe to generalize," writes Bowers, "that most classroom teachers and professors of education who keep themselves current with the most recent developments in learning theory subscribe to a cognitive interpretation of intelligence."

These same educators assume that the basic socio-cultural unit that thinks is the individual: "with regard to this last assumption, it is important to note that educators now
emphasize participation in groups as a way of faciilitating the idividual's learning potential" (p. 95).

49. Ibid., p. 199.

50. Interviews with some of the few remaining Bushmen of the Kalahari are reported by
Allen Abel in "The Lost Worlds of the Kalahari," *Saturday Night*, July/August 1998,
pp. 46–54.

51. Ibid., p. 50.

52. Ibid., p. 51.

53. David W. Orr, "What is Education For?" in *Trumpeter* 8, no. 3 (summer 1991): 101.

54. See Courtenay-Hall, "Environmental Education."

55. Courtenay-Hall, ibid., p. 378.

56. Ibid.

57. Paul Krapfel, *Shifting* (Cottonwood, Calif.: 18080 Brincat Manor Drive, Paul Krapfel,
1989). Republication forthcoming by White River Junction, Vt.: Chelsea Green.

58. Ibid., p. 11.

59. Ibid., p. 12.

60. Ibid. Krapfel provides numerous examples that would be of interest to the reader
who has a special commitment to seeking new ways of seeing the world and examples
of thoughtful encounters that inspire a rethinking of traditional approaches to environmental education.

61. Ibid., p. 35. See also Pamela Courtenay-Hall, "Environmental Education," p. 378.

62. Krapfel, *Shifting*, p. 23ff.

63. Ibid., p. 65ff.

64. Ibid., p. 80.

65. Lucie Sauvé. "Environmental Education and Sustainable Development: A Further
Appraisal," *Canadian Journal of Environmental Education* 1 (spring 1996): 7–34.

66. Ibid., p. 28.

67. Ibid.

68. Courtenay-Hall, "Environmental Education," p. 367.

69. Bowers, *Educating for an Ecologically Sustainable Culture*, p. 61.

70. Ibid.

71. Ibid.

72. J. B. White, *Heracles' Bow, Essays on the Rhetoric and Poetics of the Law*, cited in Iain Hay,
"Making Moral Imaginations. Research Ethics, Pedagogy and Professional Human
Geography," in *Ethics, Place and Environment* 1, no. 1 (1998): 55.

Appendix. Heidegger's Politics

1. The book that focused renewed attention on Heidegger's links to National Socialism
was Victor Farias's *Heidegger and Nazism* (Philadelphia: Temple University Press, 1989),
originally published in French in 1987. According to Stephen Howe, this book "was in
many ways a shoddy effort; ignorant about Heidegger's philosophy, riddled with mis-
quotation, seeking unconvincingly to indict Heidegger for anti-Semitism, in fact, the

aspect of Nazi ideology of which he was least guilty." See Stephen Howe, "A Nazi Genius," *New Statesman & Society*, 27 August 1993. Another text by historian Hugo Ott focused attention on the fact that Heidegger's break with Nazism in 1934 may not have been as complete as many of his followers believed. See Hugo Ott, *Martin Heideger: Unterwegs Zu Seiner Biographie* (Frankfurt: Campus, 1988).

2. Martin Heideger, "Only a God Can Save Us," originally published in *Der Spiegel,* 31 May 1976. Reprinted in *The Heidegger Controversy*, ed. Richard Wolin (Cambridge: The MIT Press, 1993), p. 93.

3. Ibid.

4. Ibid.

5. Ibid., p. 99.

6. Ibid., pp. 93, 97, 101ff. Incidences ranged from prohibiting the posting of the Nazis' Jewish proclamation, to refusing to comply with repeated demands to remove books of Jewish authors from the library of the Philosophical Seminar, to supporting Jews in university posts whom the Ministry officials were demanding to be removed. The *Der Spiegel* interviewer concludes: "You had Jewish students also after 1933. Your relationship to some of these students is supposed to have been quite warm" (p. 97).

7. Ibid., pp. 94–95.

8. Ibid., pp. 95–96.

9. Graeme Nicholson, "The Politics of Heidegger's Rectoral Address," *Man and World* 20 (1987): 174ff. I recommend this article to readers who are interested in better understanding the philosophical implications of this all-important rectoral address.

10. Ibid., p. 174.

11. Ibid., p. 185. Nicholson gives credit to Heidegger for taking the risk of applying his philosophy to political endeavors, because "the risk was better than the cowardice of others who took no risks and never submitted their thought to the test of praxis." Although many would argue that the failure of Heidegger's thought was that it did not direct him to avoid Nazism, Nicholson argues that Heidegger's main weakness did not lie in his philosophy per se, but in his "confusion regarding offices and constitutions. . . . To assume the rector's office and to act as a law-giver to the community" was Heidegger's final failing (pp. 185–86).

12. Martin Heidegger, "Letter to Herbert Marcuse," reported in Wolin, *Heidegger Controversy*, p. 162.

13. Heidegger, "Only a God Can Save Us," p. 101.

14. Ibid., pp. 101, 103.

15. The full quotation is: "The works that are being peddled about nowadays as the philosophy of National Socialism but have nothing whatever to do with the inner truth and greatness of this movement (namely, the encounter between global technology and modern man)—have all been written by men fishing in the troubled waters of 'values' and 'totalities.'" See Martin Heidegger, *Introduction to Metaphysics*, trans. Ralph Manhein (New York: Yale University Press, 1959), p. 166.

16. Heidegger, "Letter to Marcuse," in Wolin, *Heidegger Controversy*, p. 162.

17. Ibid., p. 163.

18. Ibid., p. 162.

19. Karl Jaspers, "Letter to the Denazification Committee," in ibid., p. 149.

20. One of the most recent publications is Rüdiger Safranski's *Martin Heidegger: Between Good and Evil*, trans. Ewald Osers (Harvard University Press, 1997). Other analyses that are more careful than many sensational alternatives include the following: Fred Dallmayer, "Heidegger, Hölderlin, and Politics," in *Margins of Political Discourse* (New York: State University of New York Press, 1989); Jacques Derrida, *On Spirit: Heidegger and the Question* (Chicago: University of Chicago Press, 1989); Karsten Harries, "Introduction" to *Martin Heidegger and National Socialism: Questions and Answers*, ed. G. Neske and E. Hettering (New York: Paragon House, 1990); Philippe Lacoue-Labarthe, *Heidegger, Art, and Politics* (Oxford: Blackwell, 1990); Jean-François Lyotard, *Heidegger and "the Jews"* (Minneapolis: University of Minnesota Press, 1990); and Thomas Sheehan, "Heidegger and the Nazis," *The New York Review of Books*, 16 June 1988, pp. 38–47.

21. Letter to Heidegger from Herbert Harcuse, reported in Wolin, *Heidegger Controversy*, p. 161.

22. Cited in ibid., p. 156.

23. Ibid.

24. Jaspers, "Letter to the Denazification Committee."

25. This criticism emerges from the work of Lacoue-Labarthe, as well as Derrida.

26. Lacoue-Labarthe, cited in Wolin, *Heidegger Controversy*, p. 286.

27. Cited in ibid., p. 157.

28. Heidegger, "Letter to Marcuse," in ibid., p. 162.

29. Nicholson, "Politics of Heidegger's Rectoral Address," p. 171.

Index